# Broadcasting
# THE BLUES

# Broadcasting
# THE BLUES

BLACK BLUES IN THE SEGREGATION ERA

# Paul Oliver

Routledge
Taylor & Francis Group

NEW YORK AND LONDON

Some material in this book is based on scripts from BBC Radio programs originally broadcast between 1956 and 1997, and is reproduced by permission of the BBC.

Published in 2006 by
Routledge
Taylor & Francis Group
270 Madison Avenue
New York, NY 10016

Published in Great Britain by
Routledge
Taylor & Francis Group
2 Park Square
Milton Park, Abingdon
Oxon OX14 4RN

© 2006 by Paul Oliver
Routledge is an imprint of Taylor & Francis Group

Printed in the United States of America on acid-free paper
10 9 8 7 6 5 4 3 2 1

International Standard Book Number-10: 0-415-97176-4 (Hardcover) 0-415-97177-2 (Softcover)
International Standard Book Number-13: 978-0-415-97176-8 (Hardcover) 978-0-415-97177-5 (Softcover)
Library of Congress Card Number 2005013957

**Library of Congress Cataloging-in-Publication Data**

Oliver, Paul, 1927-
    Broadcasting the blues : black blues in the segregation era / Paul Oliver.
        p. cm.
    Includes discography (p.  ) and index.
    ISBN 0-415-97176-4 (hardback : alk. paper) -- ISBN 0-415-97177-2 (pbk. : alk. paper)
    1. Blues (Music)--History and criticism. 2. African Americans--Music--History and criticism. 3. Blues (Music)--Social aspects--United States. I. Title.

ML3521.O445 2005
781.643'09--dc22                                                                                2005013957

Taylor & Francis Group
is the Academic Division of T&F Informa plc.

Visit the Taylor & Francis Web site at
http://www.taylorandfrancis.com

and the Routledge Web site at
http://www.routledge-ny.com

# Contents

Contents

# Preface: A Trailer

## RADIO BROADCASTING BLUES

As any farm-hand or peasant would have known a century ago, there was a time-honored method of sowing seeds. The sowers carried wide-mouthed sacks filled with seeds, which were suspended from their shoulders. As they walked over the fertile soil of the newly tilled fields, they would dip their free hands into the sacks to scoop up a quantity of the contents. With a swing of their arms in a broad arc they would "scatter the good seeds on the land"—a technique which was called "broadcasting." For many of us the method has long gone, but the term lives on in the transmission of sounds on the radio.

Who first applied it remains uncertain, but as early as 1907 the British engineer, Oliver Lodge, speaking of wireless telegraphy, observed that "it might be advantageous to start the message, speaking broadcast to receivers in all directions." Within a few years the black band-leader and composer of "Saint Louis Blues" and other blues items, W. C. Handy, is reported to have broadcast in Memphis, Tennessee. Perhaps the singer Inez Wallace had this in mind when she sang in 1923, to Fletcher Henderson's piano accompaniment, "Those radio blues, I've got those Radio Blues. The folks are raisin', they're cravin' radiophone. It makes you feel like they're thinkin' you are alone." "Now everybody jazz the blues," she added, but she obviously wasn't too happy with it: "I can't eat and I can't sleep, when it starts to moan."

By this time Duke Ellington was broadcasting in New York and both jazz bands and a few women singers were getting their music on the air. The "Queen of the Moaners," Ida Cox, made her "Broadcasting Blues," singing "Mister Radio Announcer, please listen to my plea: Turn on your radio and find my man for me," an appeal that was echoed in a number of other records. By 1930 broadcasting was so much a part of everyday experience that Walter Taylor, known as "Washboard Walter," reflected that "in the year of Eighteen Hundred and Ninety-Nine, we couldn't hear good music over the radiophone," but he added: "Listen here sweet mama, listen to my pleas to you, I want you to help me lose these broadcast blues." Exasperation drove Washboard Sam who warned, "Baby, just keep on broadcastin', and beatin' out your chops; Somebody's gonna find out the station you are on, Lord and make you lose that sweet voice you've got." Complaining that she "spread the news all over everywhere" he added, "You love to broadcast so much, oh Lord, why don't you try to get on the air?"

A number of blues singers in the 1930s had done so, broadcasting on local radio, like Lonnie Johnson with Putney Dandridge on piano in Cincinnati, or Joe Pullem with his companion "Peachey" down in Texas, where Black Ace also had a regular radio spot.

"Turn yo' radio on, turn yo' radio on" sang Leadbelly just after the War, to a popular if unrecorded gospel song theme. "If you'd heard about it eighty years ago, you wouldn't have believed it would be on the radio." In the 1950s Alec Miller, or Sonny Boy Williamson II, was famous for his broadcasts to sell Sonny Boy's Corn Meal for Interstate Grocery on "King Biscuit Time," KEIA, Helena, Arkansas. At that time Blues Boy King (later shortened to B.B. King) was a disc jockey on the highly successful Memphis radio station, WDIA—they were just two of a great many blues singers who broadcast, whether briefly or regularly, on dozens of stations. The history of, in Johnny Strauss's phrase, "Radio Broadcasting Blues," has yet to be fully researched.

So, you may ask, why a book of radio scripts on the blues that have been transmitted by the British Broadcasting Corporation (BBC) over a period of more than half a century? It's a fair question, and one that needs an answer. But it also requires an explanation of the circumstances under which the broadcasts were given, as well as their relevance to the present.

# Turn Yo' Radio on

As I explained in my book *Blues Off the Record*, my first encounter with the blues was when, as a young teenager during World War II, I was working on a farm in Suffolk, England, adjacent to the establishment of a U.S. Army camp. Two Black servicemen on "fatigues" were "digging in" the camp, and as they did so sang and called the most strange and thrilling vocal sounds that I had ever heard. "You're hearing the blues," said my friend Stan. Almost certainly, they were "hollers" and "work songs" that I was hearing, but because of my reaction Stan introduced me to his collection of blues 78s, of which a surprising number had been issued in Britain. That experience opened up a whole new world of what I then considered folk music, and sent me on a lifelong quest for finding, hearing, and making available to others all that I could acquire on the blues, its background, its significance, and its exponents.

For many years after the Second World War, I was working on a book that was concerned with the meaning of blues lyrics that I and many friends who were also collectors had heard on blues records. In this I was helped greatly by meeting and interviewing visiting blues singers in the 1950s. These included, in the early years, the guitarists Josh White, Lonnie Johnson, and Big Bill Broonzy. When Big Bill died in 1958, Brownie McGhee and harmonica-player Sonny Terry filled the gap. New Orleans–style jazz band leader and trombonist Chris Barber employed blues singers and musicians as intermission artists, pianists Roosevelt Sykes, Little Brother Montgomery, and Champion Jack Dupree among them.

From my meetings with these and other singers and musicians I learned much, as well as from the concerts and parties at which they performed. But I became aware that while many listeners enjoyed the music they did not understand what the blues lyrics were about. From 1952 on I published articles regularly in jazz magazines, but especially in Albert McCarthy's *Jazz Monthly*, for as yet there were no blues journals. Blues was seen as a forerunner of—or influence on—jazz, and as a part of the jazz idiom. I was invited by Desmond Flower of Cassell Publishers to write my first book, a monograph, *Bessie Smith*, which was published in 1959. Paradoxically, it was published in a series of "Kings of Jazz," but it enabled me to emphasize the importance of the blues. I wanted to disengage it from jazz and argued for its recognition as a distinct genre in its own right.

On reflection, I realize that I had a certain missionary zeal in those days, and I was anxious to bring the "good news of the blues" to a large and international audience. Apart from the books and records I was obtaining, I owed much to the outstanding African American author Richard Wright; I used to meet him, and his expatriate friends, in Paris in the 1950s. They helped me with problems of comprehension in some blues lyrics and in confirming my interpretation of others. Wright was very enthusiastic and, to my delight, generously offered to write the introduction to the book that I was writing, which was eventually published under the title *Blues Fell this Morning: The Meaning of the Blues*, in 1960.

The research that I did for this, and every subsequent book, was specialized and had to be tailored, to some extent, to suit publication, for clearly they addressed an unknown public as well as the enthusiasts of blues and—to quite an extent—of jazz. Yet I was conscious that the readership was not hearing the sounds of the blues, so I put together a record to go with each book; the record *Blues Fell This Morning*, compiled with the help of collector friends like the late John Mastaka, was the first blues album to be wholly initiated and issued in Britain. Even so, it wasn't enough; I had the feeling that I was "preaching to the converted." To get the message to a larger audience and to bring the music I had written about to the ears of not only those who had purchased the books, there was just one answer: broadcasting the blues.

I wasn't the first to broadcast on blues and related music. Particularly important were the radio programs by Alan Lomax, on which he played many of the recordings made by his father John A. Lomax, as well as those he recorded himself for the Archive of Folk Music of the Library of Congress in Washington, D.C. His emphasis was on work songs, and occasionally he played a field holler or two, which gave me a thrill of recognition. Lomax played little in the way of blues, but the guitarist and blues band leader Alexis Korner, who was then a trainee program director for the BBC, sometimes acted as disc jockey, from 1958, broadcasting blues records. For my part, I was interested in the social contexts and functions of the blues as an idiom, as well as the playing, singing, and content of blues as recorded by many of its singers and musicians.

Opportunities to present my research to a larger audience by way of "the wireless" (as we called the radio in those days) came at first in the *Jazz Club* and *World of Jazz* programs of the BBC. In the mid-1950s, Jack Dabbs, who produced *Jazz Club*, gave me the chance to write the scripts and present broadcasts on such subjects as "Washboard Bands" and "Urban Blues"; later, Teddy Warrick produced a number of my programs. When they were acceptable to the jazz program producers, I presented programs on "Blues in Negro Society," "Blues as an Art Form," and others discursive themes.

# RECORDING IN THE NORTH AND THE SEGREGATED SOUTH

With the publication of *Blues Fell This Morning* in 1960, I was able to broadcast about blues as a separate tradition of black music. This was reinforced the same year by being able to do extensive fieldwork in the United States, for which I was supported by a grant from the U.S. State Department, and by funding from a Blues Association organized by Robert M. W. Dixon for the purpose of recording while on the trip. I was also commissioned by the BBC to do some recordings for eventual broadcasts. Accompanied by my wife, Valerie, and with a heavy tape recorder, I interviewed and recorded many blues singers in Detroit, Chicago, and St. Louis. We made our way south to Memphis, where we met up with Chris Strachwitz, who was planning to start his own record company (which would soon be known as Arhoolie Records). Together we traveled, interviewed, and recorded in Mississippi and Louisiana, and in Texas, where we were briefly joined by folklorist Mack McCormick.

In fact, I had been strongly advised against going to the South to do research. Richard Wright and his friends supported me, but they cautioned me too, as they feared that both Val and I could be in danger. I felt sure that I'd be safe with the backing of the State Department, but I was told by its representatives that if we were in trouble, they could do little to help. Black professors at Howard University in Washington, D. C., Sterling Brown and Rayford Logan, were clearly anxious on our behalf. It was alarming. The reason for these warnings was that racial discrimination was rife in the Southern states. As this was decades ago, I think I should briefly explain the circumstances.

During the last quarter of the nineteenth century, the tensions that followed the Reconstruction period after the Civil War had increased and state legislatures in the South began to pass what were widely known as "Jim Crow laws," to separate the races. "Segregation," as it was called, was initiated in the schools and soon applied to railroad cars and just about every public facility—from theaters to barber shops, saloons to toilets and water fountains. There was, in theory, a principle of "separate but equal" facilities, but such equality was largely ignored.

It was a period of racial oppression in the South, when "lynching," or the collective murder by a mob of real or suspected offenders, contributed greatly to the fear and demoralization that Black people suffered as a result of discrimination. There was, it seemed, a need among Black people for means of expression and of communication, for personal creativity and group identity, which wasn't dependent on White culture, but enabled Blacks to give voice to their experiences, aspirations, and emotions. Gospel music met that need in the churches—and the new Blues music met it on the front porches and in the "jukes" and "barrelhouses" of the settlements "across the tracks," where the railroads divided the Black sectors from those of the Whites.

After World War II it was anticipated that Segregation in the South might end, but it didn't. Although a decade later, a number of Southern States began to comply with the Supreme Court decision to desegregate education, others didn't and mixed groups of Civil Rights demonstrators came from the North in protest, generally experiencing a hostile reception. For some of them, their trips even ended fatally. In the Deep South, segregation in most facilities persisted, as I discovered for myself in 1960, when seeking blues singers to record and interview. It was a time of "sit-ins" and race riots, so sometimes we had to use rather devious means to conceal our intentions. Fortunately, we had no serious problems, and the experience was invaluable to me in gaining a better knowledge of the segregated environments in which the blues developed.

Back in England I put together two programs from the interviews and blues recordings I'd made. Produced by Anthony Smith, the programs had no speech apart from that of the interviewees; these programs broke new ground in broadcasting and garnered a strong and—with a few exceptions—very positive and enthusiastic audience reception. Slowly I transcribed the interviews in full, ordering them to create a narrative about the singers, their music, and the contexts in which they had lived and worked. It proved to be difficult, but my book *Conversation with the Blues*, published by Cassell in 1965, was the eventual outcome, with extracts from the recordings issued on a Decca album under the same title. Some of my recordings of singers were issued in limited editions, like those of Blind Arvella Gray and Buster Pickens on the Heritage record label, while others, including those of the pianists Henry Brown and Sunnyland Slim, were issued on the 77 label.

In the meantime, I pursued some of the thematic issues I'd encountered in my listening, including the possible significance of violence and sexuality in many recordings. This study appeared as the book *Screening the Blues: Aspects of the Blues Tradition* in 1968. Each of my books had prompted some programs that brought the themes of the music to a larger audience, but this book was more contentious. In those days, some unexpurgated blues recordings could not be played on the radio, although the publication of D. H. Lawrence's *Lady Chatterley's Lover* liberated writers to a degree, and made it possible for me to quote the lyrics of these songs in an extended, one-hundred-page chapter, "The Blue Blues." I was, however, able to broadcast on other themes discussed in the book, including those of the "Santa Claus Crave" and on playing "policy" (the numbers racket).

By that time, much else had happened. The American Folk Blues Festivals had begun in 1962 and the following year I broadcast an illustrated review of the concerts. Shortly after, the American Embassy, for whom I had given many public lectures, invited me to put together a large exhibition about the blues. With the help of many collectors on both sides of the Atlantic, I assembled literally hundreds of photographs, as well as publicity and music illustrations, that were displayed on large panels over the whole ground floor of the new embassy building in Grosvenor Square, London. The *Story of the Blues* exhibition of 1964 was well reviewed in the media and attracted many people, including a number of blues singers on tour in Europe, such as Little Walter and Lightnin' Hopkins. Brother John Sellers brought the entire Alvin Ailey dance company to view it, and it was also seen by the distinguished African American author Langston Hughes. To my great pleasure, Langston invited me to contribute to some programs he was producing with D. G. Bridson for the BBC; they included my two-part feature, "The Negro Sings," reprinted in the present volume as chapter 15, "Singing the Blues." (It should be noted here that it wasn't until the early 1970s that *Black* began to replace *Negro* as the acceptable term for an African American person.)

The extensive photographic coverage of the exhibition, and the series of public lectures that I gave at the American Embassy to accompany and explain it, gave me the idea of writing a fully illustrated history of the music under the same title. *The Story of the Blues* was finally published by Barrie and Rockliff in England in 1969 and later by Chilton in the

United States. To convey the sounds of more than sixty representative blues recordings made over more than four decades, I compiled two volumes—each comprised of two LPs—which were issued by CBS; these were eventually reissued on CD.

Meanwhile, much had changed in the States. In 1964, President Lyndon Johnson signed the Civil Rights Act in which discrimination in employment or in public facilities was forbidden. Of course it was contested, but the President pledged for Blacks in 1965—two years before the shocking assassination of Reverend Martin Luther King, Jr., and the subsequent race riots in over 200 cities. By this time, interest in the blues was growing, but the music itself had changed. The aging or death of the blues pioneers, many of whom I had met personally, the migration of many blues singers and musicians to the North, the rapid adoption of electric instruments, the expansion of the urban club scene, the taking up of blues by White musicians, the international popularity of Rhythm and Blues, Rock 'n Roll, and Soul Music: All of these appealed immensely to a new generation, both Black and White. It was clear to me that the personalized and mainly acoustic rural blues that expressed in music and in verse the feelings of a repressed minority was in decline. Yet, all the new popular music forms owed so much to the blues that had flourished for well over half a century. I enjoyed the new forms too, but I got more pleasure from, and was fascinated by, the "folk blues" as they were sometimes termed; how they came about, what they meant to the singers and their listeners, and the role they played in Black communities during the era of Segregation.

It was a busy period in my life. In 1964, I'd also taught a semester at the School of Architecture in the University at Kumasi in Ghana, and for several weeks taught a course on Afro-American Music in the Department of African Studies at the University of Ghana in Legon, Accra. In fact, I had taken tapes of recordings with me to Africa, and while I was there I wrote and broadcast a series of ten programs for Radio Ghana on Jazz and Blues. Throughout this period I recorded many examples of African drumming and other music of the rainforest peoples, but it was a field trip to the savannah regions of the extreme north of the country that introduced me to African string music and the playing of the *jelli*, or *griots*: pairs and groups of singer-musicians who worked in the markets, visited the villages, and were often in the employ of a tribal chief. The implications of this experience set me on a new course of inquiry, which, after several years, was published as *Savannah Syncopators: African Retentions in the Blues* as part of the *Blues Paperbacks* series that I edited for November Books and which were published from 1970 on, later by Studio Vista in Britain and Stein and Day in the United States. Based on this experience I was able to write and present two radio programs on "Music in Ghana," and others on a broader view of African Music. My interest in spreading the news and "sowing the seeds" was also exercised in shorter radio broadcasts for the BBC Overseas Service, on both blues and vernacular architecture.

# LOOKING BACK

For a long time I had been researching an aspect of blues history that seemed to have had little attention: How did it happen, and what came before the blues? In the recordings of singers in the 1920s, there were clues that I could trace back to the "songsters"—singers with a mixed repertoire of folk songs, ballads, minstrel popular and minstrel songs—of the late nineteenth century. A period of teaching at the University of California–Berkeley in 1983 came at an opportune time. I was also interested in the origins of gospel song and the sermons of black preachers. *Songsters and Saints: Vocal Traditions on Race Records* was the outcome of this, and was published by Cambridge University Press in 1984. Here were whole new areas and aspects of the blues about which, I believed, people should know much more. It was still the era of LP records, and I compiled four albums, which were issued by Saydisc in Britain, to illustrate these themes. But, as in earlier years, I felt that this was not enough. I planned a number of broadcasts illustrating the chapters on the secular music of the songsters. Derek Drescher, producer of many radio programs that I had enjoyed, was interested in the series, which was eventually broadcast under the general title *Before the Blues*. To my surprise and satisfaction it received the first Sony Radio Award for Best Specialist Music Program of 1988.

It was now nearly thirty years since I had written *Blues Fell This Morning*, and still there was very little else published on the content of blues. But of course, I now knew much more about the music and the African American culture that gave rise to it. I thought I should revise the book, correct some of the transcriptions, and also write additional material in broadly the same categories. Cambridge University Press was interested in publishing an anniversary edition, which duly appeared in 1990. Much blues had been issued on albums, so I didn't feel the need to compile another album or two, but the need to introduce a widening audience to the significance of blues lyrics in detail appealed to me and also to Derek Drescher, I was happy to learn. So I wrote and presented a series of ten programs, *Meaning in the Blues*, which was broadcast on the BBC Third Program channel in 1991, being well received by both the reviewers in the media and, judging from their letters, the listening audience as well.

During all this time I'd also been lecturing—as well as editing and writing books—on vernacular architecture, and in 1988 I had been contracted by Blackwell Reference Books to compile the *Encyclopedia of Vernacular Architecture of the World*. It was an exciting but monumental task, which involved traveling to all the continents seeking contributors. The work took some ten years, and the encyclopedia grew so large (two million words) that it was eventually taken over by Cambridge University Press, which published it in three volumes in 1997. All this meant that I had little time to write books or radio programs on black music, but I did do some occasionally, including a two-part feature on Robert Johnson in a series titled *"Whom the Gods Loved"* (they died young), which was broadcast several years before the eventual worldwide infatuation with the man and his music. Another two-part series marked the centenary of the birth of Huddie Ledbetter, the great songster better known as Leadbelly, who had been much admired by the folk music audience but, perhaps for that reason, had been virtually ignored by blues enthusiasts.

My early programs were entirely illustrated with 78-rpm records that I'd obtained through purchases from dealers, trades with other collectors, and, in a number of instances, discoveries made in street markets and junk shops. With the advent of LP records in the late 1950s and for the three decades following, the resources were opened up greatly by specialist blues and rock record labels. In Austria, the proprietor of a handful of record labels, Johnny Parth, reissued many early blues recordings on LPs. It was his intention to reissue in the chronological order of their recording (but not of the original issue sequences), everything which was listed in *Blues and Gospel Records*. This was a comprehensive discography of the recordings, issued or unissued, made between the 1890s and 1943, which was edited by Robert M.W. Dixon and John Godrich. Except for the instances where reissues had already been made of all the recordings by specific artists, such as Bessie Smith and Robert Johnson, Johnny Parth endeavored to make everything available on LPs. Halfway through he was challenged by the compact disc revolution, however; he accepted this and proceeded to reissue everything on CD through his Document Records label.

Many items that had previously been unknown were now issued on the Document label, while the *Blues and Gospel Records* discography revealed the titles of many hundreds that had been recorded but remained unreleased, as was the case with the majority of the Library of Congress recordings. It was now that Robert Macleod began the formidable and time-consuming task of transcribing the words of all the recordings now on Document, as well as those listed in Dixon and Godrich's discography. In effect, everything related to blues and gospel music that had been commercially recorded and issued over the first fifty years, including vaudeville on the one hand and preachers' sermons on the other, together with the largely unissued field recordings of the Library of Congress, were now listed and available on CD. With the additional attempt to transcribe all the lyrics on these records, an entirely new stage in blues documentation had been attained. This, I considered, should be recognized and applauded, while some of the many questions that arose from the evidence now available needed to be examined or discussed. Accordingly I proposed a further series of broadcasts, *Documenting the Blues*, which was transmitted in 1997, shortly before producer Derek Drescher retired; through interviews with Johnny Parth, Robert Macleod, and the discographer Howard Rye, who replaced the late John Godrich, I raised and received informed replies regarding some of these issues.

## THE BOOK OF THE BROADCAST SCRIPTS

Those who were teenagers when they listened to my early broadcasts in the 1950s are probably in their mid-sixties and retired by now, while many listeners to the three long series in the 1990s are certainly middle-aged. This means that whole new generations have grown up in the meantime that may not have had access to the recordings that I played and may find the whole subject rather difficult to follow. Very often they like the blues, but what they hear is that played by the predominantly white blues bands whose music is often competent but necessarily derivative.

During the past couple of decades, further changes have taken place in the blues as an African American music, and as a major influence on the forms and styles of other genres of popular music. There have been changes, too, in the audiences to which blues have been addressed, and in the performers who sing and play the blues. This has been a period that has witnessed the death of exceptional blues artists like Muddy Waters, Howling Wolf, and John Lee Hooker, and the decline or demise of scores of others. It has also seen the closing of many blues clubs and juke joint venues, and the apparent loss of the "front porch" singers, street corner guitarists, and barrelhouse pianists. But at the same time there has been a growing awareness of the wider audience for the music, to the extent that the blues has become a positive selling point and attraction for tourists in such cities as Memphis, Tennessee, or Jackson, Mississippi, and in literally hundreds of festivals and concerts throughout the United States and Europe.

Blues has had a long history of appreciation in Europe, where the fascination with the music was possibly stimulated, to some extent, by a physical detachment from its original environment. For those in the United States who were "too close" to that environment, the blues probably did not appear as anything special, and it was principally acknowledged, when it was recognized at all, as an influence on the development of jazz. But for many in Europe it was a remarkable music, and though it may seem surprising, several of the earliest books on the subject were written in Europe—not only in Britain, but by French, Dutch, Belgian, German, and Scandinavian authors, too. Likewise, the first blues journals were published in Europe, with *Blues Unlimited* commencing in 1961 nearly a decade before the first American blues journal, *Living Blues*. And, as I've noted above, the first and most enduring attempts at a complete discography of both pre- and postwar blues were made in Britain, and the first reissue of all previously unavailable blues recordings was Austrian in origin.

Writing on blues in specialist journals and books required features that would add to existing knowledge on the subject: informing the informed, or debating finer points and issues. Inevitably, this led to a restricted readership. It had always been my intention to use my radio programs to bring new aspects of research on the blues in its many and varied forms to a wider public, with the advantage that music could be played and heard to illustrate the observations that I made. Almost all of the recordings that I played were from my own collection, which grew over the years. The problem remained that most listeners would not have access to those recordings, except as they heard them on the radio; it seemed an insoluble problem. But now, all that has changed. Every recording that I played on radio, virtually without exception, is now available on CD. The trouble is that how they relate to each other, and to the development of the music over time, can be difficult to comprehend. That's why I have put together this collection of scripts that were broadcast to the general public over a period of half a century. To illustrate the scripts by examples, I have produced for Document Records a three-CD set of recordings (Document 32-20-10), issued under the same title.

I've explained the circumstances that led to some of my books and to the broadcasts that often served to illustrate them with recordings. Their appearance on radio reflected the development of the research that I undertook. In this collection I have rearranged the programs so that the sequence of their content is, in broad terms, chronological. Radio scripts for these kinds of programs have annotations that indicate where recordings are "faded in" and "faded out," as well as the length of time that the selected extracts were to be played. The spoken texts had also to be timed, in order that the programs exactly fitted the program length. This information is of little use to the reader, so I have omitted it from the texts herein. In some instances, a few sentences had to be shortened, or deleted, to fit the schedule or to accommodate radio announcements; these I have restored here. Certain programs have been omitted, such as the two-part features on Leadbelly and Robert Johnson, as well as broadcasts on individual performers such as Sonny Terry. As for the order of the book itself, I have introduced it with a broadcast that I presented in January 1967 on the Development of the Blues, which briefly outlines blues history. For the compilation of the programs, I have divided them into four parts, which I'll summarize here.

Part I, "Before the Blues," contains the scripts of the eight programs of the radio series of the same name, broadcast in 1988, in which the traditions and the functions of African

American song at the close of the nineteenth century and in the early twentieth century are discussed. After a brief review of blues and some of the music's most famous exponents, the possible retentions of African music in blues and forerunning musical genres is debated. Africans were enslaved to provide labor in the American South, and the next program considers the persistence of their work songs and field hollers. At the close of the nineteenth century, rural "musicianers" played for dances and social functions, for both Blacks and Whites, developing instrumental skills in the process. The music of the banjo players was mimicked in the minstrel shows, but black composers and country singers adapted the so-called coon songs and altered their meaning. White ballad traditions were assimilated, but black songsters sang of the heroes with whom they could identify. Touring vaudeville troupes and traveling "medicine shows," as well as entertainments in "tent shows," provided work for many black singers, whose repertoires included comic songs and social comment. The synthesis of all these traditions helped to shape the emerging blues.

In Part II, a number of the programs from the 1950s and '60s are included; these were sometimes presented in a "series of two," or as broadcasts that were longer than usual. A couple of programs from the *Documenting the Blues* series are also included in this section, "Blues, How Do You Do?" Here the new blues idiom is considered from various perspectives, including its relationship to the repertoire of the popular vocal quartets. Recordings made for the Library of Congress Archive of Folk Song (by the Lomaxes and others) included sessions with string and washboard bands, as well as with rural blues singers. Washboard bands provided one of the links to jazz, and jazz musicians accompanied many of the women singers who dominated the early commercial recording of blues in the 1920s. They are often referred to as "Classic Blues" singers, but I propose a less generalized classification.

Many of the women singers introduced a studied presentation in their performances that was seldom evident in the rural Southern blues. Nonetheless, blues was and is creative, and its singers and musicians were essentially artists, and this led me to consider blues as an art form. In this, as in the other programs, I liked to include both well-known singers and the lesser or little-known singers who were often good vocalists and musicians. While the development of the blues as song can be traced, as it is here in a couple of programs, its importance in black society for half a century cannot be overlooked. In addition to a discussion of its social role, an introduction to the content of the blues is included in a program related to the publication of the original edition of *Blues Fell This Morning* in 1960; but this leads us to the substance of the next section.

Part III addresses the significance of the blues in the years of its growth and maturity as an expression of African American society. *Meaning in the Blues* considers, in ten programs, some of the many themes that were expressed in the blues of numerous singers. Among them were blues songs about the difficult life of Blacks during the years of segregation. This, and other programs in the series, included extracts from interviews that I made with many singers in the rural South and the urban North. Their troubled experiences were the subject of the first program; migration and the perils of hoboing were the themes of the second. The risks of gambling and the promise of good fortune in voodoo and playing "policy" were sung about frequently, as were indulgences in drinking and the returns women made from "turning tricks."

Some efforts to get money were illegal, and led to jail sentences, though their representation in blues suggests a more profound significance. In the depression years, many black people suffered, but in the era of President Franklin D. Roosevelt, some benefited from his New Deal programs. Disasters struck many African American communities as well as individuals, as blues songs that range in subject from Mississippi River floods to silicosis indicate. Yet the majority of lyrics were sung about interpersonal relationships rather than in protest or even in humor, although all are to be found in the feeling that nurtures the blues.

In part IV, "Documenting the Blues," the outcome of research into the history of blues and the recording of the music is briefly discussed in a couple of broadcasts from the radio series of the same name. These are devoted to the diverse problems of compiling a reliable discography of commercial, field, and amateur recordings, and to the comprehensive CD reissue on Document records of some 16,000 recordings. The definition and expansion of what is known as blues, and what may be termed African American music, has bearing on these enterprises. Some of the principal researchers mentioned above who have contributed to our knowledge and appreciation are interviewed on a number of issues in these final programs. If the broadcasts had been published in the past, there would still have been the problem of how readers would be able to hear the music, but now they are all available on CD, including the accompanying Document Records set, and the scripts can be read along with them.

"Stand by," as the producer would say; the broadcasts are about to commence.

# Introduction:
# The Development of the Blues

First Broadcast: 1/29/67; Producer: Teddy Warrick

I n the mid-1960s, from London to Los Angeles, pop musicians and their fans were rediscovering the power of the blues. Blues revival groups like The Rolling Stones (in their original form), The Yardbirds, Paul Butterfield's Blues Band, and John Mayall's Bluesbreakers, influenced by Muddy Waters, Howlin' Wolf, and other stars of the Chicago blues scene, were introducing the music to a new audience. As one example, the Belfast group called Them, with Van Morrison taking the vocals and playing harmonica, recorded "BABY PLEASE DON'T GO" in 1964. The song was based on the singing and playing of a guitarist from Mississippi, Big Joe Williams, who first recorded it in 1935.

♪ (Decca F12018) 12/64,* London

♪ (Bluebird BB B6200) 10/31/35, Chicago, IL

Joe Williams was a rough, burly man, a natural rambler who hoboed throughout the United States. He started playing the blues for a living in the early teens, when he worked in the sawmill camps of Mississippi's Piney Woods and found he could earn enough change performing for the other millworkers. Williams spent a few years in the penitentiary, off and on, and it was probably while in one of them that he picked up this theme. It is a work song that tells of yet another man who has gone to the "county farm" (or prison camp). Willie Turner recorded an unaccompanied version of the song under the title "ANOTHER MAN DONE GONE" in 1950.

♪ (Folkways FE 4474) 1/50, Livingstone, AL

*Note: Throughout the discography information, all dates are abbreviated in the American style of Month/Day/Year or Month/Year when no day is known.

In a way, the story of this song summarizes the development of the blues, from work songs to a new folk music to international popularization. It also summarizes a few of the problems about the music, too. William's recording isn't in the traditional blues form; it has elements that suggest that it is a standardized song; it is only partly improvised—mainly in Joe Williams's own guitar accompaniment—and there is no way of knowing to what extent even the work song version may have been influenced by Joe Williams's original record (because it was recorded after Williams made his recording).

Blues has been subject to many generalizations, and in the short space of time I shall be forced to make many myself. If the blues is a form that is shared by a great proportion of the Black community in America, its strength and fascination lies in the individual creativity of its singers and musicians. Making broad generalizations does every individual artist a disservice. I say *artist* because blues is an art form with a history, by any calculations one that has lasted as long as that of the modern movement in painting and sculpture. But it is only recently that it has in any way been recognized *as* an art form, and so its undocumented origins are already obscure.

An important source for the blues were work songs. During slavery and for some time after, Blacks worked in gangs whose efforts—logging trees, chopping out weeds in the cotton rows, even straightening the lines on railroad tracks—were coordinated by a lead singer. As they worked, they kept time with their own sung responses—a pattern that, it has been suggested, is African in origin. Although the gang-labor methods largely died out with the dissolution of the plantations, they persisted even until the 1960s in the penitentiary farms of Texas and Mississippi. In the 1930s and 1940s, John and Alan Lomax, among others, visited many of these prisons, recording songs

♪ (Tradition1020) 1947, Parchman Farm, MS

like "Katy Left Memphis" as performed by work gangs, showing how this call-and-response style worked.

A man working with a team had to follow his leader; but a man working for himself could work at his own speed. He still sang as he worked, but there was no need to follow a strict pattern. He had time to think, to sing of his troubles and of the heat of the sun, and to embellish his own words. It became, and still is, the practice for field hands to invent personal ways of singing, using vocal ornamentation as a kind of autograph. The field hollers, as they are called, have the character of the blues. Charles Berry was a particularly talented singer in this style, and was recorded in 1942 by Alan Lomax on one of his many field trips, including this "Levee Camp Holler."

♪ (Library of Congress AFS L59) 7/24/42, Stovall, MS

2

# Introduction

When the blues took shape somewhere around the turn of the twentieth century, it had the shouted declarations of the field holler and the twelve-bar, three-line structure of the later ballads—with a difference. The blues was a music of leisure, a music that was accompanied by guitar, piano, or harmonica. It was a music with an emphasis on invention and expression, and the habit of repeating the first line and rhyming with the third gave the singer time to invent his verses. But the quality of the holler is not far away from the singing of Son House, who worked on the same Mississippi plantation, Stovall's Farm, decades ago, as can be heard on his "Dry Spell Blues."

♪
(Paramount 12990) 5/28/30, Grafton, WI

Gertrude "Ma" Rainey first heard the blues in Tennessee in 1902; W. C. Handy heard them in Mississippi in 1903. Blues appeared in text collections by 1910, and the first published blues came two years later; Hart Wand's "Dallas Blues" and W.C. Handy's "Memphis Blues." The titles emphasized the widespread distribution of the blues by that date, and also the Texas and Mississippi Delta regions, where it seems to have originated. Migrant workers, casual laborers, and hoboes carried the blues; street singers spread them in the cities. Many of the early singers were blind; their incapacity denied them other work, so they played in the streets for nickels and dimes. Blind Lemon Jefferson was among the greatest blues singers, relating to the Texas tradition as Charley Patton does to Mississippi. But his technique was different: Instead of a growling voice against a steady rhythm, Jefferson sang high and piercingly, a technique suited to singing in the streets of Dallas, where he was a familiar figure until his death in 1930. His guitar acts as a second voice, answering the vocal in interpretative arpeggios.

♪
(Okeh 8455) 3/14/27, Atlanta, GA

In one of his best-known recordings, "Matchbox Blues," he sings "I'm standin' here wonderin' will a matchbox hold my clothes? I ain't got so many matches but I got so far to go." He continues, "I got a gal 'cross town she crochet all the time," and, addressing her, "If you don't quit crocheting, you gonna lose your mind." "I wouldn't mind marryin'," he sings, "But Lord, settlin' down I'm gonna act like a preacher so I can ride from town to town."

Jefferson's blues is a series of comments and, sometimes, personally addressed remarks, put together with vivid imagery; as, for instance, his line, "I'm standin' here wonderin' will a matchbox hold my clothes?" This is the blues in its maturity: the pithy expression of a creative artist who speaks through his blues of his hopes, his frustrations, and his observations on life.

Yet the blues songs that were first on record were not like this; they were compositions intended for the vaudeville stage.

♪
(Black Swan 2032) 11/20,
New York City

Lucille Hegamin's "THE JAZZ ME BLUES" is typical of this style, and was one of the first blues songs of any kind put on wax. It would be four years before any recordings were made of the rural folk blues.

In the early years of blues recordings, the emphasis was on the women singers who toured the Negro theaters in the main cities and worked in front of a row of candles in tent shows and barns throughout the South. Among the first of these was Gertrude Rainey, always known as "Ma" Rainey—a squat, even ugly, woman with a majestic voice. She sang low, impressive blues about men and moonshine against the ragged music of her Georgia Jazz Bands. Rainey's pupil was the incomparable Bessie Smith; together they defined what has been termed—erroneously, I think, as I've pointed out previously—"classic blues," blues to which they brought the conscious artistry of the stage. Tall and statuesque, Bessie Smith had an immense voice—necessary in the days when the only aid a singer had was a megaphone—and her studied inflections were an inspiration to the jazz musicians who worked with her or heard her in the touring shows and the Black Belt clubs. She was dubbed the Empress of the Blues, and she had the ability to project from the depths of her own tragic life the feeling of the blues into the even direst pop song, as can be heard on her recording of "BABY DOLL."

♪
(Columbia 14147-D)
5/4/26, New York City

Although jazz musicians were probably more influenced by the classic blues singers than they were by the country blues bands, they were imitating the vocal qualities of the blues in much the same way. Blues singers were more in demand than the old-style square-dance groups to provide music in the gin mills and juke joints, the shacks and bars that passed as dance halls in the rural South. Their instruments were often homemade: A jug could serve as a bass, a washboard as a rhythm section, and harmonicas and kazoos augmented the guitars and mandolins. The juke bands played any kind of music, including those blues that had become popularized by recording, like "KANSAS CITY BLUES," which was recorded by the Memphis Jug Band, among others.

♪
(Victor 21185) 10/19/27,
Atlanta, GA

In the more remote districts the men who reinforced the levees, sawed the timber, and maintained the railroads lived in "company towns" comprised of rough shacks. The companies maintained community saloons where the bars were planks supported by kegs of liquor and the only other piece of furniture was a piano. These were called "barrelhouses," and they gave their name to a powerful, rolling style of blues, ideal for dancing. The sawmill pianists hardly cared if the piano was out of tune: They just played louder, and if they couldn't

♪
(Vocalion 1447) 9/5/29,
Chicago, IL

♪
(Bluebird 88909) 6/26/41,
Chicago, IL

♪
(Score SLP 4022) 8/15/45,
Los Angeles, CA

sing the blues, shouted instructions to the dancers. A typical example is "HEAD RAG HOP," by Romeo Nelson.

Barrelhouse, played to a rolling left-hand bass with a rhythm of often eight beats to the bar, was one of the first blues forms to be popular in the North. In the city tenements it was ideal for the parties that the migrants from the Southern states frequently held. Chicago and Detroit became the melting pot for the blues, as Blacks, seeking work from many states, crowded into their ghettoes. During the 1930s, the guitarists, harmonica players, pianists, and singers of numerous regions were thrown together. Perhaps they felt the sense of security of being part of a group in unfamiliar surroundings; at any rate, the music of the Northern cities was generally collective in character. For example, in Washboard Sam's 1941 recording of "LEVEE CAMP BLUES," made in Chicago, there are echoes of the past in the words about the levee camp and the washboard rhythm, but the electric guitar and the assertive sound is characteristic of the Northern, urban styles of the late 1930s.

The Second World War created a gap of several years in recording, due to the rationing of the raw materials used in making records. After the war, the blues appears to have a different character. But it's an artificial break, because the music had continued to develop.

Between the wars the record companies were controlled by a few concerns based in the North, but in the postwar years a great many small record labels sprang up in the Southern states and on the West Coast, bringing local blues to a large audience. Radio programs that featured blues for eight hours at a stretch made the latest Chicago blues available to the most rural areas, and amplified instruments were soon being played everywhere—or at least, everywhere that had a power supply. And there was a reverse process: Southern bluesmen were being heard through radio programs in the North, and there was a renewed interest in what was soon known by the émigrés as "Down Home" blues. Their themes were sometimes down home, too: Lightnin' Hopkins, who began recording in his home city of Houston in the 1940s, could sing of a "SHORT HAIRED WOMAN" who bought "rats" of artificial hair, a subject that would have been taboo in Chicago.

From the late 1950s, Lightnin' Hopkins played acoustic guitar in the folk clubs of San Francisco, toured the college campuses, sang at the Newport Folk Festival, visited Britain and Europe, and made a couple of dozen albums. He was recognized as a "folk blues" singer, and in the process became a little removed from the Negro community. It was the famous Leadbelly who provided the ideal of the Negro folk singer for white audiences. Later, Big Bill Broonzy found that the songs of his childhood went down better with white audiences than did the modern Chicago blues. A succession of blues singers have been assimilated by the commercial world of "'folk music," and a generation of white imitators have mimicked them. However well-meaning, the imitations are often grotesque caricature as crude as any minstrel parody. Dave Van Ronk was a popular blues "revivalist," and in his performance of "St. James Infirmary" he gave a rather exaggerated version of a blues vocal performance.

♪
(Kicking Mule KM177)
1981, possibly Chicago, IL

Such plagiarism substituted strained voices for deep ones, crudity for simplicity. But the imitators soon discarded the folk forms. They galloped through the history of the blues in search of novelty: The techniques of the blues have become commonplace, incorporated into the playing of the derivative rhythm and blues groups of white college students, while the structure of the twelve-bar blues has been adopted by popular song. The imitations have often been successful and some of the younger musicians, who have felt themselves to be social misfits, have found in the blues a borrowed form of expression that they can share with an underprivileged minority. "I was born in Chicago in 19 and 41," sings Paul Butterfield on his original blues, "Born in Chicago."

♪
(Elektra EKL 294) 5/66,
Chicago, IL

Blues has not come out unscathed from the pressures of these interests: Its major artists were absorbed by the folk fad, and its idiom swallowed by popular song. But the blues has been particularly resilient in the past, changing as black society itself changes. Blues singers have turned to gospel song for inspiration, with their imitators, needless to say, in hot pursuit. Now it uses the mannerisms of gospel song in the vocals, while the instrumental techniques have become more elaborate, even florid, with some features in common with modern jazz. Junior Wells reflects these new influences on his performance of "Early in the Morning," recorded in Chicago in 1965. It is different—but it is still the blues.

♪
(Delmark DL612) 1956,
Chicago, IL

# I
## Before the Blues

# 1

# Blues in Retrospect

**First Broadcast: 11/4/1987; Producer: Derek Drescher**

♪
(Col. 14075-D) 5/6/25,
New York City

For most jazz lovers, Bessie Smith has always represented—as much as one person can—the art of blues singing. She was able to take a song like W. C. Handy's 1914 composition "Yellow Dog Blues" and invest it with such profound meaning that it transcended the author's rather contrived device to cast it in the form of a letter. In the publicity phrase of her day, the 1920s, she was the unchallenged Empress of the Blues. Bessie Smith was a professional entertainer, a veteran of the black traveling and vaudeville shows. Even if her technique was partly intuitive, it was molded through years on the boards and was largely deliberate. Her kind of singing is usually termed "Classic Blues."

Yet there was another side to the blues, most jazz enthusiasts realized: a tradition that was rooted in black American working-class culture. For the first blues fans, a convict epitomized this folk tradition. He was discovered in the 1930s on a Louisiana prison farm, and recorded by John A. Lomax, for the Archive of Folk Song of the Library of Congress. His name was Huddie Ledbetter, though he was always called Leadbelly.

Although "Yellow Dog Blues" was based on a twelve-bar structure, it was conceived as a song, with introduction, verse, and chorus. Leadbelly's "Alberta," however, took what we consider to be a traditional blues form. Usually, blues verses are twelve bars in length, with a standard chord progression and a three-line stanza in which the first line is repeated and rhymed with a third. Leadbelly

♪
(Bluebird B8559)
6/15/40, New York City

was a fine blues singer, but he knew a vast range of other songs. His apparently inexhaustible repertoire, his magnificent voice, and his mastery of the twelve-string guitar—not to mention his impressive build—drew the admiration of both jazz supporters and folk music scholars. They lionized him, and when he died in 1949 the authors of one jazz history wrote that "the traditional blues as a living, creative force, had come to an end."

As it happened, however, a young man recently up from Mississippi, still known by his childhood nickname of Muddy Waters, was recording in Chicago at just about that time. Among his first recordings was "I FEEL LIKE GOIN' HOME," which featured Waters on guitar and vocals and "Big" Crawford on bass, for the small Chicago-based Aristocrat label.

♪
(Aristocrat 1305) 1948, Chicago, IL

Muddy Waters was on the threshold of his career. His vibrant guitar playing may not have accorded with the image of the folk blues, but he was one of a group of migrants from the South who were to give a whole new thrust to blues music as a "living, creative force"—one that, eventually, was to have a profound influence on the popular music of the world. Muddy Waters, Howlin' Wolf, Little Walter, Elmore James, and others shaped a form of blues entertainment in the clubs and bars of Chicago and the urban North that was powerful and confident and reflected the rising aspirations of young Blacks.

♪
(Trumpet 146) 5/62, Jackson, MS

"DUST MY BROOM," by Elmore James with his Broomdusters, recorded in 1962, gives the essential Chicago blues band sound. Although he had a full band that played electric instruments, Elmore James modeled his searing approach to blues on that of the ill-fated singer Robert Johnson, whose recordings—made shortly before he was murdered in 1938, at the age of twenty-seven—were extremely influential. Johnson came from the Delta formed by the confluence of the Mississippi and Yazoo Rivers. About 200 miles north of the rivermouth delta of the Mississippi, it's flat and featureless, but it's fertile black-land country where both cotton and the blues flourished. It was where, according to W. C. Handy's song, that "the Southern crossed the Yellow Dog": the Southern Railroad tracks crossed those of the Yazoo-Delta ("Yellow Dog") line.

Until the 1960s, the South was a segregated society where Blacks were socially and economically disadvantaged. Blues offered them some release from their frustration and humiliation. Blues, many blues singers say, "is a feeling." It's also a vehicle for projecting feelings or for canalizing them. And it's a form for doing so.

♪
(Vocalion 03601) 11/27/36, San Antonio, TX

Robert Johnson's "WALKIN' BLUES" personifies the blues: He sings of blues as a state of mind, using the blues form to communicate it. He makes the guitar strings wail by sliding a bottleneck on them as he tells of his encounter with the blues.

The focus of the blues is almost invariably the singers themselves—their relationships, emotions, and experiences, real or imagined. Blues singers may sing for themselves, but they perform for their communities too, articulating the feelings of other blacks, often in vivid and poetic use of black idioms.

In the process of research, many singers of great quality and ability, and hundreds of performances of a haunting and affecting beauty, have been uncovered. Just one example is "Big Road Blues," recorded in 1928 by Tommy Johnson, a farmhand from Jackson, Mississippi, and sensitively complemented by another local guitarist, Joe McCoy.

♪
(Victor 21279) 2/3/28, Memphis, TN

To some extent Tommy Johnson fit the stereotype of the blues singer: He was gifted, but he was dissolute. He was an inveterate wanderer, taking casual work and playing music in the evenings and weekends at local juke joints. Around 1915, he was playing in the Mississippi Delta area, where he met up with the remarkable group of musicians who worked on the cotton plantations around Drew, Mississippi. Foremost was Charley Patton; born over a century ago, he had a "heavy" voice, much admired by other singers, and a remarkable sense of dynamics. The song "34 Blues" was recorded in 1934, the year of his death, but this personalized account of the effects of the Depression conveys something of his power and the compelling rhythms of his playing.

♪
(Vocalion 02651) 1/31/34, New York City

We can trace a chain of connections from Muddy Waters and Elmore James to Robert Johnson and back to Tommy Johnson and Charley Patton. It's tempting to think of Patton, Johnson, and their contemporaries hammering out the first blues in the Delta. And it's true that some of the earliest references to blues, including W. C. Handy's, relate to Mississippi. But there were parallel blues traditions in Texas and Louisiana, which may well be as old, and others in Georgia and other Southeastern states.

Blues did not arise out of nothing; nor I suspect, was it the sole invention of a few sharecroppers around Drew, Mississippi. I believe that our ideas on the origins of blues need closer scrutiny, and that the types of song that preceded it need examination. Moreover, I feel that the emphasis we have placed on the blues, in the past twenty-five years or so, has drawn attention from other song types that functioned in black communities in the South. The time is overdue for a revision of the place of the stage singers, of the collector-composers, and the so-called folksingers.

# 2

# Echoes of Africa

First Broadcast: 11/11/87; Producer: Derek Drescher

♪
(Testament T-2208)
11/24/63, Como, MS

**B**lues singer Mississippi Fred McDowell recorded a century after the emancipation of the slaves. His style of blues has often been termed "archaic"; to some it seemed that it went back to the very roots of the blues—back, in fact, to Africa. But if there are African retentions in Fred McDowell's blues, "Waiting For My Baby," what are they? How did they get there, and from where in the continent?

Writers on jazz have always been confident that their music goes back to Africa. For authority they have depended heavily on the anthropologist Melville Herskovits and the musicologist Father A. M. Jones. Herskovits claimed that the slaves came mainly from the West African rainforest: They were Yoruba from Nigeria, Fon from Dahomey, or Ashanti from Ghana. Jones, who was much quoted by Gunther Schuller in his book *Early Jazz*, analyzed the drumming of the Ewe of Togo and Ghana. When I went to West Africa in the mid-1960s, I was thrilled to hear, and

♪
(Document 32-20-1)
4/30/64, Legon, Ghana

record, on Ewe drum orchestras, playing "Abkekor" music, led by Ladzekpo on *atsimeru* drum.

There's no doubt that rainforest music did survive the diaspora when slaves were shipped to the Americas. Ashanti and Ewe captives were dispatched to Surinam, in what is now Guyana in South America, where African-based religion and customs, stories, and crafts still exist. The exciting multilayered rhythms of the drums of Ewe music can be directly compared with an

♪
(Folkways FE4502) 1950s, Surinam

example of "DJUKA DRUMS" recorded in Surinam in the 1950s by the Djukas, descendants of escaped slaves.

My Ashanti students at the Department of African Studies at the University of Ghana were interested in these links to their own traditional music. But they literally collapsed in laughter when I played them examples of jazz, which they found rhythmically elementary, and of blues, to which they couldn't relate at all. I had to agree; the music of the rainforest was far removed from that of the Deep South.

♪
(CBS.52799) 5/64, Navrongo, Ghana

A month later, I was working on a field project in the savannah grasslands several hundred miles to the north. One night I recorded a "RING DANCE" of Mamprusi tribesmen gathered in a slowly moving circle, counterclockwise around a central drummer. The dancers wore anklets that jangled; they blew whistles, shouted, and sang. My recordings of the Mamprusi tribesmen were strongly reminiscent of the recent recordings of drum-and-fife trios in Mississippi and Tennessee. Here, I thought, there did seem to be a link between African music and North American. Although some of their instruments were homemade, the drums of these country bands were of a familiar type: bass and snare drums. Perhaps they were a regressed form of military band? Or perhaps they picked up the instruments when the Southern regiments were disbanded after the Civil War? As there's no record of these bands before the end of the nineteenth century, we're left in doubt as to their origins.

♪
(London, LTZ-K15209) 1959, Como, MS

One such trio, the Young Family of Mississippi, was recorded by Alan Lomax in 1959 performing the traditional song "HEN DUCK." Yet there's a problem. During the slavery period, Blacks in the South were usually forbidden to play drums; Congo Square, in New Orleans, was a rare exception. Drum rhythms, though, probably persisted in the foot stamping of the plantation ring dances. Also danced counterclockwise, they were accompanied with complex hand clapping and "patting," beating the resonant parts of the body. Early travelers in the South often described the awesome sounds of the ring dance coining from the slave quarters. They continued until the late 1930s; a rare example, "MY SOUL IS A WITNESS,"was recorded in 1934, in Jennings, Louisiana, performed by Austin Coleman and companions.

♪
(Library of Congress LBC 1) 7/34, Jennings, LA

There may well be a connection between the African ring dancers and the drum-and-fife bands, but neither were playing anything like the blues. It was while I was on the same field trip, in 1964, that I glimpsed an answer to the problem of African retentions in blues. Two Fra-fra musicians, one

14

playing a monochord fiddle, the other throwing a calabash rattle between his hands to provide a bass rhythm, were playing in the village of Nangodi where I was working, close to the border with Burkina Faso (which was then called Upper Volta). They were *jelli*, or in the French term, *griots*: professional historians, satirists, praise singers. They sang "YARUM"—salt songs—in praise of the chief; these were called salt songs, they explained, because salt was good to taste.

Kunaal and Sosira—these Fra-fra musicians—brought back vivid memories of two singers I'd recorded a few years before in Louisiana, James "Butch" Cage and Willie Thomas. Butch Cage played fiddle, like Sosira, holding it low against his chest. Willie strummed the guitar, not with the rhythmic complexity of Kunaal's calabash, but performing the same function. Listening to the *griots*, I recalled Butch sawing at the strings, bothering the notes, repeating his phrases while he and Willie sang in the same parched voices, with descending vocal lines. But what *they* were playing *was* blues, the "FORTY-FOUR BLUES."

Griots or jelli, like Kunaal and Sosira, are to be found across two thousand miles of arid savannah, from Senegal to Chad. Well north of the forests, there isn't wood for making big drums; instead, gourds and calabashes are used for drums and for making small stringed instruments.

They are bowed like Sosira's, or plucked, like the *halam*, which generally has three to five strings. The instruments are fretless, though sometimes a player puts one finger under the string to act as a fret. Such stringed instruments are not found in the rainforest regions. Yacouba Bukari recorded "KOUCO SOLO," played on the *kouco*, a boat-shaped form of the halam, in Mali.

The short notes and staccato rhythms of the kouco are very like those of the banjo, the one authenticated African instrument widely used in North America. Eighteenth and nineteenth century writers—including President Thomas Jefferson, himself a Virginia plantation and slaveowner—described the making and playing of the *bania*, or *banjar*. Wrote Jefferson, "The instrument proper for them is the 'banjar,' which they brought hither from Africa, and which is the original of the guitar, its chords being precisely the four lower chords of the guitar." One hundred and fifty years after Jefferson's observation, a Virginia farmer and old-time square dance musician, John Lawson Tyree, played "HOP ALONG, LOU" on the banjo in similar fashion.

Black musicians played fiddle and banjo for Whites as well as Blacks, even in the slave period. With the suppression of drummers, the string players from the Savannah regions were

♪
(CBS 52799) 5/64,
Nangodi, Ghana

♪
CBS 52799) 8/9/60,
Zachary, LA

♪
(Nonesuch H-72074)
c. 1973, Gao, Mali

♪
(BRI 24088) n.d., Virginia

in favor, and soon dominated; they passed their skills on to their sons. Any retentions from Africa in the blues are not intuitive; they're not "in the blood." They are cultural, handed down through successive generations in a society that was largely, but not wholly, segregated from that of Whites.

This applies, I believe, to the so-called blue notes. It has often been suggested that they arose from the meeting of African pentatonic with European diatonic scales, leading to a flattening of the thirds and sevenths. But such notes are widely employed among the jelli musicians, and the influence, I would suggest, is far more direct. So is the use of the falling contour in melodies: the high attack to a vocal phrase and the descending steps of the vocal line. One example can be heard in a recording of Makai, a griot in Niger, playing the three-string *gouroumi* lute to accompany his singing of "BABAI."

♪
(CBS 52799) 3/7/63,
Dogondoutchi, Niger

It wasn't until the late nineteenth century that cheap guitars became widely available and began to replace the banjo. They allowed the players to achieve, by sliding the strings, the desired flattened and "bent" notes, with their strong associations with the human voice. When Hawaii was annexed to the United States in 1898, the Hawaiian style of guitar playing with steel bars laid on the strings became popular. Black musicians may have borrowed the technique or developed it independently. The composer W. C. Handy heard a Mississippi guitarist using a bird bone as a slide as early as 1903. Fred McDowell used the same technique on his performance of "Waitin' for My Baby," with his guitar tuned to an open chord, which opened the program. His subtle rhythms, the pulsating beat, the bent notes on the crying strings, the repeat phrase in vocal and guitar, and the descending contour of his vocal line: In these he revealed a cultural inheritance, which, I believe, had its origins in the music of the griots of the West African savannah.

# 3

# Go Down, Old Hannah

First Broadcast: 11/18/87; Producer: Derek Drescher

**I** have discussed the extent to which African retentions could be traced in blues expression on the banjo and guitar, and in blues vocals. But Blacks were not brought to North America to play music; they were there for one purpose only—to provide slave labor on the plantations of the South. Although the Africans who were captured and shipped across the Atlantic to the Americas may have numbered several millions, recent analyses suggest that fewer than half a million slaves were imported to North America before the Civil War. That's less than 3 percent of the total number of Blacks living in the United States today. The slaves were encouraged to have large families so they could stock the plantations with children who would be slaves, too. They learned the skills and traditions of their parents and grandparents—including the custom of accompanying work with song.

Many observers of slave life—like the English actress, Fanny Kemble—described hearing the slaves performing work songs. One diarist wrote, "While at work in the cotton fields the slaves often sing some wild, simple melody, by way of mutual cheer, which usually ends in a chorus in which all join with a right, hearty will, in a key so loud as to be heard from one plantation to another." John Lomax recorded a group of convicts at Parchman State Farm prison in 1947 singing one of these work songs, called "ROSIE."

♪
(Nixa NJL 11) 1947,
State Penitentiary,
Parchman, MS

Work songs like this were used to set the pace for loading steamboats, packing cotton bales with the jackscrew, shucking

**17**

corn, rowing boats, hoeing the fields—and in fact for every other activity that called for coordinated labor. That applied to virtually every job that the field slaves had to do. The tradition was again an African one, but it, too, did not come from the rainforests—the cultivation of forest fruits doesn't require this kind of synchronized work. But it *is* characteristic of the savannah regions, where crops such as rice or groundnuts are cultivated by long rows of workers who sing in unison. One acted as a lead singer, calling the words of a song; the company of farmers responded in chorus, keeping the time of their flashing hoes. A group of Diola rice farmers were recorded in the Casamance region of Southern Senegal singing a "RICE FIELD WORKSONG," while collectively using their hoes.

♪ (Folkways FE4323) c. 1963, Casamance, Senegal

Slavery, of course, was abolished after the Civil War, and in theory work songs should have gone with it. But they persisted where occupations required coordinated work. One that survived until recently was "track lining." Crews of men armed with "Jim Crow bars" straightened the railroad tracks that had warped in the Southern heat. Singing to the lead of the section boss, they levered them with bars that were made by the firm of James A. Gandy, giving them the name of "gandy-dancers." In a recording made on location near Demopolis, Alabama, the section boss, Joe Warner, sings snatches of work song, "LET's MOVE IT," while the captain of this branch of the Frisco line gives directions to the gandy-dancers from a distance.

♪ (Folkways FA 2659) n.d., Demopolis, AL

Inevitably, the kind of work undertaken influenced the way a work song was employed. But the conditions of slavery, both in working and in a brutal discipline, continued in the penitentiaries of Louisiana, Mississippi, Arkansas, and Texas. These prisons operated immense farms that were, until the 1960s, cultivated by gang labor. There are thirteen farms in the system of the Texas Department of Corrections still, with around 12,000 prisoners, of whom a disproportionate number are Black. In the 1930s, many black work gangs were recorded in the prisons, on field equipment for the Library of Congress. A recording was made in Brazoria, Texas, by Clyde Hill and gang. The pace is slow: In the oppressive heat and humidity of the Brazos River bottomlands, it was important for the lead singer to establish a steady rate that the men could maintain throughout the working day.

Leader Clyde Hill sang to the white captain, "Captain I'm due in Seminole, Okla—," and the group responded by completing the name of the state: "—homa." This was followed by "Captain, I'm gonna walk and talk with Al—," and the chorus sang "—berta," hanging on the name, and following it with,

(Library of Congress AFSL3) 4/16/39, Clemens State Farm, Brazoria, TX

"Oh, in them long, hot summer days. . . ." One man cried, "Go down, Old Hannah", using a slave name for the sun; with the sun down, the day's work would be over.

This seems to have been an extremely old work song, sung in the call-and-response unison style often described in accounts of plantation life. But new forms developed. In the 1950s, a team of four men were recorded "double cutting"—that is, standing in pairs on either side of a tree, and synchronizing their axes dangerously to the complicated rhythms of their song as they felled the tree. They were recorded on the Parchman, Mississippi prison farm, "a great institution in a great state," as a sign outside the prison proclaimed when I was there in the 1960s! Rejoicing in nicknames like Little Red, Tangle Eye, and Hard Hair, they sang the syncopated lines of "KATY LEFT MEMPHIS," exhaling sharply with their efforts.

(Tradition 1020) 1947, Camp No. 10, State Penitentiary, Parchman, MS

Not all work songs were collective; there were solo songs too. Hollers, as they were called, were much more free in their structure. With the breakup of the plantations after the Civil War, many slaves were allocated the standard "forty acres and a mule" (though many more were not). Those who had them set about farming their smallholdings, singing hollers as they worked. The custom of singing them seems also to have stemmed from Africa, and was common throughout the South until the 1940s; and the introduction of mechanization. It can be heard in a recording of a "LUCKY HOLLER," by a field hand named Ed Lewis, in Lambert State Penitentiary, Mississippi, in 1959. Lewis's singing has the same introspective character and attenuated elaborations to the vocal line as the traditional African song.

(Atlantic LP 1346) c. 7/59, Lambert State Penitentiary, MS

One of the most popular blues singers on record in the 1920s was Alger "Texas" Alexander, who came from Jewett, Texas, not far from the prison farms. There's a rumor that he was an inmate of one of them, and certainly work songs are frequently recalled in his blues. He never attempted to play an instrument, so the Okeh record company employed Lonnie Johnson and Eddie Lang to accompany him—somewhat uncertainly, it must be admitted. He disregarded them anyway, and followed his own time as he sang his "PENITENTIARY MOAN," with verses about "Uncle Bud" Russell, the "long-chain" man who brought convicts to the Texas prisons. Russell was notorious for the beatings he administered, which were said to make the Red River flow red with blood.

(Okeh 8640) 11/16/28, New York City

Prison farms were known to many blues singers, and so were the chain gangs, in which shackled prisoners were leased out to the county for road or bridge building. Texas Alexander's cousin, Lightnin' Hopkins, told me about his experience on the chain gang in his slow, laconic fashion:

> Working out on the road gang—it ain't no easy thing, I tell ya. Every evenin' when you come in they would chain you, they'd lock you with a chain aroun' your leg. Lock you up to this post, next one to that post; all the way down, till they lock *all* o' ya up. So therefore you'd be locked that night, and next mawnin' when you get ready to go out to eatin' breakfast, man come to unlock you. You go out, eat your breakfast, catch the mules, hitch the wagon, git right on down to the work. Two hundred days . . . that was a long time.

Another long-term prisoner was Robert Pete Williams, an inmate of the Louisiana State Penitentiary at Angola, where Leadbelly had been a prisoner in earlier years. Williams was serving a life sentence for shooting a man when he was recorded singing about his unsuccessful appeal to the pardon board. His "PARDON DENIED AGAIN" is a long, freely extemporized song that has the extended, meandering, loosely structured character of the holler, held together with his finely poised guitar playing. The conventional blues form wasn't far away.

♪
(Folk-Lyric 109)
1959, Angola State
Penitentiary, LA

# 4

# Old Country Stomp

First Broadcast: 11/25/87; Producer: Derek Drescher

♪
(Fly-Mat/FLYLP 259)
6/13/36, State Farm,
Lynn, VA

In 1936, veteran banjo player Jimmie Strothers was recorded for the Library of Congress at the Lynne State Farm in Virginia performing a banjo solo he called "THOUGHT I HEARD MY BANJO SAY," a typical country breakdown, known in many white hillbilly versions as "Cripple Creek." It was just one item in the shared tradition of rural dance music known to both Whites and Blacks.

In the slavery period and after, black musicians played for white dances, learning the tunes and earning a little "spending change." A boy could make a banjo out of a gourd, pan, and broomstick in the days when playing music—rather than the phonograph or the "ghetto blaster"—was every black child's ambition. If he hadn't an instrument, he improvised one. Wash Wilson, an ex-slave, recalled that "they'd take a buffalo horn and scrape it out to make a flute. That sure be heard a long ways off. They take a mule's jawbone and rattle a stick across the teeth." Or they would make some other instrument. "In my childhood I saw many sorts of 'quills,'" wrote Thomas Talley of Fisk University in 1920. "The quills were short reed pipes closed at one end, made from cane found in our southern canebrakes." They were "whittled with a jack-knife and then wedged into a wooden frame, and the player blew them with his mouth."

♪
(Vocalion 1230)
6/13/28, Chicago, IL

Henry Thomas, a Texas singer who was born in 1874, recorded what he called an "OLD COUNTRY STOMP," calling sets and giving

21

instructions to the dancers in couplets, accompanying himself on both guitar and "quills".

Calling sets to the tunes of "Sourwood Mountain" or "Old Joe Clark" was common to the dances of both races. But black dancers were noted for their solo dancing, "cutting capers" in bewildering, loose-limbed jigs—the nineteenth-century equivalent of breakdancing. During his famous tour of America, Charles Dickens witnessed in New York the spectacular black dancer Juba, whose performance was electrifying as he did the "double-shuffle, single-shuffle, cut and cross-cut, snapping his fingers, rolling his eyes, turning in his knees, presenting the backs of his legs to the front, spinning on his toes and heels," dancing, as Dickens observed, "with wire legs, and no legs at all." Sometimes solo dancers performed on a wooden box to amplify the drumming of their feet, or they spread sand over the floorboards to do a shuffle. Some dances imitated bird movements, like the "buck and wing," which involved holding the neck stiffly while hopping with syncopated steps and flapping outstretched arms to "stop time."

♪
(Reprise R2012)
6/8/61, Houston, TX

Mance Lipscomb, a Texas sharecropper who was born in 1895, played for dances since he was a boy. He recorded an instrumental called "BUCK DANCE," created to accompany the buck and wing. Of course, he couldn't read music; his music just came to him, as he told me, "from the air." Mance's background was typical of his generation, with roots in his music that went well back into the nineteenth century. In spite of his technical accomplishment, he was strictly a weekend musician. For Blind Blake it was different: As a sightless musician, he had to live by his playing. In spite of his disability, he traveled from Florida to Detroit by way of Georgia and Kentucky, playing for construction camp dances, perfecting his relaxed technique by competing with other musicians. His "DRY BONE SHUFFLE" is a typical dance instrumental, with the suspensions and stop-time that permitted displays of inventive footwork. Clift Moore accompanied Blake with clappers made from bones.

♪
(Paramount unissued)
c. 4/13/27, Chicago, IL

Several of the dances performed by Blacks were written down and published at the close of the nineteenth century. Some were animal imitations, like the Elephant Squat, the Grizzly Bear, or the Turkey Trot; others were notable for their novelty steps, like the Bombashay, the Pas-ma-La, or Falling off a Log. They enjoyed a popularity that moved from colored hops and low-down dives to the more raffish urban dance halls. A black composer, Ernest Hogan, published "Pas ma La" as a tune in 1895, with words that referred to a number of these dances. It slipped back into the folk idiom and a Mississippi singer, Jim Jackson, incorporated it into one of his recordings, "BYE BYE POLICEMAN," made over thirty years later.

Jim Jackson, Blind Blake, and Mance Lipscomb all played guitar. Cheap guitars were manufactured by firms like Lyon and Healy, Washburn, and Gibson in the 1890s, and the mail-order companies responded; by 1908 Sears-Roebuck was marketing a standard guitar, complete with extra strings and a chord book, for less than two dollars. The guitar was well-suited to the slides and shuffles of black dances of the day. Rural dances weren't subtle affairs, and the music was rugged and often coarse-grained. Peg Leg Howell's Gang was a vital, if raw, band that played for dimes in the streets of Atlanta, and for barbecues in rural Georgia. Howell's recording of "TURKEY BUZZARD BLUES" has the syncopated swing that black dancers liked, but the tune was based on an old favorite that was known at least as early as the 1830s, "Turkey in the Straw." In the vocal they make reference to another old dance tune, "Sugar in the Gourd," and the Hootchy-Kootchy, the belly dance, that caused a scandal at the Chicago World's Fair of 1893.

A good black fiddle player, like Eddie Anthony, would be in demand for both black and white dances, and might even be invited to play with white musicians. The skill was passed on through families, and some formed their own string bands—like the Bookers of Black Ridge, in Kentucky's Jessamine County. James Booker Senior was born in 1837 and was a noted fiddler before the Civil War; his son Jim, born in 1872, followed his style, and his other children were also musicians. Jim Booker led the Booker Orchestra, but he also worked with a white banjo player, Marion Underwood, and even recorded with a white string band, Taylor's Kentucky Boys. On "GRAY EAGLE," Jim Booker plays brilliantly in the hoedown style associated with the white string bands.

A smoother style was adopted by the Mississippi Shieks, a black string band from Jackson, Mississippi. It was a large family band, with more than a dozen musicians in all. Each member played several instruments: brothers Bo, Edgar, Harry, and Lonnie all played violin. With the string band, they augmented their meager earnings as tenant farmers on the Dupress plantation, and gained a statewide reputation. Bo, as Bo Carter, recorded blues with his guitar, so did the family's adopted brother, Walter Vincson. Lonnie Chatmon plays fiddle and Walter plays guitar and sings the vocal on the Mississippi Shieks's recording of "THE JAZZ FIDDLER." Sings Walter, "We got the fiddle, shake the bow, this is the tune all fiddlers ought

♪
(Victor V38505) 9/7/28, Memphis, TN

♪
(Columbia 14382) 10/30/28, Atlanta, GA

♪
(Gennett 6130) 4/26/27, Richmond, IN

♪
(Okeh 45436) 2/17/30, Shreveport, LA

to know—it's too bad. Boy, this is something you never have seen—a man playing jazz on a violin...."

When the guitar became popular, banjos and fiddles fell somewhat into decline. But in the country districts, string bands continued to thrive, with fiddles, mandolins, guitars, and basses. There were still hundreds of them in the 1920s, playing for dances all over the South—bands like Sid Hemphill's in Mississippi, Willie Walker's in the Carolinas, and the Wright Brothers in Texas. But very few were recorded, leaving us with an unbalanced view of black popular music. One of the few was the Dallas String Band, led by the mandolin player, Coley Jones. They played for dances, and serenaded in the streets of Dallas, Texas. Like the Mississippi Sheiks, they were among the last representatives of a long tradition, surviving into the 1930s by adapting, with a little ironic humor, to what they termed "THE HOKUM BLUES."

♪
(Columbia 14389)
12/8/28, Dallas, TX

Part of the appeal of blues lay in its suitability for dancing. If the tempo of many blues numbers was leisurely, it was still ideal for "slow dragging" on the front porch or in the local juke joint. Blues singers may have developed the blues as an expressive and personalized idiom, but they were also accustomed to playing for dances in both country barrelhouses and urban rent-parties. The influential guitarist Big Bill Broonzy and the equally celebrated pianist "Georgia Tom" Dorsey recorded "COME ON MAMA," a typical dance blues; Hannah May offered the enthusiastic vocal.

♪
(Perfect 169) 9/16/30,
New York City

Among the dances mentioned in the song and the cheerful banter are the Mississippi Rub, the Shimmy Shake, the Blacksnake Wiggle, Mess Around, and Snake Hips. At least two of these dances, the Possum Trot and Scratching the Gravel, had been in currency for a century when "COME ON MAMA" was recorded in 1930.

# 5

# Ragtime Millionaire

First Broadcast: 12/2/87; Producer: Derek Drescher

♪

(Paramount 3022)
5/27, Chicago, IL

♪

(Victor 31642) 5/20/07,
New York City

**S**id Harkreader and Grady Moore, two white hillbilly musicians from Tennessee, recorded their version of "I'm Looking for the Bully of the Town" in 1927, by which time the song was over thirty years old.

The story goes that in 1896 a sports writer and amateur guitarist named Charles E. Trevathan was traveling by train to Chicago from San Francisco. To while away the journey, he entertained other passengers with this and other "Negro melodies" he'd picked up, which he probably heard at Babe Connor's notorious joint in St. Louis. Also on the train was a singer, May Irwin, with the company of her show, *The Country Sport*. She was fascinated by the song and, back east the following year, introduced it in her new show, *The Widow Jones*. It was an outstanding success, with its narrative of the razor-toting black "bully." Irwin went into the studio to record "The Bully Song," and her version was issued in 1907.

With their stereotypical images of Blacks, the words of May Irwin's "Bully Song" were characteristic of the songs of the period. But the tune was catchy, and it inspired a spate of "bully" songs, like "De Bully's Wedding Night" and "Dere's a Bully Gone to Rest." May Irwin's song remained the most popular of them all, and it was rapidly taken up by hillbilly singers and string bands, such as Gid Tanner's Skillet Lickers. Surprisingly, it was very popular with African Americans, too. A fragmentary version was recorded in 1940 for the Library of Congress by two "troubadours," as they

♪
(Flyright LP260) 10/9/40,
Shreveport, LA

called themselves, in Shreveport, Louisiana—Kid West, who played mandolin, and guitarist Joe Harris, this version was called "BULLY OF THE TOWN."

The "Bully Song" had been published nearly forty-five years earlier, when Kid West and Joe Harris were boys. At that time, "coon" songs were in vogue; the term may have referred to the minstrel tune of the 1830s, "Old Zip Coon," or it may have been a derogatory comparison of a black person with the white eyes, black face, and unpredictable behavior of a raccoon. Whatever the case, over six hundred "coon songs" were published, depicting African Americans as violent and ostentatious, lazy and irresponsible, or loveable and childlike. Paul Allen's "New Coon in Town" of 1883 probably started the craze, and its theme of a strange, black newcomer remained a favorite. It was the subject of "MYSTERIOUS COON," sung by the minstrel Alec Johnson in Atlanta. He told the story of a wealthy stranger who was brought up before the judge for alleged stealing. The song probably appealed because of the way the mysterious "coon" turns the tables, peeling off a thousand dollar bill to pay a hundred dollar fine, and telling the judge to keep the change.

♪
(Columbia 14378)
11/2/28, Atlanta, GA

Alec Johnson's accompanists played havoc with the stereotypes of the kind of music played by blues musicians. The violin was played by the blues singer, Bo Carter; the guitarist was Joe McCoy, who later formed the Harlem Hamfats; and his brother Charlie McCoy, who accompanied such seminal bluesmen as Tommy Johnson and Ishman Bracey, played mandolin. The songwriter isn't known, but it may have been Chris Smith, because Alec Johnson also recorded "Next Week, Sometime" by the entertainer Bert Williams and composer Chris Smith. Smith was born in Charleston, South Carolina, in 1879. He started work in a bakery, but he was a natural wit and soon formed a vaudeville duet with another black youth, Elmer Bowman. In 1903, when he was just twenty-one, he composed a comic song, "NEVER LET THE SAME BEE STING YOU TWICE." It was recorded later by Richard "Rabbit" Brown, a black boatman from New Orleans, who seems to have regarded it as a serious piece of homespun philosophy.

♪
(Victor 24175) 3/11/27,
New Orleans, LA

Chris Smith went on to compose "You're in the Right Church but the Wrong Pew," which was adapted by many black singers; he also wrote the well-known dance number "Ballin' the Jack," and in 1912, with Elmer Bowman, "I Got de Blues"—one of the first songs to be published with "blues" in the title.

Many songs of the period filtered through the black communities, to be taken up by the songsters. It was customary in the South to identify an instrumentalist who did not sing as a "musicianer," and one who also took vocals as a "songster." Songsters prided themselves on the breadth and variety of their repertoires, and they were much in demand as local entertainers. They form a distinct generation, born in the decades that pre-ceeded the generation of blues singers. A number of songsters made records, and though they have been largely overlooked in favor of the blues, they give us a picture of the songs popular at the turn of the century. Many preserved the old songs intact, but if they'd partially forgotten them they made composite songs. Lil McClintock, a songster from Clinton, South Carolina, combined Thomas Allen's typical Southern plantation melody "Lindy Lou—By the Watermelon Vine" published in 1904, with Jack Drisdane's sentimental song of 1905, "Keep a Little Cozy Corner in Your Heart For Me," and an unlikely fragment of an English music hall song, written coincidentally by another McClintock, C. W., in 1904, "Everybody Works but Father." But the song that gave the medley its title, "DON'T THINK I'M SANTA CLAUS," written in the same year, was by a black composer, Irving Jones.

♪
(Columbia 14575)
12/4/30, Atlanta, GA

Black composers like James Bland, Ben Harney (who passed for White), Ernest Hogan, Sam Lucas, Cecil Mack, and Chris Smith all wrote coon and ragtime songs. Many found their way into the repertoires of the country songsters, but none seem to have been as popular as the songs of Jones, who had a knack of being able to pick up black idioms and incorporate them authentically in his lyrics, so that eventually they were re-absorbed into popular usage. He was a stage performer, but he was unable to write music and reputedly lost a lot of songs to the "cuff boys," white composers who pirated black songs and then published them. But he got others to write up his musical ideas, and, as early as 1894, he'd published his "Possumala" dance (a pun on "Pas-ma-la"), and in 1897, he had a big hit with "Take Your Clothes and Go." It inspired a rejoinder that he also wrote, "Let Me Bring My Clothes Back Home," which was collected as a folk song in the Deep South only a few years later. Henry Thomas, also known as Ragtime Texas, whose dance calls and quills (panpipes) playing made him a distinctive per-former, recorded part of it as "ARKANSAS." But he bowdlerized the wife's declaration in the song, "Honey, I'm tired of coon; I'm goin' to pass for White," to a rather meaningless, "Honey, I'm done with beans; I'm goin' to pass for green."

♪
(Vocalion 1286) 6/30/27,
Chicago, IL

Songsters were rarely literate and they couldn't read music. To learn these songs, let alone adapt them, they had to have the time and the opportunity that dances and barbecues seldom provided. One of the traditional centers for the exchange of musical ideas was the barbershop. Every black barber kept a guitar in the corner of his shop for the use of clients awaiting their turn. William Moore was a barber who was born in 1893 and raised at Tappahannock, on the James River in Virginia. A versatile musician who played guitar, fiddle, and piano, he also farmed and ran a barbershop at Tappahannock and another at Warsaw. He was in demand to play at local dances, and this is reflected in the strong dance rhythm of his recording of "RAGTIME MILLIONAIRE," another Irving Jones song composed in 1900. Moore kept the irony of the man who claimed to be more popular than "the man in the President's Chair," but he updated the song with fantasies of Henry Ford giving him a brand new Model T Ford. He incorporated a few words from another Jones song, "My Money Never Runs Out": "Every tooth in my head is solid gold, makes those boys look icy cold. I brush my teeth with diamond dust, and I don't care if the bank would bust. All you little people take your hats off to me, 'cause I'm the Ragtime Millionaire."

♪
(Paramount 12636) 1/28, Chicago, IL

Why did black composers write coon songs? Why did the songsters learn them and remember them for so long afterward? And why were they popular with black audiences? These are questions that are not easily answered. But I believe that the composers chose to work in the popular idiom of the day, and the best of them, like Chris Smith or Irving Jones, subtly deflected their emphasis. By sharing the jokes in the coon songs they defused them; and by writing them better they established a foothold for the black songwriters.

The songsters and their audiences were first of all attracted by the fact that many of these songs had good tunes. But they enjoyed the humor and the irony of the lyrics. Though I have been unable to trace its composers' names, "THE TRAVELING COON" is one of the most widespread of these songs. The traveling coon is a "trickster," a "superblack" who outmaneuvers or outwits his opponents. When he dives off the Titanic, he is dismissed as an idiot, but then when the ship strikes the iceberg, he's shooting craps in Liverpool. Luke Jordan, a songster and odd-job man from Appomatox, Virginia, recorded a version of the song. In it, the Traveling Coon is sentenced to be hung, but as the spectators pray, he shoots up in the air and escapes. Audiences identified with the cunning hero; it's probably no accident that he is called a "traveling coon" at the beginning of the song, but a "traveling man" at the end.

♪
(Victor 20957) 8/16/27, Charlotte, NC

# 6

# Doctor Medicine

First Broadcast: 12/9/87; Producer: Derek Drescher

♪
(Paramount 12518)
8/27, Chicago, IL

It's curious, but we know more about black song of the slave period than we do of the Reconstruction years that followed the Civil War. No one seems to have studied black song again until the early years of the twentieth century. But if we compare the field notes made then with the earliest recordings made by the songsters in the late 1920s, we find that many of the same songs were being sung. What is more, they were sung over a vast area of the South, from the Carolinas to Texas. There were local variants, but the songsters obviously drew upon a common resource of songs that had been in general currency for a long time. But, in the days before radio or recordings, how were they circulated, and by whom?

It's possible to find some clues. Take the song recorded by a Memphis blacksmith and noted songster, Frank Stokes, which he called "You Shall"; its proper title was "You Shall Be Free"; perhaps the record company didn't like that, or some of the verses. One stanza was collected frequently: "Some folks say that a nigger won't steal. . . . But I caught twenty in my cornfield. . . . Stokes cut out the offensive term and shifted the target; he sang, Some folks say that a preacher won't steal. . . . I caught about eleven in a watermelon field. . . ."

They've been altered, but some of Stokes's verses can be traced back at least to 1846 and the publication of *The Negro Singers Own Book*. This was a *songster*, in the original use of the term: a collection

29

of song lyrics, intended for the use of minstrel show entertainers. They sold for a dime apiece, and thousands of these pocket-sized books were printed. The minstrel shows that used them date back to the 1830s. These entertainments, which continued for nearly a century, parodied black folkways, dancing, and humor. Many were racist, but they were tremendously popular. The shows became formalized with a chairman, called Mister Interlocutor; the endmen, Mister Tambo and Mister Bones; and a line of banjo players and other showmen (and later, showgirls). It seems incongruous now, but from the mid-1850s on there were a great many black minstrel performers, too. Like the white minstrels, they blackened their faces with burned cork, whitened their eyes, painted their lips an exaggerated pink, and wore the regulation white gloves and "long-tailed blue" frock coats. Shows like Brooker and Clayton's Georgia Minstrels, Haverly's Colored Minstrels, Hicks' Georgia Slave Troupe, and scores of others toured the South. They were still touring in the 1930s, the bright, clattering sound of the banjo line contrasting with the rasping bass of a seven-gallon jug and other novelty instruments. Earl McDonald's Original Louisville Jug Band, which recorded "SHE'S IN THE GRAVEYARD NOW," is but one of many groups who continued to perform in this style well into the 1920s and '30s.

♪
(Columbia 14255)
3/30/27, Atlanta, GA

Many of the twentieth-century minstrel shows featured women singers, but they were rare. Generally, it seems, good female singers tended to join the churches, but some became professional entertainers, working under canvas and touring with minstrel shows, circuses, and carnivals. One of the best-known shows was Silas Green from New Orleans; another was the famous Rabbit Foot Minstrels, managed by F. S. Wolcott from Port Gibson, Mississippi. Will "Pa" Rainey and his better-known wife, whom he married in 1904, Gertrude "Ma" Rainey, worked on this show, as did many others; Ma Rainey had a stout figure and homely features, but she was a great favorite of black audiences with her glittering necklace of gold pieces, her earthy humor, and her robust songs. One of her popular recordings was "MA RAINEY'S BLACK BOTTOM," sung to the accompaniment of a rough-and-ready band.

♪
(Paramount 12590)
12/27, Chicago, IL

Some of the big white circuses had a "Number 2 Show," or what was disparagingly called a "jig show," which was Black. But White or Black, they all played a part in disseminating songs. Black audiences could watch the white shows from the "Jim Crow" benches, and because of their general popularity, there was an exchange of songs among the segregated companies. John Queen, for instance, was a white clog dancer and

♪
(Riverside RLP 12-611)
5/29/50,
Charlottesville, LA

minstrel from New Orleans who wrote a song, "I Got Mine," in 1901 that rapidly became a favorite among Blacks. The verses relate how the singer makes the best of a number of situations, but in every performance at least one verse makes rueful reference to a jail sentence or a beating from an angry lover.

A popular version of "I've Got Mine" was recorded by Pink Anderson, whose whole life was spent entertaining on the show circuit, but not with the big minstrel companies. He played in the medicine shows, working with Dr. W. R. Kerr's show for well over thirty years. Medicine shows traveled through the rural South, selling "cure-alls" of sometimes dubious quality to people who often had little access to more traditional medical services. For Blacks in the South, access to good medical services was almost nonexistent; even at the end of World War II, there were only seventy-five hospital beds available to meet the needs of a million Blacks in some parts of the South. Hospitals were still segregated until the 1960s. As such, medicine bags and charms were relied upon; people visited the "conjure doctors"; and herb doctors—some of whom were skilled and some charlatans—made up potions that they sold in the streets. To attract a crowd, they'd put on entertainment, and numerous songsters got their start this way. Gus Cannon, a Mississippi-born banjo player, told me of some of the doctors he had worked with and the places they'd visited: "I worked for Dr. C. Hangerson, I worked for Dr. Stokey right here on South Parkway, Memphis. I worked with a man out of Louisville. I worked through Mississippi, I worked through Virginia, I worked through Alabama, I worked through Mobile, Gulfport Bay, St. Louis—far as I been down, playin' my banjo on them doctor shows. . . . And I worked right back here to Memphis."

Another singer, an albino piano player named Rufus Perryman—whose mottled pink skin earned him the name of Speckled Red—expressed his opinion of the doctor shows: "One medicine good for a thousand things—and wasn't good for *nothin'*. "Right String, but the Wrong Yo-Yo" was typical of Speckled Red's barrelhouse and medicine show entertainment.

♪
(Brunswick 715) 4/8/30,
Chicago, IL

Jim Jackson was Red's companion in the Red Rose Minstrels, and he was responsible for getting Speckled Red on record. Jackson, like his namesake Papa Charlie Jackson and other singers like Frank Stokes and Henry Thomas, made many recordings that together give us a good impression of the range of the songsters' repertoires. He was a well-known singer in Memphis, Tennessee, whose songs were typical of the minstrel

♪
(Victor 21387) 1/30/28,
Memphis, TN

and medicine shows. "I HEARD THE VOICE OF A PORK CHOP" combines irony, humorous fantasy, and—obliquely—comments on poverty in lines like "my stomach sent a telegram to my mouth: 'There's a wreck on the road somewhere.'"

I consider the minstrel and medicine shows to be important to our understanding of black music and song before the blues, because they maintained a tradition that extended well back into the nineteenth century. Yet they also continued well into the present one, providing employment for songsters and blues singers, and being essential to the process of spreading songs. Companies like the Florida Cotton Blossoms or Sugar Foot Green's continued to play to large crowds even in the 1950s. The medicine shows continued even longer, but if it wasn't for field work done by Bruce Bastin and Pete Lowry, none of them may ever have been recorded. In 1972 they recorded what may well have been the last medicine show in the South. Its doctor was Chief Thundercloud, a full-blood Potawatomi Indian from Oklahoma; its entertainer was a one-legged singer, dancer, and harmonica player named Arthur Jackson, known as Peg Leg

♪
(Flyright LP507-508)
9/15/72, Pittsboro, NC

Sam. Sam's routine of stories and performance of "HAND ME DOWN" for a black crowd in Pittsboro, North Carolina, conveys the rough-hewn rapport between entertainer-musician and rural audience that no studio can ever capture.

# 7

# John Henry and the Boll Weevil

**First Broadcast: 12/16/87; Producer: Derek Drescher**

♪
(Heritage HLP 1004)
7/11/60, Chicago, IL

One of my most enduring memories is of getting off the streetcar at Maxwell and Halstead Streets on Chicago's South Side and almost colliding with a tall, burly, blind man who was singing on the sidewalk. He had a tin cup pinned to his jacket for tips, and he was playing a steel-bodied National guitar in open tuning, a glass bottleneck slipped over the middle finger of his maimed left hand. He was bellowing above the traffic noise seemingly endless choruses of "JOHN HENRY," and to me he was the archetypal street singer. His name was Arvella Gray, and I wasted no time in recording him.

Arvella had led a hard life, but though he'd been blinded by a gunshot that also shattered his hand, he was proud that, as he said, he had "come through with his skin on." Slowly I realized that he identified closely with John Henry. The ballad hero had been a steel driver, a man who drove metal spikes with his nine-pound hammer into mountain rock so that dynamite charges could be placed in the holes. In the nineteenth century, when the great transcontinental railroad lines were built, this was part of the tunneling process. However, when a steam-powered mechanical drill was introduced on the C & O Railroad in West Virginia about 1870, the black drilling crews were threatened. As the story goes, John Henry competed with the steam drill, valiantly attempting to beat the machine at its own game, but he died from exhaustion during the contest; his wife, Polly Ann, took up his hammer and carried on. Soon after the contest in the Big Bend Tunnel, a ballad about it was in circulation. It was sung by both Blacks and Whites, although it probably originated among black workers. When segregation laws and the Black Codes came into force, John Henry's unequal struggle became of their own.

The contest inspired a slew of John Henry songs. To Mississippi John Hurt, he was a failed hero who laid his hammer beside the road and walked off the job. Hurt, who was from Avalon, Mississippi, and had once been a track liner before recording his version of the song in 1928, called "SPIKE DRIVER BLUES," sings gently but defiantly, "This old hammer killed John Henry, but it won't kill me. . . ."

(Okeh 8692) 12/28/28, New York City

Ballads are song narratives, with stanzas that usually have eight or sixteen bars. In Britain they have a history going back to the mid-sixteenth century, but they flourished in the Appalachian Mountains of the United States among the white mountain folk, beginning in the 1700s. New ballads on American themes were composed. The British ballad "Lady Isabel and the Elfin Night" probably didn't mean much to Blacks, and the newer white ballad heroes may not have appealed greatly, either. With John Henry, though, a whole new vein of black ballads emerged, with heroes and themes that did have meaning for them.

One of the best-known ballads was "Casey Jones," which was composed by a black engineer and wiper at the Memphis railroad roundhouse, Wash Saunders. Casey Jones was the white driver of the Cannonball Express, which crashed into another train on May 1, 1900, in Canton, Mississippi. A commercial version of the ballad was published in 1909, called "Casey Jones, The Brave Engineer," and rather oddly described as "the greatest comedy hit in years." When Furry Lewis, a Memphis songster, recorded the ballad under the name "KASSIE JONES (PART 2)," it lacked the note of heroism that other popular versions had. He quotes Casey's widow as saying, "Children, children, won't you hold your breath? Draw another pension from your daddy's death." With a final glimpse of the driver dead beneath the boiler of the engineer, Lewis states, from where he stands, "Had it written on the tail of his shirt, 'Natural born Easeman, don't have to work.'"

(Victor 21664) 8/28/28, Memphis, TN

Casey Jones was indisputably White; what is more in dispute among folklorists is whether this was the crash that was the subject of the ballad, or whether it was another driver on another line. Most ballad stories have been challenged: "Frankie and Albert" is another. It was also popularized by being published later—as "Frankie and Johnny"—by the Leighton Brothers, who picked up one or two ballads and exploited them in this way. The strongest claim for the identification of the couple seems to be for Frankie Butler of St. Louis, an "ebony hued cake-walker," according to a newspaper account. She stabbed her young lover, Al Britt, in October 1899—although in the song she always shoots him.

Then there's "Stack O'Lee." Sometimes called "Stackerlee," "Staggerlee," or "Stagolee," he appears to have been the mulatto grandson of Jim Lee, founder of a Mississippi riverboat line. He is said to have shot Billy Lyons—or "Billy the Lion" as John Hurt calls him—around the turn of the century. While that ballad is known mainly in Mississippi, "ELLA SPEED" is known to Texas singers, although the incident may have occurred in New Orleans. According to Leadbelly, she was shot with a Colt 41 by Bill Martin, who was "long and slender, better known by being a bartender." Leadbelly's version of the ballad features his own powerful twelve-string guitar accompaniment, with unusual accompaniment on zither by Paul Mason Howard. The mourners in this song wear red, once the common color for black funerals in the South, perhaps a holdover from African ceremonies.

It was probably the unjustified brutality in some of these ballads that carried a double meaning for the songsters and their audiences. But the appeal of Railroad Bill may have been different. His identity is certain: he was Morris Slater, a black turpentine worker in the piney woods of Escambia County, Alabama. Slater was credited with a number of shootings and daring train robberies in the early 1890s. Sheriff E. McMillan tracked Railroad Bill—as he was now called—in 1895 to a house in Bluff Springs, and opened fire. Bill wasn't hit, but McMillan was killed. Two years later, after many escapades and just as many escapes, Railroad Bill was ambushed at a grocery store in Atmore; his killers claimed the bounty of $1,250. In the violent and repressive early years of segregation when lynchings were frequent, the outlaw's anarchic independence, his defiance, his miraculous escapes and eventual defeat only by ambush excited the admiration of many Blacks. Will Bennett, a songster from Loudon, Tennessee, recorded an interesting version of "RAILROAD BILL" in 1930. Instead of describing incidents about the bandit, Bill becomes the subject of the song himself. Bill's independence is celebrated in verses like: "Railroad Bill, Railroad Bill. He never worked, and he never will. Ride, Bill, Ride."

Perhaps it was because the story of Railroad Bill fitted one stereotype of Blacks that it was also popular with white singers. More white artists recorded it than black, although even as late

♪ (Capitol H639) 10/4/44, Hollywood, CA

♪ (Vocalion 1464) 8/28/29, Knoxville, TN

as the 1970s it was collected from black singers in the field. The same applies to another ballad, one of the most popular of all, although it was only rarely recorded commercially. It was about an insect, little more than a quarter-of-an-inch long, with a pointed "bill": the cotton boll weevil. This pest laid its eggs in the cotton "square," or bud; when the larva hatched, it consumed the cotton boll from within. The boll weevil first appeared in Mexico, and by 1892 it was in Texas. By 1905, it was devastating fields all over the South and hundreds of thousands of farmers lost their crops. Every attempt to destroy the bug seemed to fail, and Blacks began to identify with the irrepressible brown insect that endured all attempts to demolish it and won out. Mance Lipscomb, a Texas sharecropper, witnessed the destruction created by these insects; his "BALLAD OF THE BOLL WEEVIL" shows great respect for the "little brown bug."

♪
(Reprise 2012) 7/8/61,
Houston, TX

Among the most widely known black ballads was one of the last, which concerned the loss of the Titanic in 1912. According to Leadbelly's version of the Titanic ballad, "Jack Johnson [the famous black prize fighter] wanted to get on board, but the captain hollered 'I ain't haulin' no coal.'" Other versions may not mention Jack Johnson, but it was widely known that the wealthy and poor were segregated on board, and the poor suffered the most. While the songsters sympathized with those who lost their lives, they and their audiences seem to have taken comfort in the destruction of what had seemed to be an invincible symbol of white power and supremacy. Pink Anderson was still singing his version of "THE SHIP TITANIC" in traveling medicine shows during the 1950s.

♪
(Riverside RLP 12-611)
5/29/50,
Charlottesville, LA

There were a few ballads that came later than that of the Titanic, but the majority seem to date from the twenty years that preceded the outbreak of the First World War. This was also the period when twelve-bar blues gained its hold on black song. As I mentioned earlier, black ballads often took the traditional stanza form, sung in four- or eight-line verses over eight or sixteen bars, such as we heard in "John Henry" and "Casey Jones." Sometimes, though, they were built of pairs of couplets, like "Ella Speed" or "John Henry." But a popular form of black ballad was a couplet and refrain sung over twelve bars—"Railroad Bill" was of this type—with the couplet occupying eight bars and the refrain another four. "Frankie and Albert," "Stack O'Lee," and the "Boll Weevil" often took this twelve-bar form. Mississippi songsters Papa Harvey Hull and Long Cleeve Reed recorded their "ORIGINAL STACK O'LEE BLUES" in this form. It's just another piece in the musical mosaic that gave shape to the blues.

♪
(Black Patti 8030) 5/27,
Chicago, IL

# 8

# Yonder Comes the Blues

First Broadcast: 12/23/87; Producer: Derek Drescher

In the past few programs I've tried to identify some of the types of secular black song that existed in the Southern United States before the appearance of blues. These old traditions continued well into the present century, and were recorded commercially or, in some instances, by researchers in the field. I've also indicated some of the ways in which they may have had some influence on the shaping of the blues, such as the dominance of strings, the use of certain flattened notes, and the falling contour of the vocals in the music of the griots of the West African savannah that seem to have been retained in blues. We have heard examples of work songs, which represented a tradition—African in kind—that survived from slavery times in the collective songs of the Southern penitentiaries and as free solo improvisations, or "hollers" in the cotton fields.

Then there was the tradition of playing for dancing on banjo and fiddle, and the subsequent popularity of the string bands; these were little recorded, but thrived until the 1960s. The stereotypes portrayed in the "bully" and "coon" songs of the 1890s raised the question: "Why did Blacks also compose them and many black songsters perform them?" Later we heard recordings of entertainers who played on the minstrel and medicine shows, taking their music to all parts of the rural South. And we heard some of the black ballads that told of the exploits of heroes, and antiheroes, with which the singers and their audiences identified. But there

♪
(Okeh 8679) 3/13/29,
Atlanta, GA

♪
(Okeh 8693) 3/14/29,
Atlanta, GA

♪
(Pye/NixaNJL2) 1/31/56,
London, England

♪
(Brunswick 7166)
2/20/30, Memphis, TN

were also songs with a lively sense of the ridiculous that challenged figures of authority or status and brought an element of realism or sometimes of caricature to them. A songster from Brownsville, Tennessee, known as Hambone Willie Newbern sang one of them, "Nobody Knows What the Good Deacon's Doing, Lord When the Lights Go Out."

Willie Newbern was a veteran of the medicine shows, and though I've been unable to trace the precise origin of his song, it's typical of the ironic humor popular with medicine-show audiences. At that same time in March 1929 he recorded "Dreamy-Eyed Woman"—or, as it says on the label, "Hambone Willie's Dreamy-Eyed Woman Blues"—for an Okeh field unit in Atlanta, far from his home. It was, of course, a twelve-bar blues.

Compared with the previous song, it is immediately apparent that this one is far more personal, and with its small points of detail—his dreamy-eyed woman lives on Cherry Street; she answers him with her hands on her hips—it was probably a fragment of his own life that he was recounting. The relationship with his woman is far more convincing than the stereotype of the wayward deacon. As a songster, Newbern may have picked up blues as he gathered other types of song on the traveling shows. And similarly, he—or other songsters like him—could have been instrumental in spreading the new form, which offered to young musicians a structure for song and a means of self-expression.

Yet there remain some fundamental questions: How did the blues take shape? When did it emerge as a form in its own right? Unfortunately, there are no clear answers to these questions. Although Ma Rainey and W.C. Handy heard blues being sung at the turn of the century, there are no transcriptions of the music or verses they heard. Later, in 1908, John Lomax collected a song from a Mississippi woman named Dink, who had been shipped out to Texas with a levee-building crew. She was "washing her man's clothes outside their tent on the bank of the Brazos River," he recalled. Her song has appealed to many white women singers, but there are few versions by black singers on record.

Josh White, like other singers who have recorded it, called the theme "Dink's Blues," though John Lomax referred to it as "Dink's Song," and admitted that the tune to Dink's eight-bar blues was "lost." On the music transcription, Lomax noted that it should be performed "slow and intense," and Josh White sang it this way. The song does occur in more forceful form on a few early records, under the title "Fare Thee Well Blues." Joe Calicott,

a songster from the hill country of northern Mississippi, recorded his version in 1930. Its directness of approach, reminiscent
of Willie Newbern's, makes Josh White's recording seem man-
nered and theatrical by comparison.

Is "Fare Thee Well Blues"/"Dink's Blues" a prototype of the
blues form? Perhaps, for it has the eight-bar sequence, with
the two-line-plus-refrain form that was typical of many black
ballads. But it links with other "fare thee well" songs of the
turn of the century, including "Fare Thee Honey, Fare Thee
Well," by the white clog dancer and composer of "I Got Mine,"
John Queen. Queen of course, may have collected it from black
singers on a traveling show.

It seems that there were several blues songs in circulation
early in the century that lent themselves to improvisation or
the addition of personal stanzas. "Make Me a Pallet on the
Floor" is one; "Joe Turner Blues" is another. Among the most
widely distributed was "POOR BOY, LONG WAYS FROM HOME."
Medicine-shown performer Gus Cannon learned it in the early
1900s from one Alec Lee, who played it Hawaiian style (in open
tuning, using a metal bar or glass bottleneck to fret the strings).
In fact, all versions of "Poor Boy" appear to be played with
a slide, and Gus adapted the technique to the banjo, laying it
across his lap.

♪
(Paramount 12571)
11/27, Chicago, IL

In the earliest collections of black song that give any hint
of blues, compiled between 1903 and 1910, reference is sometimes made to "over-and-overs," or the use of repeated lines.
Some collections made in Georgia and Texas group the stanzas
noted under the general heading of "Railroad Blues," which
seems to reflect the migration of the singers and their songs.
"TRAVELING BLUES," by Blind Willie McTell from Statesboro,
Georgia, suggests this formative stage in the blues with its
over-and-over lines, vocal and railroad imitations on guitar,
and personal account of begging rides, money, and food as he
hoboed across, as he terms it, "South Americas." In one verse
he addresses the train driver: "Mister Engineer, let a poor man
ride the blinds"—meaning the baggage cars—and gets the
reply, "I wouldn't mind it feller, but you know this train ain't
mine." In McTell's account, he "begin to sing 'Poor Boy' to
him," playing a snatch of the tune on his twelve-string guitar,
and thus earning himself a ride.

♪
(Columbia 14484-D)
10/30/29, Atlanta, GA

The hardening of the blues into the familiar twelve-bar,
three-line structure only occurred slowly in the rural tradition.
Even in 1930, the great and influential singer Tommy Johnson
could sing his "COOL DRINK OF WATER BLUES" with irregular stanzas of varying lengths and rhyme schemes that are, in

♪
(Victor 21279) 2/3/28,
Memphis, TN

order: A–A–A; A–A; A–B; A–A; A–B; B–B; B. His final verses are also an exchange with a railroadman: "Lord, I asked the conductor, could I ride the blinds?" He is told, "Son, buy your ticket, buy your ticket, cause this train ain't none of mine." It is, of course, very similar to the dialogue on Willie McTell's "Travelin' Blues," and is an example of the use of formulae in lines, part lines, and stanzas, and the common pool of "floating verses" that encapsulated a common experience or emotion on which blues singers drew.

The publishing of blues helped fix its form, at least among bands and professional singers. Hart Wand's "Dallas Blues" was published in 1912; Leroy "Lasses" White published "Nigger Blues" in 1913; and the following year saw the appearance of W. C. Handy's "St. Louis Blues." They had to wait until after World War I before recordings of the blues could reach an eager market. The story of Mamie Smith's first recording date in 1920, secured for her by Perry Bradford, has often been told. Her "CRAZY BLUES" "made it possible for all of us," said Alberta Hunter, who—like Smith herself—was primarily a stage and vaudeville singer. "Crazy Blues" was a composed song, but Bradford included twelve-bar stanzas on an A–B–C structure. The original recording had accompaniment by Johnny Dunn's Jazz Hounds, featuring Dope Andrews on trombone, and Smith's youthful, spirited vocal. It had the crowds standing impatiently in their hundreds outside the record shops.

(Okeh 4169) 8/10/20, New York City

Blues emerged at the turn of the century, when the "Jim Crow" laws were enacted by every Southern state to segregate Blacks and Whites. In 1896, the Supreme Court had upheld the doctrine of "separate but equal," and Blacks were debarred from public facilities that were open to Whites throughout the South. The frustration and humiliation that they felt found release in the blues. Nineteenth-century idioms had been important, even essential, to the shaping of the blues, but they were gradually displaced over the years as countless thousands of Southern Blacks adopted the new music. There were losses, of course—in variety of song form, in ragtime virtuosity, in humor. But there were great gains in power, in poetry, and in emotional depth. In the words of Ma Rainey, one of the great exponents of the new music, who recorded "YONDER COME THE BLUES" in 1925, "There was no holding it back." Eventually it was to influence the popular music of the world.

(Paramount 12357) 12/25, New York City

# II

# Blues, How Do You Do?

# 9

# Anticipatin' Blues

First Broadcast: 10/25/87; Producer: Derek Drescher

♪
(Columbia 14331-D)
4/13/28, Atlanta, GA

Robert Hicks, known as Barbecue Bob, blues guitarist and country cook, recorded in Atlanta, Georgia, in April 1928, "Chocolate to the Bone." He was rejoicing in his color, casting doubts on those who were darker or lighter than he was. The boastful lyrics include, "So glad I'm brownskin, so glad I'm brownskin, chocolate to the bone, an' I got what it takes to make a monkey man leave his home." A young man, and color conscious, he died of pneumonia before he was thirty, but left some sixty recordings accompanying his rich voice with twelve-string guitar, frequently using a slide on the strings.

Where did he get his ideas for blues? Clearly, he listened to records, for in the same song he sings, "I'm like Miss Lillian, like Miss Lillian, I mean Miss Glinn you see; she said 'A brown-skin man is just all right with me.'" Bob was referring to Lillian Glinn's "Brownskin Blues," recorded a few months earlier; he might also have heard her when she appeared at the 81 Theater in Atlanta.

♪
(Okeh 8033) 3/2/22,
New York City

Had he also heard the Excelsior Quartette, or even heard them in Mamie Smith's touring company several years earlier? Their "Kitchen Mechanic Blues," recorded in March 1922, asks in harmony, "Ain't you glad you're brownskin, honey, chocolate to the bone?" Did Barbecue Bob pick up the line from the record, or was it in general currency at the time he recorded? In the same song, the Quartette sing of "the kitchen mechanic in the White folks' yard" who would bring you "chicken, biscuits, honey, and

43

all of your ham," a version of a verse that was sung before the Civil War, which referred to the pickings that the house slaves slipped to the field hands in the slave quarters.

Yet, who were the Excelsior Quartette? We do not know much about them, but they appear to have come from Virginia and were popular enough to tour on the black theater circuit after World War I. By the time they recorded, vocal quartets had been popular for at least forty years. Recent research has led to the recovery of a number of early records of these groups. One such group, the Unique Quartette, is known to have recorded some twenty sessions between 1890 and 1894. A single Edison cylinder made in late 1893, "MAMMA'S BLACK BABY BOY," has been found from these sessions. It tells of a doting black mother who "gave me ten cents to buy me some gum; I slipped in a saloon and I bought me some rum. I staggered and strutted all over this place—and the mud it was splattered all in my face. And the people all say I was a disgrace." Despite his bad behavior, the protagonist remained his "mamma's black baby boy."

Among the other titles recorded by the Unique Quartette are "Camp-Ground Jubilee" and "Negro Shout," or "Who Broke the Lock on the Hen Roost Door?" If these recordings are found, they may help to establish the missing links among the late-nineteenth-century African American song traditions, the repertoires of the songsters, and hence, the blues. The Dinwiddie Colored Quartet recorded a decade later, in 1902, after a few years of singing to raise funds for the John A. Dix Industrial School of Dinwiddie, Virginia, where they were believed to have been students. One of their songs was "POOR MOURNER," also known as "Po' Mona," a widely known song in the minstrel shows, of which some verses were published in the *Negro Singers' Own Book* as early as 1846. It was doubtless popular for the implications of its refrain, "You Shall be free, you shall be free, when the Good Lord sets you free."

The quartets have been largely overlooked until comparatively recently, even though they are unquestionably the oldest of the African American song tradition of which we have recorded evidence. More than fifty CDs of the quartets are available in the Document record label series, while the latest edition of the seminal blues discography *Blues and Gospel Records* has doubled its coverage of them. By far the majority on record sang spirituals and gospel songs, but it is noticeable that secular songs were prominent until the mid-1920s. Writing at that time, noted Harlem Renaissance poet and song collector James Weldon Johnson emphasized their spontaneity: "Pick up four colored boys or young men anywhere and the chances

♪
(Edison Cylinder) c. 1893, probably New York City

♪
(Monarch Cylinder) c. 10/02, New York City

are ninety out of a hundred that you have a quartet." Johnson believed that "all male Negro youth is divided into quartets." When he was a small boy around 1880 his pleasure was listening to the "crack quartets made up of waiters at the Jacksonville hotels." These hotels would have been just the place to hear the Old South Quartette's close harmony version of "OYSTERS AND WINE AT 2A.M."

♪
(QRS R7006) 8/28,
New York City

"In the days when such a thing as a white barber was unknown in the South, every barber shop had its quartet, and the men spent their leisure time playing on the guitar—not banjo, mind you—and harmonizing," added Johnson. He described the excitement when these vocalists' explorations in the field of harmony produced a new chord, and the backslapping when a new chord was discovered and repeated until it was mastered.

It is usually assumed that the quartets were trained in the manner of the Fisk Jubilee Singers, and that they performed mainly for white audiences. But reports in the African American press show that this is erroneous. Even some quartets in the educational institutions were untrained, as Natalie Curtis-Burlin discovered while doing field work at the Hampton Institute in Virginia during the First World War. "Black singers made up the parts themselves extemporaneously," she insisted; they "sang together with the same spontaneity that individuals feel when gathering with a group—they fall in line and keep step as they walk." She is known to have made recordings on an early portable machine, but it is not known whether they survived. These were of a quartet that comprised a tenor who was a tinsmith, an plowman who was the lead, a schoolmaster baritone, and a bricklayer bass. Explaining how they performed, one said, "We just feel it"—a description that would be familiar to many who have interviewed blues singers. Among their songs were cornfield and cotton-picking work songs, which may have sounded like the "SAD BLUES" recorded by the Norfolk Jubilee Quartet. "SAD BLUES" was clearly based on a field holler, and its shadings could only have come from direct experience. This recording, it should be noted, was made some fifteen years before cotton and cornfield hollers were recorded for the Library of Congress.

♪
(Paramount 12054) 4/23,
New York City

Norfolk, Virginia, was a breeding ground for quartets, no doubt inspired by the success of this particular group, which recorded secular items as the Norfolk Jazz Quartet and religious ones as the Norfolk Jubilee Quartet. Of their first thirty titles, only three were religious, but the group continued to record regularly until 1940, eventually making about 150 recordings, of which the majority were in the "Sacred" category. This seems to have been a policy decision of the record companies, because, in the second half of the 1920s, country blues singers were recorded in large numbers. The compilers of record catalogs liked to differentiate, and the secular items sung by the quartets were greatly reduced. A few experimented with the blues form, even borrowing verses from blues records. One example is the Monarch Jazz Quartet's version of Bessie Smith's "Backwater Blues," recorded under the title "WHAT'S THE MATTER NOW?" in Richmond, Virginia, in 1929.

♪
(Paramount 12844) 2/29, Richmond, VA

As a blues number this recording wasn't successful; the song structure and the personalized nature of blues is simply unsuitable for harmonizing quartets. The Birmingham Jubilee Singers from Alabama were one of several groups who continued to perform secular songs into the 1930s, but "Raise a Rukus Tonight" or "Who Stole the Lock" were performed more excitingly by the jug bands. Such old-time songs were going out of style with the dominance of blues, whereas gospel song permitted the groups to develop complex part singing. Nonetheless, further examination of the songs of pre-1920s close harmony groups reveals important connections between their repertoires, that of the songsters, and the lyric foundations of the blues.

# 10

# In the Field

First Broadcast: 10/18/87; Producer: Derek Drescher

**I**f you're flying across the United States, it's likely that you'll have a little packet of Pure Cane Imperial Sugar served with your coffee, its place of origin reading Sugarland, Texas. But Sugarland has connotations for those at all familiar with the recordings made for the Library of Congress—connotations that are far less sweet. "Ain't No More Cane on This Brazos" ("they done grind it all in molasses") was recorded at the Central State Farm, Sugarland, Texas, by John Avery Lomax for the Archive of Folk Music of the Library of Congress. It was a group work song by a team of convicts at the penitentiary farm, led by Ernest Williams.

♪
(Library of Congress AFS 13) 12/33, Central State Farm, Sugarland, TX

Since early in the century, collectors such as Howard Odum, Newman White, Dorothy Scarborough—and Thomas Talley, who was the sole African American song collector, wrote down the songs of black workers. Recording in the field opened up new possibilities that the commercial companies recognized, instituting location recording sessions in the South, in addition to their studio sessions, from the mid-1920s on. These reflected current tastes in blues and in gospel song. Then, in 1928, the Archive of Folk Music was established at the Library of Congress. Though the names of John and Alan Lomax are for many virtually synonymous with the archive, many collectors contributed to it, including its first archivist, Robert Winslow Gordon. Before and during his tenancy he recorded over 900 cylinders and discs and transcribed ten thousand manuscripts, mostly of white song, until

47

he moved to Darien, in south Georgia. There he recorded a number of black singers, including a former shanty man, J.A.S. Spencer, who had sailed from nearby Doboy Sound. Spencer sang the old sea shanty "BLOW BOYS BLOW" for Gordon, who recorded it on a cylinder in 1926.

♪ (Library of Congress AFS L68) 5/11/26, Darien, GA

Gordon recorded extensively, and much of this material has never been issued on either LP or CD. In 1926, Gordon traveled to the Georgia Sea Islands, where he recorded Mary C. Mann, a black deaconess, who recalled many of the early Sea Island slave songs. Her recording of "FINGER RING," a rowing song, is one of only three of the seventy-six cylinders she made that was issued.

♪ (Library of Congress AFS L68) 4/26, Merrian, GA

Disagreements with the administration led to Gordon's resignation from the Folk Music Archive in 1932. Soon after, the Texas folklorist John Avery Lomax was in Washington, D.C., checking out library collections for a new book. He was retained by the archive's music division to make recordings. Backed by funding agencies, which supported his work for several years, John Lomax and his son Alan embarked on their first field trip with 500 pounds of recording equipment in their car. In six months they covered some sixteen thousand miles, an achievement in itself considering the state of the roads in the 1930s. Their main objective was to record "the folk songs of the Negro—songs that, in musical phrasing and in poetic content, are most unlike those of the white race, the least contaminated by white influence or by modern Negro jazz," John Lomax explained. "Our best field was the southern penitentiaries," he wrote in his autobiography, *Adventures of a Ballad Hunter*. "We went to all eleven of them and presented our plan to possibly 25,000 Negro convicts. Most of these men and women saw in us hope that once more they might get out into the free world." One that did, and whose parole the Lomaxes may have effected, was Huddie Ledbetter, better known as Leadbelly, whose story has been told and retold in biography, novels, film, and on scores of record albums. Many of his songs were learned from records, while others were in the white tradition.

The Lomaxes' intention to seek "uncontaminated" folk song was often compromised by the singers, such as Jimmy Strothers, whose "TENNESSEE DOG" combined elements from the white mountain song "Cripple Creek" with the Hokum Boys' record "Beedle Um Bum." It doubtless also reflected his experience performing in medicine shows.

♪ (Library of Congress LBC 11) 6/13/36, State Farm, Lynn, VA

The chief of the Library of Congress Music Division, Harold Spivacke, wrote at length to congratulate John Lomax on his preparation of the singers at the session, which he attended. But when I interviewed him in the 1960s, Spivacke told me that he sent the Lomaxes on subsequent trips as soon as he could, to get them "out of his hair." The drive that enabled them to cope with the constant traveling, hostile prison officers, disapproving academics (especially African American ones), and frequent bouts of sickness, made the Lomaxes unique. It also tended to eclipse the work of many fieldworkers on whose help they depended for finding singers and setting up sessions outside the penal systems.

One of these independent fieldworkers was a resident of Sumter County, Alabama, Ruby Pickens Tarrt, who was a tireless researcher. Born in 1880, she collected the narratives of ex-slaves for the Federal Writers Project, as well as innumerable song texts. When she sent a short story to John Lomax based on her work, he eagerly sought her help, which, because she had no access to recording equipment, she gladly gave. The Lomaxes made four visits to Sumter County, where Ruby Pickens Tarrt arranged for them to meet and record many singers, including Richard Amerson, Dock Reed, Vera Hall, Enoch Brown, Harriett McClintock, and a score of the local songsters, including Blind Jesse Harris. Amerson, an ex-steamboat worker, claimed to be a "double-jointed man" capable of carrying five-thousand-pound bales of cotton. He had been a section hand, a well digger, a minstrel, a mule skinner, a minister, a farmer, and a voodoo doctor. Lomax recorded Amerson bragging about his "Steamboat Days" as well as performing a loading holler.

♪
(Library of Congress AFS L53) 11/1/40, Livingston, AL

John Lomax wrote enthusiastically about Amerson, describing him as a "vagabond, drunk (when he can find alcohol)," but nonetheless unforgettable. Of his hollering friend Enoch Brown, and of Dock Reed and Vera Hall, no mention is made in his autobiography. Nor did he refer to Jesse Harris, although Lomax recorded the accordion-playing Harris's version of the popular song "Railroad Bill." Undoubtedly this performance was too "contaminated" for Lomax to describe in his autobiography, and the original recording remained in the Library of Congress vaults until it was issued on CD some decades later.

♪
(Library of Congress, unissued) 7/24/37, Livingston, AL

With her fascination for black song undiminished, Ruby Pickens Tarrt was in her seventies when she helped Harold Courlander and Frederic Ramsey Jr. with their field recordings in the region after World War II. She was a white woman, rather patronizingly described by Lomax as being "fond of her Negroes." This "fondness," however, enabled her to win the trust of dozens of performers who Lomax would never have been able to record without her help.

♪
(Library of Congress
Fly SDM257) 6/20/35,
Eatonville, FL

Zora Neale Hurston was an African American born in the all-black town of Eatonville, Florida. She studied in the North, and the noted anthropologist Franz Boas secured a grant for her to study black culture back in Florida where, as she wrote, "songs are born out of feeling, with an old beat-up piano, or a guitar for a midwife." Mary Elizabeth Barnicle—the names of the women collectors seem to come in threes—invited Neale Hurston to join her in a field study in Florida. "I was to select the area and contact the subjects. Alan Lomax was joining us with a recording machine," Hurston recalled. She introduced them to "the best guitarist" Alan Lomax had heard since Leadbelly: Gabriel Brown. In June 1935, Lomax recorded Brown singing his "EDUCATION BLUES," with Rochelle French on second guitar. Brown played in what folk guitarists call "cross-note" or "Sebastapol" tuning, an open tuning that allows for a particularly resonant sound, with a knife laid on the strings.

Later, the Library of Congress team moved on to the Florida Everglades, where, they recorded a country jook band, at Belle Glade. (A "jook," or "juke," band was a small group of country musicians who would entertain in an elementary rough saloon also known as a "jook" or "juke," which was the only resort for Blacks in the most rural parts of the Deep South. Later they were replaced by phonographs or "juke-boxes.") Zora Neale Hurston was responsible for the success of the trip, but some African American academics disapproved of her on-site field work, which even led to her being initiated as a voodoo priestess in New Orleans. She wrote novels, articles, and her autobiography, but by the late 1940s she could only find work as a housemaid; she died forgotten and in poverty in 1960.

Other African American collectors and scholars of black music gave increasing attention to recording in the field, and had a more positive approach to the blues. John Wesley Work, the third in the dynasty of Work academics at Fisk University, recorded some forty items for the Library of Congress in 1941 at the Fort Valley Festival in southern Georgia. He was interested in string bands, which had not been of interest to the Lomaxes, and the following year even recorded the Nashville Washboard Band in his own home performing the jug band song "OLD JOE." The band included James Kelly on mandolin, Joe Dalton on guitar, and Tom Carroll on what was described by John Wesley Work as a "cord-can, one-string bull-fiddle" (but more commonly known as a washtub bass). The spirited washboard player was one Theopolis Stokes.

♪
(Library of Congress
LBC3) 7/15/42,
Nashville, TN

A few days later, Work joined his Fisk co-professor, Lewis Jones, to make a study project of black culture in Coahoma

County, Mississippi. It was sponsored jointly by Fisk and the Library of Congress, with Alan Lomax and his sister Bess doing the recording. In Lomax's recollections of the trip Work's contribution is ignored, but credit is given to "the unflappable bronze Dante" and "much-admired friend" Jones for finding the singers and arranging the sessions. At Clack's Store on Lake Cormorant, they recorded the veteran blues performer Eddie "Son" House, who had recorded commercially for Paramount Records a dozen years earlier. House was the mentor of a young guitarist and field hand, McKinley Morganfield, who they recorded on Stovall's Plantation, singing "COUNTRY BLUES." Morganfield, as Muddy Waters, was to become one of the most celebrated of all blues singers.

♪
(Testament 2210)
7/22/42, Clarksdale, MS

Morganfield's recordings for the Library of Congress, like those of Son House, have been much reissued because of their historical importance. But blues enthusiasts have been responsible for the reissue of a great many Library of Congress archive recordings that would otherwise have remained unheard. During the 1970s, a series by Bruce Bastin in England on his Flyright-Matchbox label, edited by John Cowley, made many recordings from the archive available for the first time. A few have been reissued on Bastin's Travelin' Man compact discs. Others have been reissued on Johnny Parth's Document label, together with some Library of Congress items that may not otherwise appear on CD. Even so, this leaves the majority—perhaps 90 percent—of the Library of Congress field recordings remaining unknown and unplayed—or, more than likely after this amount of time, unplayable. As just two examples, over sixty recordings were made of Richard Amerson, but only three of these have ever been issued; similarly, Dock Reed made more than seventy, yet just seven of these were available on LP. What have we lost of this valuable documentation?

It is telling that the recordings made by other fieldworkers for the archive, whose interests and perceptions differed from those of the Lomaxes, are largely unavailable. Among these are recordings made by B. A. Botkin in the Carolinas, Henry Faulk in Texas, and Herbert Halpert in Mississippi and Georgia. If it were not for Bastin and Cowley we would never have heard the blues of Peach County, Georgia, singer Buster "Buzz" Ezell, recorded in March 1943 by the black folklorists Willis Lawrence James from Atlanta and Louis Jones from Nashville. "I done some o' everything: sawmill, road gangs, played in circuses, hoochie coochie shows," Ezell claimed. Among his songs, they recorded him performing a patriotic blues about World War II, "ROOSEVELT AND HITLER."

♪
(Library of Congress, unissued) 3/5/43, Fort Valley, GA

Currently, the postwar recordings made by Alan Lomax, and a few of the prewar ones for the Library of Congress made with or by his father, John A. Lomax, are being reissued on over 100 compact discs. But there appear to be no plans to issue the majority of the prewar recordings of the Archive of Folk Song, and none that were made by other collectors, to my knowledge. There is no question that the scale and quality of the field recordings made by the Lomaxes will ever be forgotten. But there is a serious possibility that hundreds of recordings made by African American singers in the rural South a lifetime ago may be lost forever. Moreover, it is likely that the other collectors in the field who had the perspicacity and the motivation to preserve these songs in the difficult circumstances of the segregated South of the 1930s will not get the recognition that is their due. Surely, what remains of this priceless heritage of African American culture should be made available while it is still possible to retrieve it, so that future generations can be assured of its survival, for both pleasure and research.

# 11

# Playing the Boards

First Broadcast: 8/3/56; Producer: Jack Dabbs

So you're a musician. "Tell me, what instrument do you play?" you may be asked. But although you try to be casual, it's hard to sound convincing when you reply, "Oh, I play a washboard." It must be admitted that the common scrubbing board, gray perhaps with the residue of soap suds and worn by rough brushing of hard bristle, does not appear very musical. The washboard is, well, seldom taken seriously, and that is a pity, for it is a righteous instrument with a jazz ancestry as long as that of any of its more orthodox musical brethren. True, in the hands of a poor player, it remains a common scrubbing board, but played by a musician who appreciates its possibilities—Bruce Johnson of the Washboard Serenaders, for example—it becomes a vital and flexible rhythm instrument. Early jazz and "hokum" (novelty) ensembles often featured the instrument, in their names as well as their music. The Washboard Rhythm Kings were one such group, and in 1932 they recorded a spirited performance of "Tiger Rag" that featured the washboard's distinctive rhythm.

♪
(Victor 24059) 7/6/32, Camden, NJ

Fundamentally, the washboard is played by scraping across its corrugations as a child would drag a stick across a picket fence. But then, the drums, castanets, or xylophone are basically just as simple; some form of these instruments have long existed in Africa, where performances on them achieved exceptionally high standards. The musical antecedents of the washboard may also be found there in the notched gourds and sticks gouged with channels that so often form part of the rhythm.

It was probably those stalwart and indispensible African American women sold into slavery on Southern plantations who first appreciated the rhythmic possibilities of the washboard. Besides caring for the white children and raising their own (not inconsiderable) families, they coped with the immense laundry occasioned by the extensive use of linen in the Southern Plantation homes. Many observers in the nineteenth century noted the extended, improvised songs of the black washerwomen. They were called "Rubbing Songs" and were sung to the rhythm of the scrubbing brush on the washboard. The women eased the burden of their work by performing these songs, although observers do not tell us how much the linen suffered in the process!

African Americans have a talent for improvisation in the instruments they make as well as in their music, and when the washboard lay idle, some must have picked it up to find, in scraping it with a piece of wood, a rhythmic accompaniment to singing. Guitar pickers and banjo players must have welcomed its superiority over the customary "pat" accompaniments. These "pats" were rhythmic backgrounds to songs and dances made by slapping and striking the thighs, knees, and ribs; by using the fingers, the palm, or the ball of the thumb, a variety of sounds could be made. But the "pat" was soft in tone, while the washboard was crisper in sound and louder in volume, giving, with a similar technique, a more driving support to the singer.

Talented players brought the found instrument to new heights. One notable virtuoso was a South Carolina musician with the improbable name of Oh, Red—surely the only person with a comma in his name! (His real name was the equally improbable George Washington.) He was an itinerant player who accompanied a number of folk singers and who recorded a great many times with the talented guitarist Blind Boy Fuller. One of Fuller's and Red's best-known recordings was of the novelty blues number "STEP IT UP AND GO."

♪
(Columbia 37230) 3/5/40, New York City

Some washboard players used to scrape their instruments with a nail, but Oh, Red, in common with many others, used the pat technique and played with his fingers, wearing thimbles on them in order to increase the volume of his instrument and to avoid wear and tear on his fingertips. By striking the board in different places and/or by adding pieces of wood beneath it, a player could vary its tonal qualities. Generally he would increase the range of his instrument by affixing cowbells and pieces of iron to the wooden frame, carefully selected for their notes when struck. Robert "Washboard Slim" Young used such

♪
(Okeh 06437) 5/22/41,
Chicago, IL

a set-up on his accompaniment to Brownie McGhee's recording of "Key to My Door."

Many black folk musicians seemed to be aware of the musical potentialities of the most unlikely pieces of household equipment, and sometimes a washboard player would surround himself with other equally procurable articles—skillets, bottles, plowshares—and include these in his playing. Others would join in with rudimentary instruments adapted from pieces of domestic hardware, aided perhaps by a harmonica, a cheap and fairly common instrument in the South. The harmonica that takes the lead on "Sonny's Jump," is played by the distinctive and hugely talented musician Sanders Terrell, also known as Sonny Terry, who is accompanied by a bass made from a washtub, a broom handle, and a length of wire; a pair of castanets fashioned from pieces of hollow bones; and a zinc washboard embellished with cymbals made from frying pans and saucepan lids.

♪
(Folkways FLP 6) 1952,
New York City

Pretty rough and primitive it is, but this was the music of the cottonwood loggers, the oil drillers, and the turpentine pressers—men whose environment was rough and primitive. Such bands were popular in black communities throughout the South, not only in the country districts but in the towns, too—including Birmingham, Atlanta, and especially the river ports of Memphis and New Orleans. One-string fiddles made from cigar boxes, string basses made from barrels and tea chests, musical saws, and jaw's harps supplemented the other homemade instruments. Many a New Orleans musician first played in such a band, begging for money on the sidewalk until he could afford a trumpet or trombone. If the range of the instruments and the abilities of the players were often somewhat limited, there was always the strong rhythm of the washboard to carry them over the weak spots. Guitarist Bobbie Leecan had no illusions when he called his group the Need More Band. This amusingly titled ensemble recorded the aptly named "Washboard Cut-Out" in 1927.

♪
(Victor 20660) 4/5/27,
Camden, NJ

No washboard band "took Chicago by storm" as the books say of the bands of Tom Brown, Freddie Keppard, or King Oliver, but when jazz moved north the washboard made its unobtrusive appearance there. New York rent-party pianist Lem Fowler led one of the first groups to record, proudly naming his band Fowler's Washboard Wonders. Even though there are orthodox instruments on his recording of the popular novelty "Salty Dog," this is strictly an amateur performance—jazz from a tenement back room, not from a dance hall on Fifty-second Street or Lexington Avenue.

♪
(Columbia 1411 ID)
10/28/25, New York City

In the classic New Orleans band structure, there was no place at first for primitive instruments, but by the mid-1920s a number of musicians—Charlie Irvis, Cecil Scott, Jimmy Blythe, Natty Dominique, and many more—began to appreciate that the crisp, staccato tonal qualities of the washboard could give an ideal rhythmic impetus to a jazz band. They still liked to think of it as a folk instrument, though, so these groups took "backwoodsy" names, calling themselves the Dixie Jazzers Washboard Band or the Beale Street Washboard Band. Popular jazz producer-pianist-arranger Clarence Williams was a fan of the instrument, as is apparent through the scores of recordings he made with various lineups, many of which gained their drive and vitality from his use of washboard players. One of these assembled-for-the-studio groups was the colorfully named Blue Grass Footwarmers, who recorded Williams's "CHARLESTON HOUND."

♪
(Harmony 248-H)
6/16/26, New York City

Jasper Taylor scrubbed the boards on "Charleston Hound," but Williams also discovered the talents of such remarkable players as Floyd Casey and Willie Williams. Casey was a spirited player, as can be heard on Clarence Williams's Washboard Four recording of "CANDY LIPS." On this record he provides admirable support for Williams's exuberant scat vocals, a lively rhythm behind Ed Allen's clean trumpet and Benny Moten's incisive clarinet, and brings the tune to vigorous conclusion with his syncopated breaks.

♪
(Okeh 8440) 1/29/27,
New York City

Although Johnny Dodds played clarinet with Louis Armstrong and King Oliver, he liked to play with small, informal groups, and would suddenly appear with a jug or washboard band. He tried to convey his enthusiasm for the rhythmic texture of the washboards to his brother Baby Dodds, and made him supply the rhythm in his Beale Street Washboard Band. Baby Dodds complained that the thimbles hurt his fingertips, but—sore fingers or not—his sympathetic use of different rhythmic patterns chosen to accord with the work of the lead instruments is an object lesson in technique, as can be heard on "FORTY AND TIGHT," recorded by Johnny Dodd's Beale Street Washboard Band.

♪
(Vocalion V1016) 7/24/29,
Chicago, IL

Some drummers scorned the boards, but others were as happy with them as with their elaborate drum kits. Jimmy Bertrand was one of these, and he would even change from one instrument to the other while playing in a performance. At one time he played with Erskine Tate, the "hot" violinist who led a big band for eight years at the Vendome Theater on State Street in Chicago. Few of the big bands used a washboard, however, and one can imagine that it would look a trifle too domestic among the gleaming array of instruments, the satin draperies, and the proud bandsmen sleek in their tuxedos. Henderson and Duke Ellington had no use for the instrument, but that the boards could swing a big band was proved by McKinney's Cotton Pickers. Listen to Cuba Austin's rhythms behind John Nesbitt's fiery trumpet on their recording of "MILENBERG JOYS."

♪
(Victor 21611) 7/11/28, Chicago, IL

When the smooth efficiency of the swing bands temporarily dominated jazz, the washboard returned to its folk origins, flourishing obscurely in Southern country bands or with the urban blues singers and musicians in the cities of the North. One of the players most sought after was Big Bill Broonzy's Memphis-born half-brother Washboard Sam. Sam's guttural voice was powerful enough to compete with his washboard, an instrument embellished with cowbells and a gramophone turntable. Sam, Big Bill Broonzy, and pianist Memphis Slim made a formidable group, as can be heard on their 1941 recording of "FLYING CROW BLUES."

♪
(Bluebird B-8844) 6/26/41, Chicago, IL

Then the inevitable happened: The washboard became a novelty instrument, appearing on the music hall circuit in variety acts and as a major comic item in bands such as Spike Jones and His City Slickers. Its comic potential is explored on Jones's recording of "HOTCHA CORNIA (BLACK EYES)." The revival of interest in traditional jazz came in time to rescue the washboard from this pitiful fate, but it is still employed for its novelty appeal, as a variation for a couple of numbers in an evening's program.

♪
(HMVBD 1099) 7/42, n.p.

The washboard is the one folk instrument of a truly improvised nature that has passed through every phase of jazz, and the current appearance—a little self-consciously, perhaps—of numerous washboard bands throughout the country is an encouraging indication of interest in that venerable and homey instrument. In the 1930s, English bands failed to exploit a golden opportunity when the Washboard Serenaders visited London. It is doubtful whether any skiffle groups succeed in recapturing something of the inspired frenzy, the irrepressible gaiety of that wonderful band, as it played "THE SHEIK OF ARABY."

♪
(Parlophone F428) 7/19/35, London, UK

# 12

# Declassifying the Classic Blues
First Broadcast: 11/4/87; Producer: Derek Drescher

♪
(Okeh 8434) 11/17/26,
Chicago, IL

**I**n this series I want to reconsider some of the built-in assumptions that influence our perception and understanding of the blues and related musical forms. One of the records that helped launch the issue of so-called "Race Records" (or 78-rpm discs that were for sale to African Americans, identified as being for black purchasers by having numerically distinct series) was Mamie Smith's "Crazy Blues." It was to the benefit of many other black women singers that a black woman had at last broke into what had previously been an exclusively white market. During the decade after the release of this record, more than 200 women singers were recorded and their songs issued on Race Records. Several of them made more than a hundred titles each, and a great many made a few dozen. In addition, there were those who made just a handful of titles that were often of great interest, nonetheless. Some, like Hattie McDaniels, had a remarkable career as a singer in black show business, and later as a film actress (famous for her role in *Gone With the Wind*). She made just six titles on record, including "Boo-Hoo Blues" with Lovie Austin's Serenaders accompanying her.

These many female recording artists are known today as "Classic Blues Singers." But what does the term *Classic Blues* mean? How did it come into use, and is it adequate to embrace so broad a range of artists?

♪
(Paramount 12252)
10/16/24, New York City

"With Gertrude Ma Rainey, greatest of all blues singers, came the classic blues," wrote the jazz historian Rudi Blesh, unequivocally, over fifty years ago. His book *Shining Trumpets: A History of Jazz* was first published in 1949; it included two chapters on blues that preceded a chapter titled "The Beginnings of Jazz." Blesh made a distinction between "Archaic Blues" and "Classic Blues," using Ma Rainey as an example of the latter. She "never surpassed the unadorned tragedy she achieves here. Nor can a more perfect fusion of voice and instruments be found anywhere else in recorded blues literature," he wrote of her recording of "SEE SEE RIDER." Blesh rhapsodized, "In the coda, the cornet responds like the voice of Rainey herself, singing phrases of overpowering, regretful sadness that rise unexpectedly to a moment of deceptive triumph on the high tonic only to sink back to the blue third interval as if overcome by despair." The cornet was played by Louis Armstrong.

Blesh applied his discerning ear and lush writing style to his division of the blues. Among the "Archaic" singers he discussed were Blind Lemon Jefferson, Charley Jordan, Jesse James, Mama Yancey, Lucille Bogan, Montana Taylor, and Robert Johnson—his romantic image of Johnson as a troubled loner has persisted to the present day. So has his identification of the "Classic" blues singers, who included, as might be expected, Bessie Smith, as well as Bertha "Chippie" Hill, Hociel Thomas, Sippie Wallace, and—less likely—the great jazz pianist and composer Jelly Roll Morton. Blesh castigated the exponents of what he termed the "Postclassic" blues, which he subdivided into the "contemporary blues, with a falling off of power but not of sincerity," which included the work of Roosevelt Sykes and Lonnie Johnson; and "decadent or sophisticated blues," which included Jazz Gillum, Josh White, and the venerable Billie Holiday, whom Blesh called "not a real blues singer but merely a smart entertainer." (Well, he couldn't be expected to get everything right!)

Bearing in mind the state of blues knowledge at the time, Blesh's attempt—among the very first—to classify the blues was an important step. He was an art historian, and his criteria were partly historical, partly aesthetic. Fortunately, his terms "archaic" and "postclassic" were soon replaced, but the notion of "Classic Blues" has lasted until the present. With over 200 singers and their work now available to us, a revision is overdue. The range of material recorded by these women is amazing, encompassing folk and traditional song, minstrel and medicine show singing, vaudeville and popular song, as well as blues. Edith Wilson's "RULES AND REGULATIONS: 'SIGNED RAZOR JIM'"

♪
(Columbia 3653)
6/92, New York City

reprised a popular stereotype in African American entertainment that had endured since the 1890s and the days of the "'coon song": the razor-toting bad man who controls the dancers at a respectable ball.

This is not a blues number, nor even song with blues expression, but a spirited performance by a professional entertainer with able backing by Johnny Dunn and his band. The term "Vaudeville Blues" has been used recently to avoid the "Classic Blues" tag, but it is not appropriate here. Edith Wilson was a musical-show and revue singer who was only fifteen when she replaced Mamie Smith in the all-black musical *Put and Take*. Soon she was singing in a succession of Lew Leslie musical shows such as the *Plantation Revue, From Dover Street to Dixie, Chocolate Kiddies*, the *Blackbirds Revue*, and so on, at the Lafayette in Harlem Theatre in Harlem, the Alhambra Theater in downtown New York City, and with the *Blackbirds* shows at the London Pavilion. Like Alberta Hunter, Ethel Waters, Josie Miles, and many others, she was not a blues artist but a revue artist. It's a cliché of popular music theory that the audience defines the authenticity of an act; although I question this, I do believe that the artists and the audience in the performance context define the genre. Vaudeville entertainment was somewhat different from blues.

More typical vaudeville performers were Jodie and Sue Edwards, known on the black vaudeville stage as Butterbeans and Susie. Their "MAMA STAYED OUT THE WHOLE NIGHT LONG" is a typically robust, suggestive, and confrontational exchange that belied their long and harmonious life together: They had been married on stage when they were mere teenagers. Theirs was a low-down, even grotesque, comedy performed in ludicrous costumes with strutting dancing and exaggerated posturing, and the vaudeville audiences loved them. George Williams and Bessie Brown, Coot Grant and Kid Sox Wilson, Biddy Paige and Popo Warfield, were just a few of the vocal comedy duets who worked the Theater Owners Booking Agency venues and other black vaudeville circuits. Sometimes they ventured into the blues arena, but their form of vaudeville blues and entertainment gained its effect from parody and innuendo. Many women blues singers joined them on stage, but the blues they sang had to be in similar vein. Some preferred to tour with traveling shows that "barnstormed" across the South, working in vacant farm buildings, in movie theaters, and under canvas tents—wherever they could obtain a venue. Some of the road shows were those of updated minstrel companies, like the celebrated Rabbit Foot Minstrels, operating out of Port Gibson, Mississippi, or

♪
(Okeh 8319) 3/10/26, New York City

Ephraim Williams's Silas Green from New Orleans minstrel show, which actually came from North Carolina.

Lizzie Miles was one of the singers on record who spent many years with the road shows and circuses. Her recording of "You're Always Messin' Round With My Man" is typical of the slightly racy blues songs that were popular on the show circuits.

♪
(Victor 19083) 5/23/33, New York City

By the time it was recorded in 1933, the New Orleans–born singer had worked for several years with the Cole Brothers Circus, singing, dancing, doing a high wire act, and even working with the elephants. With her husband, J. C. Miles, she worked with the Alabama Minstrels; the two later formed their own company. Numerous women singers had long careers with the road shows and stock companies, including Edmonia Henderson, who sang with the Drake and Walker Stock show; Ida Cox, who was long associated with the Florida Cotton Blossoms minstrel show and later had her own Raisin' Cain company; and Hattie Burleson, whose show was still on the road in the 1950s. Some of the most famous so-called "Classic Blues Singers" had a similar background—not the least of them Ma Rainey, whose Ma and Pa Rainey show was the training ground for many young talents.

However, some singers could not adapt to the restless life of the traveling show, and preferred a more intimate relationship with their audiences. One of these was Mattie Hite, who was a club—or as they preferred to call them in Harlem in the 1920s, a "cabaret"—singer. Her recording of "Texas Twist" is typical of the cabaret repertory.

♪
(Columbia 14503-D) 1/27/30, n.p.

Mattie Hite sang at Barron Wilkins's Astoria Cafe, the Nest, Pod's and Jerry's, and many other nightspots where blues was the principal fare. Her friend Mary Stafford, and the gruff male impersonator Gladys Bentley, were among these blues club-cabaret singers on record. Bentley's "Ground Hog Blues" is typical of her low-down style.

♪
(Okeh 8610) 8/28, New York City

Apart from all these, there were the jazz singers like Eva Taylor who had no aspirations toward blues singing at all, but who still are lumped together under the rubrics "Classic Blues" or "Vaudeville Blues."

In my view, the problem lies in the use of global terms that inevitably work against singers who were fully professional, but did not aspire to be regular blues singers, though they may have included a blues number or two in their nightly shows. A classification based on where the material was performed may help to differentiate them. Of course, it is based on function rather than stylistic analysis, but this will follow if, as I believe, the genre is defined by the artist and her audience within the specific performance context.

# 13

# Blues as an Art Form, Part I: Playing the Blues

First Broadcast: 2/28/68; Producer: Teddy Warrick

There are a few lines by Rudyard Kipling that rather appeal to me:

> Our Father Adam sat under a tree and scratched with a stick in the mould,
>
> and the first rude sketch that the world had seen was joy to his mighty heart.
>
> Till the Devil whispered behind the leaves "It's pretty, but is it art?"

I have a suspicion that if he had ever heard a blues song, Kipling would have played the Devil to Charley Patton's Adam. But the point is valid: While humankind creates, there'll always be those who will question the aesthetic merit of the work. If we agree with Leo Tolstoy that art is the transmission of feeling that the artist has experienced, or that it is the duty of the artist—as Socrates demanded of the sculptor—to "give concrete expression to the workings of the soul," then blues is an art form and the blues singer is an artist. So I don't intend to try and justify an argument that the blues is an art form—I only intend to discuss it as one. But exactly what kind of art form is it?

♪
(Columbia 14438)
4/10/29, Atlanta, GA

♪
(Chess 1936) 5/23/65,
Chicago, IL

♪
(Ducretet-Thomson TKL
43094) c. 1958,
Seville, Spain

♪
(Modern 20-746) 1/50,
Detroit, MI

I can imagine an orchestral violinist, listening to Peg Leg Howell's "Broke and Hungry Blues," wincing at the fiddle technique—"alley fiddle," as the blues singer calls it. And I can hear the protests of the concert soloist at Peg Leg Howell's abrasive singing, which was a familiar sound in the streets of Atlanta, Georgia, for forty years. Peg Leg's singing was rough-hewn, bearing a relationship to the voice of his contemporary Fyodor Chaliapin as, say, a Breton peasant blanket chest would to a Louis Quatorze commode (the one with the marks of the adze, the other with its polished kingwood veneers and gilt bronze embellishments). One is forthright, spontaneous, direct; the other has wit, elegance, pleasurable conceits. This isn't to say that one is better than the other—but they are very different.

But what do we mean by *blues*? If Peg Leg Howell's Atlanta street singing is blues, so too is Buddy Guy's Gospel-influenced, modern city blues of the Chicago nightclubs, as we can hear on his recording of "Leave My Girl Alone."

From the turn of the century, blues developed over six decades, having moved from deeply rural origins to intensely urban contexts, and is now spread over an area the size of Europe. It is a music that has been well preserved in most of its phases through recording, and it's one that has been more subject than most to commercial pressures. So how does it compare with other musical forms?

It is illuminating to compare blues with another popular form, familiar through recordings and concert performances: the Spanish *cante flamenco*. For example, listen to Pepe el de la Matrona singing a "Soleares" of the kind that spread from Triana to Cádiz and Juarez.

"The day of the earthquake the water rose high, but it could not reach the level of my anxiety"—these words wouldn't be out of place in a blues song. Pepe el de la Matrona embellishes his words, extending his syllables in an abstract and expressive manner, while the guitar supports the vocal with flourishes, descending phrases, and punctuation of emphatic chords. The blues singer too, elaborates his words or hums and moans for expressive effect. Often, as on "Wednesday Evening" by John Lee Hooker, the guitar playing is close to the voice. The guitarist "bends" the notes by pushing the string sideways against the fret, and slides his fretting finger up and down the neck to make the strings whine. Hooker—a Mississippi-born singer who lived for twenty years in Detroit—raises his notes by "hammering-on": fretting the string a fraction after picking it.

Both flamenco and blues are recognizable within their respective idioms, having formal and expressive qualities that help to define their individual characters. Blues has more variety than flamenco (and I'm speaking as a lover of both); the range of instruments used and the different styles of blues songs are far greater. But there is a similarity in the development of regional styles and traditions in both styles. The regional styles of blues are unified by the common elements in technique and the use of the basic blues forms. Most common of these is the twelve-bar blues. In its most usual form it consists of twelve bars divided into three lines of four bars each. The vocal often occupies only two bars in each line, the concluding bars allowing room for an improvised instrumental answer to the words, which generally form iambic pentameters. Though the chord sequence of tonic–subdominant–dominant is related to that of the simple ballads and hymns, it provides a certain inevitable resolution to the blues. Some people may find this monotonous; the blues singer delights in it. As we've heard in many examples, the stanzas are frequently of A–A–B verses that leave room for the improvisation of new lines during the song.

With his spare, bony lines and startling verses, Blind Lemon Jefferson was the archetypal Texas singer, his guitar acting as a second voice. His "Hangman's Blues" is a remarkable projection into the mind of a condemned man.

♪
(Paramount 12679) 8/28, Chicago, IL

It's the predetermined sequence that allows the blues performer the freedom to improvise and create. And it's one that he can alter if he wishes. On "Waiting for My Baby" by Mississippi singer Fred McDowell, notice how he builds up the tension of his blues by a pounding beat of the bass strings of his guitar against the ringing treble, and how he fragments the lines into an irregular but cohesive extension of the blues form.

♪
(Testament T-2208) 11/24/63, n.p.

The singing sound of his guitar was produced with a bottleneck; it's annealed in a flame so that the edges aren't jagged, and worn over the third or fourth finger. When he plays, he strokes the strings to produce a crying, wailing sound. In blues the association of the instruments with the voice is fundamental; blues is a vocal music. The harmonica is an excellent example of the way the blues instrumentalist has devised a technique to meet his needs. In order to get a greater range from his instrument, he plays a harmonica that is tuned in the subdominant chord of the guitarist's key; if the theme is in *E*, he plays on an *A* harmonica. This, known as the "crossed harp" technique, enables him to "bend" the notes as much as the guitarist slides the strings. Cupping in the hands, fluttering the fingers, and unorthodox tongue work increase the range of a ten-cent instrument. Alec

♪
(Trumpet 139) possibly 3/51, Jackson, MS

Miller, also known as "Sonny Boy Williamson, No. II" shows how it's done on his recording of "Do It if You Wanna."

It's the blues form that enables blues musicians to work together without rehearsal, and the use of the flattened notes, the "bent" notes, that are consistent in the idiom. Some theorists have suggested that the diminished thirds and dominant sevenths, which blues singers and musicians favor, are the result of placing a European diatonic scale on an African pentatonic. Be that as it may, the blues singer shows a distinct preference for these flatted notes and for deliberate dissonance. His extension of the instruments applies to the making of them, too, as I have mentioned with regard to the jug and washboard bands. On "Good Feeling Blues" by the South Carolina singer Blind Boy Fuller, the wailing harp of a young and also blind Sonny Terry and the brittle sound of Oh, Red's washboard are totally integrated with guitar and voice.

♪
(Okeh 06231) 3/7/40,
New York City

Of course, the problem is much greater for the blues pianist, because the piano's keys are positive and do not allow for bending the notes. Blues pianists have achieved equivalent effects by "crushing" the keys: striking adjacent keys at a fractional interval to produce a grace note equivalent to the "blue notes" of the guitarist. The percussive role of the piano in the blues is no doubt partly due to this limitation of the keyboard. Jimmy Yancey, born in Chicago in 1898, was one of the earliest blues pianists in that city. Both in the treble and in the bass figures of his slow boogie "Eternal Blues" he demonstrates the blues pianist's use of clusters, crushed notes, and dissonances.

♪
(Session 12-001) 12/43,
Chicago, IL

# 14

# The Blues and Black Society

Original Broadcast: 2/15/68; Producer: Teddy Warrick

On a field trip in the South in 1960, I met a singer in Houston by the name of Edwin Buster Pickens. He was a small man, worried looking, and he appeared rather incongruous in a derby hat and faded tuxedo that was green with age. When he took off his hat—and the neckerchief he wore underneath it—he showed a quiff of hair on the front of his forehead. It was a kind of insignia worn by the Texas barrelhouse pianists that told the sawmill operators that he was a piano player and not a mill hand. The blues was, quite simply, the focus of Buster Pickens's life. As he explained to me, "The only way that anyone can ever play blues— he's got to have them. You got to have experienced something in life. You been troubled, you been broke, you been hungry, no job, no money, the one you love is deserted you—that makes you blue. Blues don't derive from a person's say, just get up and just say, 'I'm gonna sing the blues' without he's got to have a feelin'; he's got to have some thing within, that he can bring it out. Just how he feels about it."

Buster Pickens wasn't a great blues singer, but he was a typical one—typical because he was one of untold numbers of men for whom singing the blues was an essential part of their lives. He'd never had his name on a record label; he wasn't known to blues collectors. But he *was* known from Arkansas to the Mexican border along the Santa Fe Line, which linked the sawmill and cotton towns—and the barrelhouses. He'd spent a rough life hoboing on the freight trains and playing in the juke joints in the country, until later curfew laws closed them down. His music was simple—elemental—and very moving, as can be heard on this recording I made of him singing "COLORADO SPRINGS BLUES."

♪
(Decca LK 4664) 7/60,
Houston, TX

A couple of years later, in 1962, Pickens was murdered over a dollar debt in a bar-room squabble. He was a lonely, rather tragic figure in his last years, when work had become scarce; it wasn't an enviable life. Pickens had never even stepped as high as the bottom rung of the social ladder, and the blues was the way in which he found relief from the pressures that continually bore on him: poverty, ghetto housing, rootless traveling, woman trouble. He sang the blues because he had to. The pressures in his life he shared with a great many bluesmen; they are the blues, and they can become frighteningly real. "I've got the blues so bad I can feel them in the dark," sang Blind Willie McTell. For the tormented spirit of Robert Johnson, the blues was an aching heart disease; like consumption, it was killing him by degrees, as he sang in his "PREACHING BLUES."

♪
(Vocalion 04630)
11/27/36,
San Antonio, TX

This is the blues at its most expressive: an outpouring of fears and frustrations. Blacks in the United States are members of an underprivileged class, and it makes no difference if their standard of living is far higher than that of most people in Africa, India, or much of South America. For them, being below the poverty line in the world's richest nation means suffering. Ernest attempts to play the blues by white imitators notwithstanding, the blues is, inescapably, the music of the African American, and it seems undeniable that it is a cultural expression that relates back to the circumstances of segregation. It's true that racial discrimination is seldom blatantly the theme of the blues—but it's never far away. "I can hear my black name ringin' all up and down the line," sang Sonny Boy Williamson in his aptly titled "MY BLACK NAME BLUES."

♪
(Bluebird B8992) 7/30/42,
Chicago, IL

In Sonny Boy's blues it's clear that "black" is an epithet. In the blues Negroes are often angry about their color: "Black is evil"; things become "too black bad"; another sings "I'm blue, Black and evil—and I did not make myself." White people are rarely the direct subject of blues, but there's no doubting that it's a white man's world, as is evident in the verse of Robert Wilkins's "FALLING DOWN BLUES," in which the singer indicates that treating a girl as if she were White means that she gets the best possible attention. "I'll certainly treat you just like you was White. That don't satisfy you girl, I'll take your life."

♪
(Brunswick 7125)
9/23/29, Memphis, TN

In Afro-American society, a class system developed that was based on color, a tragic stratification that generally put the black-skinned person at the bottom, and the lightest-skinned, the nearest to White, at the top. But a light skin could also be suspect *because* it was near White; superstition said that a yellow-skinned girl would soon show a stripe of black color. "A brownskin woman is the best brownie after all," sang Barbecue Bob in his blues "BROWN SKIN GAL." He added an ironic, "ashes to ashes, dust to dust; if you can't ride the train, catch the ginger bus."

♪
(Columbia 14257-D)
6/15/27, New York City

There's a note of acceptance in Barbecue Bob's song. "People, if you hear me humming on this song both night and day, I'm just a poor boy in trouble, trying to drive the blues away," sang Walter Davis. In other words, some of the anger that might have found more direct expression in the 1920s and 1930s was dissipated in the blues. Often, though, the blues, if not actively defiant, expresses a disregard for events, born of a fatalistic pride and suspicion of the promises for the future. Jesse James, reputedly a convict on parole, made a powerful statement of an "outsider" one day in June 1936 in his recording of "LONESOME DAY BLUES," singing, "Now the day's been a long ol' lonesome day; d'ya hear me talkin' to ya, d'ya hear what I say? Lord the day's been a long ol' lonesome day, and now tomorrow will be the same ol' way." He continues, "You better stop and listen see what tomorrow bring, it may bring you sunshine, Lord, and it may bring rain."

♪
(Decca 7213) 6/3/36,
Chicago, IL

In this tough slice of "barrelhouse" blues, Jesse James was his own central theme. I have attempted to show how the blues replaced the earlier African American ballads with the blues singer himself standing in for the ballad hero. But there's a fundamental difference: Blues singers may introduce a boasting line or two, but they usually described the situation without glamor. They sing, both for themselves and the black community. If the content is often far removed from the experience of the population as a whole, it's real for those to whom the blues is addressed.

♪
(Columbia 14491-D;
DOCD 5147) 11/15/29,
Chicago, IL

The themes of Henry Townsend's "MISTREATED BLUES"—separation and migration—are characteristic of the blues of any period, a direct reflection of the unsettled nature of the black family in a rootless society. Thirty years after he made that recording, he talked to me about the underlying honesty of the blues, saying, "If the blues is delivered in the truth, which most of them are, they are told exactly as the story go and as the feelin' that they have—so I think it'll touch. And as I was sayin', if I sing the blues and I tell the truth, what have I done? What have I committed? I haven't lied. So it's just a tone—I mean it's just a frame of mind that people are in."

Many blues are about minor incidents: slivers of life drawn from the immediate experience of the singer. The details are often explicit and the personalities are named, almost as if the singer assumed that all who heard his blues would know who they were. Sleepy John Estes, for instance, has drawn a picture of his native Brownsville, Tennessee, in his songs, which are populated with the personalities of the colored sector of that city, like Marthy Hardin; Al Rawls, who ran the funeral home; or Vassie Williams, the car mechanic. Or he sings of notable white people like Lawyer Clark or Mr. Pat Mann. There's no hint of protest; Estes respectfully names the white men as "Mister," while acknowledging the Blacks without formal title. His "Brownsville Blues" offers a mix of personal biography (he tells us that he was raised in Lawther County and schooled on Winfield Lane), news (he's planning to get his car repaired at Vassie Williams's shop), and his standing in town (although he rues a wasted life in Brownsville, he reassures himself that there are people who believe that he's all right) taking comfort, perhaps, in the paternalistic relationship between Whites and Blacks that was typical in Southern communities in the 1930s.

♪
(Decca 7473) 4/22/38,
New York City

There are blues, of course, that *do* play a ballad role, that narrate a particular event that seems to have gained special importance. The terrible fire in Natchez, Mississippi, in April 1940, that caused the death of 200 people, including the band of Walter Barnes, is a case in point. It's been the subject of blues by Baby Doo, Howling Wolf, John Lee Hooker, and Gene Gilmore, who recorded a particularly interesting version called "The Natchez Fire."

♪
(Decca 7763) 6/4/40,
Chicago, IL

Perhaps Gilmore knew the band or some of the people who died in the fire, giving this event special significance for him; it's hard to say. Generally, blues songs that tell of disasters are about something that the singer has probably witnessed, and something that is familiar to his audience. The tornadoes that sweep up from the Texas coast as far as St. Louis and beyond are one such subject, described by Kokomo Arnold in his song "Mean Old Twister." Typically, he relates it to himself and draws a personal moral from the actual events.

♪
(Decca 7347) 5/30/37,
Chicago, IL

The 1930s were probably the richest period for the blues on social themes, beyond the immediate personal dramas of disintegrating love affairs. There are blues songs about high rents and low wages, about working in steel mills and on the slaughterhouse killing floor, about the Public Works Administration and Public Relief, about Welfare Projects and the Red Cross. There are blues songs about popular heroes—President Franklin D. Roosevelt or Joe Louis—and others on the death of blues singers, including Leroy Carr, Doctor Clayton, Bessie Smith; and about crime, about prison, about sickness and death. Some are on universal themes; others are essentially "in-group" numbers: Who else in the 1930s cared about the death of Leroy Carr beyond the small coterie of his fellow blues singers and the purchasers of his records?

Typically, in-group songs were about the "policy" racket, like Cripple Clarence Lofton's "POLICY BLUES." They are almost incomprehensible unless one knows the special code of this inner-city phenomenon: The "policy" is the "numbers" gambling racket; the "Interstate" is a gambling wheel; a "gig" is a bet; and the "policy writer" takes the bet. The bets are laid in number combinations, normally of three numerals.

(Session 10-014) 12/43, Chicago, IL

On this recording, Lofton refers to "getting tired of these policy writers 3-6-9-in' for me." This is another use of a special code, as "3-6-9" is the number combination for excreta; by applying it to the policy writer, Lofton was wishing a particularly nasty curse on him. With a dream book to guide him as to the number combination of every kind of subject and event, the blues singer had an opportunity to express the most illicit of subjects in a form that only those who play the numbers could understand. It was a splendid vehicle for protest, but characteristically in the 1930s this potential was never realized; the target of most policy blues is the policy writer. Where the policy blues *did* function was in providing a sense of belonging to a tightly knit group for those who understood its words and numerals.

Yet the policy blues is a special case; by and large the blues is about commonplace themes, and the most familiar are those of love and sex. Platonic, ideal love has no place in the blues, though. Love inevitably means sexual love, as Texas Alexander, who spent a lifetime in the cotton fields—and penitentiaries—of Texas, sings in his "NINETY-EIGHT DEGREE BLUES" with typically forthright imagery.

(Okeh 8705) 6/15/29, San Antonio, TX

There are certain songs, however, that have a special significance even though their meaning seems innocuous enough. These are sexual songs with lyrics—once we understand their coded imagery—that would be inadmissible on radio even today. Even so, the recorded versions are totally unlike the exchange of obscenities of extreme violence and crudity that can be heard in the unexpurgated "SHAVE 'EM DRY." In putting them on record, blues singer Bessie Jackson played a game with the censor, but even in this form its purpose was catalytic.

(Melotone M13442) 3/5/35, New York City

Obviously, Jackson's song and other songs like it had considerable value in being released from constraints. They are not blues songs in the strictest sense, but they are the kind of songs that barrelhouse pianists would sing, and they allowed for a discharge of aggressive emotion. They substituted for protest until the World War II years, when violence could be given a legitimate outlet.

When the war involved the United States, the blues became noticeably more optimistic and extroverted. Roosevelt's Executive Order 8802 against job discrimination ensured better wages for those at home, and those drafted into the armed forces felt they had a chance to prove their worth. African American fighting units were reckless in their disregard for personal safety; the tone of Sonny Boy Williamson's "WIN THE WAR BLUES" is characteristic of the mood of the times: "I want a machine gun, I want to be hid out in the woods, I want to show ol' man Hitler that Sonny Boy don't mean him no good. I want to drop a bomb and set the Japanese city on fire."

♪ (Bluebird 34-0722) 12/14/44, Chicago, IL

Yet many black servicemen who were trained for combat found they were to be employed as service troops, as stevedores, and pioneers. Their morale was damaged, and when they returned to the United States after the war, they found that although they had fought—and many had died—for their country, segregation was to remain. African Americans were embittered by the experience, and Williamson's almost naive patriotism was now replaced by an expressed reluctance to fight in the Korean War of the early 1950s. In "THE WORLD IS IN A TANGLE," Jimmy Rodgers, a guitarist in Muddy Waters's band, sang, "You know the Reds are messed up yonder and we ain't gonna be here long. That's why I'm gonna build myself a cave move down in the ground. You know when I go into the Army darlin' there won't be no more Reds aroun'." Jimmy Rodgers was opting out.

♪ (Chess 1453) 1950, Chicago, IL

In the past, the blues had largely been accommodative, helping the singer to adjust himself to conditions of which he was often the victim. This passivity has often irritated Black intellectuals who have disowned the blues, seeing it as being too closely related to the submissiveness of Southern African Americans in the years between the wars, which they greatly resent. Now, however, signs of definite political concern were appearing in the blues. The ascent of President Dwight D. Eisenhower and the Republican Party in the early 1950s was a cause for alarm among many blues singers, including J. B. Lenoir. In his "EISENHOWER BLUES," he declared simply his conviction that he was heading for the welfare rolls: "I've got those Eisenhower Blues. What on earth are we gonna do?" he asked.

♪ (Parrot 802) 1954, Chicago, IL

Lenoir was too outspoken; his record was banned, and the censors firmly clamped down on protest blues. This raises the question of whether the lack of songs like these being released during the 1930s was in fact the result of rigid censorship, but on this there is no information. Once started, however, the blues of the 1950s often had a distinctly critical tone, hidden sometimes in the brashness of the music. Two witty singers, Bo Diddley and Chuck Berry, led an advance guard of popular rhythm and blues in which the message was often camouflaged by lively, danceable music. But Chuck Berry's black listeners would not miss the stringent irony of "IT WASN'T ME," in which he paraded a catalog of national, racial, and even college sorority prejudice in the context of a typical R and B tune. He sings, "I met a German girl in England. She was going to school in France. Say we danced in Mississippi at an Alpha Kappa dance. It wasn't me, uh-uh boys it wasn't me."

♪
(Chess CRL 4506) 9/1/65, Chicago, IL

It could be argued that Chuck Berry's music is not the blues, that his brand of R and B is closer to rock and roll. It's true his songs have a sophistication not to be found in the blues of an older generation, which was represented in the 1960s by the tough and uncompromising music of Muddy Waters and Howlin Wolf. Their fierce, aggressive music may not have had much significance as far as the words were concerned, but their delivery, often accompanied by violent action, had a wealth of meaning. Form was dominating content, but their expressive technique reflected the spirit of the period, investing old words with new power, as can be heard in Wolf's forceful performance of "SMOKE STACK LIGHTNING."

♪
(Chess 1434) 1956, Chicago, IL

The blues does not speak for the whole of black society. There are no blues songs about black professional men—scientists, professors, lawyers, architects. There are no blues songs about the National Association for the Advancement of Colored People, the Congress on Racial Equality, or the Student Nonviolent Coordinating Committee; and none about black writers or leaders—not even those of the black Muslim movement—as they work *for* the black masses. The blues is the music *of* the black masses. In its words and music—and frequently in both—it has offered at each stage of its history an effective mirror to the prevalent feelings and attitudes, not of the black intelligentsia, but of ordinary black men and women at the time. And what of today?

Most of the singers I have mentioned were active in 1970s, but the most influential blues singer was B. B. ("Blues Boy") King, who had a host of followers who have developed—like King himself—a remarkable rapport with audiences. King has scarcely to open his mouth to have his audience roaring with him; the impression of unity and of mass hysteria barely held in check is very real, as can be heard in recordings like his 1966 release "DON'T ANSWER THE DOOR." The words may not *seem*

♪
(Bluesway 6001) 11/5/66, n.p.

to matter, but the callousness, the rejection of outside aid to which the crowd responds is indicative of the mood that set Los Angeles alight in the famous late-1960s riots—"Burn, baby, Burn"—it's no coincidence that the catchphrase that excited the fire raisers of Watts came from a black blues disc jockey.

# 15

# Singing the Blues
Original Broadcast: 10/2/64 and 10/9/64; Producers: Langston Hughes and D. G. Bridson

♪
(Pye GGL 0205)
c. 1958, New York City

♪
(Royale 18131)
2/17/43, New York City

Immediately after the Civil War, a group of ex-slaves sold their own fetters to raise sufficient funds to build a schoolroom and, in doing so, founded the Fisk University in Nashville, Tennessee. But the school quickly ran short of funds, so the students brainstormed about ways to raise additional money. They came up with the idea of forming a choir to sing traditional African American spirituals, calling themselves the Fisk Jubilee Singers. The success of this group brought black spirituals and plantation songs to the ears of white America. The Fisk Jubilee Singers established beyond a doubt the fact that Blacks possessed great talent in music and song, but they also set the pattern of arrangement and dilution of the spirituals that has persisted for nearly a century.

Josh White is an accomplished performer of traditional African American song, but his arrangement of a chain-gang song called "Going Home Boy" is hardly convincing as an interpretation of the authentic article.

He is a balladist—an advocate, if you like—who has brought black song traditions to the concert platform and the television screen. In the late 1930s his clean guitar playing, smooth voice, and refined appearance won him large audiences and recognition, so much so that in 1941 he played a goodwill tour in Mexico for the U.S. government. Though his repertoire drew from many sources, at his best he revealed the simplicity of the folk tradition, as in his version of the well-known ballad "House of the Rising Sun."

A curious gender shift is apparent, for the song is a lament by a prostitute in a New Orleans brothel, which "has been the ruin of many a poor girl, and me, Oh, Lord, for one." In fact, he learned it from the "torch singer" Libby Holman.

Outside the black world, the audience for the more fundamental, apparently untamed folk song was a small one, but it grew dramatically in the 1940s with the appearance of Leadbelly (Huddie Ledbetter) in New York. Discovered by John Lomax in a Louisiana penitentiary, Leadbelly brought a new dimension to black song. Twice jailed—for murder and for attempted homicide—he was himself a figure out of a folk legend, a seeming anachronism, larger than life, who was the sole guardian of an old tradition. Brought to New York on parole by his discoverer, he thrilled his listeners with his powerful, even demonic performances. His version of "The House of the Rising Sun," which he called "IN NEW ORLEANS," was less studied, less embroidered than Josh White's, but to his audience it was more forthright, closer to the folk.

♪
(Royale 18131) 1943,
New York, NY

Leadbelly was a remarkable figure who unconsciously set a standard against which every succeeding folksinger who might have broken the color/culture line has been compared. His appearances at colleges and clubs could have set a pattern to be followed by many other African American singers, but paradoxically his seemingly inexhaustible repertoire and many-sided abilities frustrated any natural succession. In 1949, on a brief visit to France, Leadbelly fell ill, and shortly after his return to the United States, died. Folklorists and jazz enthusiasts mourned the passing of the "last great Negro folk artist." No other singer on record has left as rich a legacy of song as did Leadbelly. His ballads fed the skiffle craze in Europe in the 1950s and sustained the folk-song boom in the United States in the 1960s.

There was no immediate successor to Leadbelly, but in 1951 the blues singer Big Bill Broonzy was invited to Europe and unexpectedly revealed an extensive repertoire of ballads and songs learned in his youth. He gave up the electric guitar that he had been playing in Chicago blues clubs, took up his old acoustic model and—returning to the States—found increasing interest in his early music. He was encouraged by young, white college students, many of whom saw in his music eternal values of equality and a common folk heritage. Pete Seeger, who had been a member of the Weavers, joined him on tours and recordings. Broonzy's recording of "JOHN HENRY," made with Seeger's rhythm banjo, shows the influence of both his country childhood and the folk boom itself, as he shaped his performance to fit the expectations of his audience.

♪
(Folkways FA 2328) 1956,
Chicago, IL

"They tell me I'm singin' folk songs. I guess they must be right. I guess my songs is folk songs: I ain't never heard a hoss sing," Broonzy used to say. It was one of his favorite jokes, and it summed up meaningfully the dilemma of the blues singer who has been embraced by folk music; blues singers were sought after for their recollections of songs of their childhood rather than the blues.

In turn, Broonzy's death in 1958 opened the way for Brownie McGhee and Sonny Terry. Though McGhee was lame and Sonny Terry was blind, they made a strong professional team. Having appeared on Broadway in small roles, they were used to "sophisticated" white audiences. Terry's virtuosity on the harmonica proved that in the black tradition there could be found technical skill of a high—if unorthodox—order, and his impressions of the "Fox Chase" won him wide admiration.

Although the black folksingers who were to be heard in the early 1950s could be numbered on the fingers of one hand, within a few years there were several others. Elizabeth Cotten, maid to the Seeger family, was found to be a talented ragtime-influenced guitarist; San Francisco-based Jesse Fuller was a one-man band who performed outside the entrances of jazz festivals and was soon invited in. But the purists noticed that the singers were being weaned away from black audiences altogether, and in the apparently inevitable process of decanonization the authenticity of Leadbelly, Broonzy, Terry, and McGhee was held in question. Conscious efforts to seek out early-recording folksingers led to the rediscovery of such artists as Walter "Furry" Lewis, whose repertoire included many old ballads, among them "Casey Jones."

Furry Lewis was known from his recordings of thirty years earlier, but hitherto unknown singers were also being found. In Texas, Chris Strachwitz, Mack McCormick, and I recorded a sharecropper named Mance Lipscomb, who sang ballads that he had learned in his childhood and during a somewhat dissolute youth. His version of "'Bout a Spoonful" is a classic folk blues song. Recorded also by Papa Charlie Jackson and Howling Wolf, Lipscomb's is an individual interpretation.

A man of great dignity and talent, Mance Lipscomb was able to build a new home for his family from the money he earned during subsequent engagements at colleges and folk festivals. His new audiences were no less appreciative of his repertoire than those at the country suppers in East Texas where he normally played.

During the 1960s, several veteran singers had been found. The lyrics to "Avalon Blues," recorded by Mississippi John Hurt

♪
(Bluesville BVLP 1002) 12/59, Englewood Cliffs, NJ

♪
(Folkways FS 3823) 10/3/59, Memphis, TN

♪
(Arhoolie F1001) 8/13/60, Navasota, TX

77

in 1928, led to his rediscovery. Hurt was a gentle, withdrawn man of seventy who had preserved, for over thirty-five years, the remarkable finger-picking style that has made his old records collectors items. His distinctive version of "CANDY MAN BLUES" was a particular audience favorite.

♪
(Piedmont PLP 13157)
3/26/63, Washington, D.C.

The folk music revival brought a new awareness of the richness of African American song. In presenting their music to the large audiences of festivals and mass media, African American singers have tapped their own wedges into the splintering barrier of segregation. They have won new regard for black performers and their art, but young Blacks might be forgiven for holding the trend in some contempt. For them, these performers are still playing the old role of entertaining the white folks; the music these men are playing is the folk music of the past rather than of the present. Their songs are borrowed, rearranged, and rerecorded by popular groups of young, white, so-called folksingers. If these older Blacks have earned respect for their music, the younger ones suspect condescension.

Nonetheless, the folk-song movement built an appreciation of the black contribution to American culture through the 1950s and '60s, and this played a small role in the integration struggle. Big Bill Broonzy, it will be remembered, was one of a number of black singers who became, through their interpretations of the rich variety of their musical traditions, ambassadors for the black cause. Aware of this added responsibility, Broonzy composed a number of songs that made their point. "A black man is called a boy, I don't care what he can do," he sang in one song; "I wonder when I will get to be called a man." In another, "BLACK, BROWN AND WHITE," he sang unequivocally against racial discrimination: "If you're White, you're all right, if you're Brown, stick around, but if you're Black—Oh brother, get back, get back!"

♪
(Vogue 134) 9/20/51,
Paris, France

Though Broonzy was basically a blues singer, "Black, Brown and White" was not a blues number. It was not until he was accepted as a folksinger that he was able to sing this song in the United States—and then only in folk-song circles. Its first commercial recording was made in Paris in 1951, but he had previously cut a version in a Texas recording booth and had tried to hawk the test pressing to the commercial record companies. It was direct and outspoken, and they weren't interested. At the same time, however, a piano-playing sharecropper from Texas, Mercy Dee Walton, was able to record blues songs that were, in their way, as effective an indictment of a segregated system as was Broonzy's more self-conscious composition, notably in the song "DARK MUDDY BOTTOM."

♪
(Specialty 481) 10/4/53,
Los Angeles, CA

The essential difference between Walton's and Broonzy's songs lies in the nature of the blues itself. The blues is a highly individual form of expression, and Mercy Dee, as a blues singer who never attempted to perform on the folk song circuit, sings in purely personal terms. True to the blues tradition, there is no direct accusation or appeal, scarcely a note of complaint. With the matter-of-fact quality that is so marked in the blues, he makes a statement of conditions and leaves the listener to draw conclusions. This is typical of the blues, which is not a vehicle for emphatic protest. The blues singer is seldom concerned with events outside his immediate experience, and emotional declarations are most frequently in terms of love, infidelity, and sex, or problems in which he is personally involved.

In the black song traditions, the ballads and folk songs in ballad form speak for the group: The triumph of black people over adversity is symbolized in the epic story of John Henry or the invincible insect, the boll weevil. In the blues, on the other hand, the singer speaks for himself, and it seems that the blues has developed as Blacks have become aware of their own identity. The blues singer sings of his observations on his known world, and his listeners identify themselves with him rather than—as in the ballads—with the hero of the song. There is little call to the group: no appeals to the racial minority, no demands for concerted action. The blues has played little active part in the civil rights campaign in summoning support, although indirectly it has helped the individual in self-assertion. The blues singer does give voice to the anxieties and frustrations of a member of an underprivileged group.

New hope was given to African Americans when the administration of President John F. Kennedy declared its determination to face squarely the civil rights issue. The president's evident sincerity won him the support of the black press, and although the enactment of the Civil Rights Bill seemed a long time coming, the rulings of the Supreme Court justices against segregation were recognized as more than gestures. These advances in legislation were personified, by Blacks, in the president himself, and when he was assassinated in Dallas the profound shock that was felt by so many millions greatly affected the black community. In a moving blues called "SAD DAY IN TEXAS," Otis Spann sang of his keen sense of personal loss.

♪
(Testament S-01) c. 12/63, Chicago, IL

Characteristically, Spann expresses an individual's sorrow. The blues singer's reaction to the tragic and brutal incidents that occurred in Little Rock, Arkansas; Jackson, Mississippi; or Birmingham, Alabama are in a sense predictable, because

♪
(Vee-Jay 538) 1963,
Chicago, IL

few blues singers could have experienced such incidents first-hand, and it's unlikely that any blues song so based would have secured commercial release. But the tension, the humiliation, and the fear with which Blacks have had to learn to live is evident in John Lee Hooker's frightened, impassioned, angry "Birmingham Blues."

"I know one thing: A man is just a man," Hooker bitterly declares. A man, whatever his color, is a man, not something less than a man nor a boy to the end of his life. Hooker's throbbing guitar and the punctuation of the drums was the folk blues of the city—coarser and tougher in the spirit of the blues of the 1960s. Increasingly, the blues have evolved from the contemplative playing and singing of the solo guitarist to the assertive, full-bodied support of the group that underscores the verses of the singer. The threat of "the fire next time" as the African American author James Baldwin had warned, was implicit in the aggressiveness of modern blues. "I'm a man!" shouted one of the finest—and fiercest—of urban blues singers, Muddy Waters, with almost terrifying effect, in his classic song "Mannish Boy." I'm a man, he sang in effect, and I demand to be treated as one.

♪
(London RE-U 1060)
5/24/62, Chicago, IL

# 16

# Blues as an Art Form,
# Part II: Expressing the Blues

Original Broadcast: 3/7/68; Producer: Teddy Warrick

♪
(Chess 1620) 1/56,
Chicago, IL

Rural blues groups and their counterparts in the city led to the blues bands of Chicago, Illinois, and Detroit, Michigan, which evolved from the late 1930s to the present. In a group of the kind led by Big Bill Broonzy, Elmore James, Howling Wolf, Sonny Boy Williamson, or Muddy Waters, a rhythm section of drums, string bass, and piano may support a front line of two guitars and a harmonica. But in the blues band the melodic and rhythmic parts are interrelated with the instruments of the whole group playing both roles, as can be heard on Muddy Waters's classic mid-1950s recording of "FORTY DAYS AND FORTY NIGHTS." Waters is accompanied by Walter Horton on harmonica, Jimmy Rodgers on second guitar, and Otis Spann on piano.

Though there is no doubting that this is essentially a blues band, its structure brings it close to that of small group jazz. From King Oliver through Charlie Parker to Sun Ra, the blues has been fundamental in jazz; in fact, it may well be argued that the blues is the only consistent element in the changing forms of the music. It's the ability to play the blues by which any jazz musician of any period is judged: Without jazz, the blues would flourish happily; without the blues, jazz would wither and die. In jazz, which is primarily an instrumental music, the intonation and phrasing of the blues singer has been the basis for its sound qualities. Both the jazz musician and the blues musician use their instruments to carry the expression and the emotional intensity of the vocal. This vocalized quality of the blues instrumental can be heard in the playing of a twenty-six-year-old Louis Armstrong accompanying Bertha "Chippie" Hill on "Pratt City Blues." She was five years his junior, but her voice was full and, in contrast with the trumpet patterns, stark, grand, and monumental.

♪
(Okeh 8420) 11/23/26, Chicago, IL

This is the "low-down" blues. The term *low-down*, like most blues terms, is not easy to define. It doesn't mean "low in character," nor "low in pitch," but "searching to the depths of feeling"; in the words of the artist, Paul Klee, "our pounding heart drives us down, deep down to the source of all." It's a quality of the greatest blues singers that is not related to the depth or power of their voices. Curiously, blues collectors often equate the deeper, heavy voices with sincerity and creativity, but the preference of blues singers doesn't necessarily bear this out. Among the best-loved of all blues singers was Leroy Carr, a pianist who worked in Indianapolis and who had a relatively light voice. His involvement with his material was complete, and the poetry of his words struck a chord with his audience. One of Carr's best loved recordings was "Blues before Sunrise."

♪
(Victor 02657) 2/21/34, St. Louis, MO

When Leroy Carr died of nephritis in 1935, he was mourned throughout the African American world. The influence of his blues can be heard in the work of scores of singers right up to the present day. But if the influence of blues singers is any indication of the qualities that the black audience might admire, then Tommy Johnson, a Mississippi singer who made a handful of recordings in 1928, must rank highly. Johnson does not appear to have improvised his blues—at any rate, on record—but to have carefully refined his personal expression with a studied use of falsetto syllables against a simple rhythmic pattern. One of his best-known recordings is "Big Road Blues."

♪
(Victor 21279) 2/3/28, Memphis, TN

Tommy Johnson's "Big Road Blues" is by no means totally original. It has verses that appear in many other blues songs, and some of them were in circulation many years before he recorded his version. In fact, Jesse James's "Long Lonesome Day Blues" and Howling Wolf's "Smokestack Lightnin'" are links in a complex chain of blues numbers that relate to Tommy Johnson's original. Most blues singers draw from a common pool of "floating verses," which they modify and adapt to suit their personal requirements as they compose new songs. Many take on a shorthand significance with a wealth of unstated associated meanings, permitting a maximum of content with a strict economy of means. The importance of Tommy Johnson's blues song—and others like it, of course—lies in the apt marrying of words, music, meaning, and personal expression to create an artistic whole. Other singers recognize this and, when the appropriate resolution has been achieved, are happy to reinterpret within the form established. So, nearly forty years later, a street singer in Chicago, Blind James Brewer, sang his version of "Big Road Blues," which is clearly based on Tommy Johnson's.

♪
(Flyright LP 549) 7/11/60, Chicago, IL

Such influences as these are due in part to the effects of recording; a blues becomes "set" when it is released on disc. But recording is a fact in the history of blues and could be an important indication of the significance of the blues in black life. Within a year or two of their introduction in the early 1920s, blues records were selling at a rate of several million a year, even though they were relatively expensive. They were sold as "Race" records, marketed exclusively to the black community and—in lieu of any other study of the values placed on blues—they give us the most effective gauge available to the audiences' taste. Of course, the availability of records was conditioned by distribution methods and the type of blues recorded by the singers who were located by the talent scouts. But it still seems clear that a number of singers who are not favored by collectors today were much appreciated at the time their discs were issued—Tampa Red, Jimmy Gordon, Joe Pullem, and Jazz Gillum among them.

William Bunch, a guitarist and pianist who called himself Peetie Wheatstraw, the "Devil's Son-in-Law," was one such highly popular blues singer. Other singers called themselves Peetie's Boy, Peetie Wheatstraw's Buddy, or The Devil's Daddy-in-Law in open admiration. Obviously, William Bunch represented some ideal, but his negligent manner; casual, thrown-away lines; and blurred enunciation was introspective, as can be heard on his recording of "Long Lonesome Dive."

♪
(Vocalion 02712) 3/25/34, New York City

Peetie Wheatstraw came over as an individual, as a real being, one of themselves. For his black listeners—there weren't any others—who bought his records, his integrity as a man was important. Like many popular blues singers, he had a turn of phrase, a rough poetry, that was immediately identifiable. There have been many attempts to write poetry in the blues idiom: Richard Wright, Langston Hughes, Sterling Brown, Fenton Robinson, and even the white poet W. H. Auden have composed poems in the blues form, and with blues imagery. But somehow they have failed to achieve the simplicity of lyric expression of the best blues songs, which sometimes look bleak

♪
(Decca 7171) 2/4/36,
Chicago, IL

in print, but are a total creation in song. One moving example is Red Nelson's "CRYING MOTHER BLUES." With Cripple Clarence Lofton accompanying him on piano, Nelson sings of the death of his mother: "Dear mother's dead and gone to glory, my old dad gone straight away, only way to meet my mother, I will have to change my lowdown ways. Tombstone's my pillow, graveyard gonna be my bed, blue skies gonna be my blanket, and the pale moon gonna be my spread. Stop your crying, do away with all of your tears. If you can't stay with me, mother, it must have been your time to leave from here."

♪
(Bluebird B9037) 2/20/42,
Chicago, IL

Another fine example of the rough-hewn beauty of the country blues is Tommy McClennan's "BLUES TRIP ME THIS MORNING." It's an unfortunate fact that, for the majority of collectors, the appeal of the blues lies mainly in the music and the voice, and very little in the content. But let's listen again: What does McClennan mean when he sings "the blues got up on one Sunday morning; they tripped me, they throwed me down"? A folksinger seldom sings needlessly—and the blues is a form of folk song. The blues is a means of expression and communication, and it is my contention that one cannot enjoy it to the fullest extent by listening to its musical qualities alone; one must also try to understand what the singer is trying to say through the medium of the blues. The singer was addressing himself to an audience who understood and shared with him many common experiences; to appreciate the significance of what he sings, one must learn something of his world.

It has been asserted that the blues is a folk song of protest—correctly I think, but only to a certain extent. Jimmy Gordon expressed it succinctly when he sang "Well, I drink to keep from laughing, and I laugh to keep from crying; I keep a smile on my face so the public won't know my mind." The blues singer seldom registers his or her protest in such undisguised terms as does Gabriel Brown in his recording of "I'm Gonna Take it Easy": "You can have an old job, maybe it's hard or soft; You try to save something, and then they lay you off. Now what your bosses are doing, you can never tell; they're always tryin' to cut the personnel," he sings, adding the refrain "Now, I'm gonna take it easy, babe, that's what I'm gonna do."

Sentimentalists would speak of the irrepressible gaiety of the blues, but the blues is not gay. There is humor in black music taken as a whole, and the blues has its measure of tough, ribald humor. But the jokes are wry, the amusement often cynical and never without meaning, as can be heard in Lonnie Johnson's recording of "HARD TIMES AIN'T GONE NOWHERE," on which he sings: "People ravin' bout hard times, I don't know why

♪
(Decca 3378) 11/8/37,
Chicago, IL

they should. If some people was like me, they didn't have no money when times was good."

The blues has no definable length. The three-minute 78-rpm record—used to record most of the classic blues performances until the coming of LPs— has been an unfortunate tailor for blues songs, extending some and abbreviating others. In a sense, all blues are one extended composition; in another sense, a blues song may only be a verse or two in length. There is often an internal logic, however, even in apparently unrelated verses. Bob Campbell recorded "STARVATION FARM BLUES," a typical migration song, which declares unequivocally that he is going to Detroit to get himself a job because he is tired of staying round on a starvation farm. And, he adds, "Going to Detroit, gonna work in Mister Ford's place, say my woman told me last night, 'you won't even stand Mister Ford's ways.'"

♪
(Vocalion 02798) 8/1/34,
New York City

The reference was clearly to the Ford Motor Company's use of black labor to block the organization of labor unions within the firm. But then the song seems to change direction: "I know my dog when I hear him bark. I know my rider [my woman] when I feel her in the dark. You better stop your woman from smilin' in my face, if she don't stop a-smilin' I'm sure gonna take your place."

If the literal content seems irrelevant, the words are symbolically appropriate, referring first to the singer's security and then leaving no doubt that with an inducement he will assume a new role. It may be subconscious imagery, but it's singularly apt.

I have tried here to show how the blues relates in the context of the total black society, and how it functions as a vehicle of personal self-expression. Are blues singers born or made? A little of both I think, being born into the culture-producing society and learning to express within the blues idiom through hearing others. In a wooden one-room shack in Zachary, Louisiana, I recorded a seven-year-old boy singing a little song called "ROOSTER BLUES." It was a social blues of the kind used for dancing, and its words had typical folk allusions. They also had a sexual meaning, and the elders suppressed giggles while he sang, as one coaxed him along by playing gently on a fiddle.

♪
(Unissued) 8/7/60,
Zachary, LA

Later—perhaps not much later—this young boy would understand the song's double meanings, and by that time he would have learned more blues songs from similar sources. He was too young to go into the juke joints, of course; he picked up the words from the record of "ROOSTER BLUES" by a popular local blues singer who lived a few miles away in Baton Rouge—Lightnin' Slim Hicks.

♪
(Excello 2169) 9/59,
Crowley, LA

Blues is the music of the community, to be heard on the radio networks that beam to the black consumer market, on the front porches, and from records in the jukeboxes at the local cola bars. Young boys still fashion instruments out of fencing wire and lard cans or cigar boxes, and save up to buy an electric instrument. Or they play the piano at the home of a deacon of a local church, like Georgia Talbert, a fourteen-year-old girl whom I recorded playing "BOOGIE AND SLOW" blues in Clarksdale, Mississippi.

♪
(Unissued) 8/60, Clarksdale, MS

In other words, blues is accessible to the members of the community, and it plays an important part in that community's total life. It is a very functional art; it's one in which technical perfection and immaculate execution have little place; where techniques arise directly out of expressive needs. It's an art that provides an opportunity for the least gifted to have some kind of structure for creative effort, and affords the true original with a form that does not hamper inspiration. It is emotionally rich and communicates powerfully across cultures, while within the African American world it performs cathartic, ritualistic, symbolic, and aesthetic roles. In all this it seems to me to be a very perfect art both for the individual and for the group.

If I were to make a comparison between the blues and another art form in order to define its character, it would probably be with a tribal art, with sculpture of the Sepik River in New Guinea, or of the Yoruba in western Nigeria: It is repetitive in the broad identification of the forms, but powerfully expressive, intensely charged in its individual creative manifestations. "What a right little, tight little, round little world it was when Greece was the only source of culture," wrote Roger Fry when commencing an essay on African sculpture. For many of us, the world of music has been a tight little one of the Western European tradition, but the blues, a folk music of our own century and perhaps the last folk music that may ever appear, has helped change that. Now the blues shows signs of cultural decline; the florid exaggerations of its most recent forms suggests that it has already entered a decadent phase in its history. Perhaps, surprisingly; perhaps not. It is this phase that has most powerfully influenced popular music today, but the implications of its approach to qualities of expression and of sound in all its stages of development have a significance for every kind of music. But now there are few, if any, of the first generation of bluesmen, of the second or third generation even, who remain with us. In a period when the values of Western music are everywhere being re-examined, we may all too easily forget the black sharecroppers, sawmill hands, truck drivers, and foundrymen whose burning desire to speak through the blues has enriched our whole musical experience.

# III
# Meaning in the Blues

# 17

# Blues and Trouble

First Broadcast: 5/25/91; Producer: Derek Drescher

Some years ago, I was sitting in the noisy back room of a record store on Twelfth Street in Detroit. Twelfth Street had become the main artery of the black sector after the more famous Hastings Street had been removed to make room for an expressway. My companion was a blues pianist named Vernon Harrison, although he was known locally only by the nickname Boogie Woogie Red. I asked him why he played the blues, and what the blues meant to him. He didn't hesitate to reply, but just started to play and talk while I wrestled with my tape recorder. To me, Boogie Woogie Red's spontaneous reply was a remarkable definition of the blues: "It's something that you play when you are in a low mood; it has to come from the heart. But, there's so much good feeling in the blues that comes from playing it."

In other words, blues is a condition, and it's a way of expressing and relieving it through music. It was the well-known blues singer John Lee Hooker who put me in touch with Boogie Woogie Red. Hooker was, of course, a professional singer who had to perform blues on demand: in the club, on the bandstand, in the recording studio, and not just when he was "alone to himself." I wondered if he had a different view of the blues. He told me, "There's a lot of things that give you the blues, that give me the blues, that give any man the blues: it's somewhere down the line that you have been hurt some place. I mean it's no certain type of hurtin' but you have been hurt some place and you get to playin' the blues that reaches. And so that's why when I sing the blues I sing it with the big feelin'. I really means it."

Like many blues, John Lee Hooker's "Two White Horses" borrowed an image from another blues—Blind Lemon Jefferson's in this case—but it was based on an event in his youth. It had occurred in Clarksdale, Mississippi, where John Lee Hooker was raised by his mother before he moved to Detroit. Shortly after talking with him, I was myself in Clarksdale. It's the main town of the lowland region, the Mississippi Delta. Lying a few hundred miles north of the mouth of the Mississippi, it's always regarded as the heartland of the blues. There I met a guitar-playing tractor driver named Robert Curtis Smith from the nearby plantation called Council Spur. He'd never recorded before, and when I asked him why and when he sang the blues, he giggled nervously, replying, "The most reason I sing the blues is because most things in my life and coming up was so difficult, it seemed like I had a harder time than most people. I worked in the fields. . . . I lived in Clarksdale, way up to Jackson, working, working, and it mostly keeps me with the blues because everything I go to do turns out backward."

Robert Smith endured a hard life in Mississippi. He was then only just over thirty years of age, but he found it almost impossible to provide for his large family at the Council Spur plantation. Like most black sharecroppers, he was exploited, as he made clear in his pointed "Council Spur Blues." The song tells about Mr. Walker, the plantation owner who nearly shot him, and Mr. Roy Flowers, who told him to hunt rabbits if he needed food.

A blues narrative such as Smith's, directly related to an aspect of the singer's experience that was shared by many in his audience, epitomizes the blues as an expressive idiom. But it hasn't always been like that, and it isn't today. Boogie Woogie Red believed that blues had been "going on for centuries and centuries" and that it "would always last," and the feelings that inspired it undoubtedly have, and will. Yet blues as a musical form is less than a century old. In the first series, "Before the Blues," I discussed the kinds of black song—ballads, minstrel songs, work songs, and the like—that preceded blues and that fed into it in the first decade of this century. The earliest noted blues songs were made of random verses, often quite arbitrary in their sequence. The songster Henry Thomas, who was born in 1874 and is believed to be one of the oldest black singers on record, made several blues of this type. To his own archaic accompaniment on the pan pipes and strummed guitar, he stitched together a number of already traditional verses in

♪
(Guest Star LP1902)
7/7/61, Miami, FL

♪
(Bluesville 1064) 7/60,
Clarksdale, MS

♪
(Vocalion 1137) 10/5/27,
Chicago, IL

♪
(Columbia 14491)
11/15/29, Chicago, IL

his song "Red River Blues," including "Poor Boy, long ways from home" and "Which-away do the Red River run?"—both of which were collected in the field before 1905.

Two years after Thomas made this recording, Henry Townsend from St. Louis, just twenty years old, made his first recordings. The great Wall Street crash had occurred only three weeks earlier, but Henry was already a victim of economic pressures. Out of work, he was still bitter about being turned out on the streets by the young woman with whom he had been living. His "Poor Man Blues" was focused around a theme rather than sung as a narrative, but it was characteristic of the later, far more personalized blues.

Much of the emotional impact of Henry Townsend's song came from the contrast between his guitar playing—with its apparently repetitive, but subtly changing phrase—and his high, hurt voice. Ironically, when I met up with him in St. Louis over thirty years later, he had a job as a collector of bad debts, presumably from people who were as broke as he had been. He confirmed that he had been penniless and depressed when he made "Poor Man Blues." I asked him whether all his blues arose from similar feelings, and he answered,

> I tell you, in most cases the way I feel, the song will come to you when you are really depressed, you know. I mean, words'll come to you and you feel them and you decide you'll do something about it, so the thing that you do about it, is more or less to put it in rhymes and words and make them come out. It gives you relief—it kinda helps somehow.

That you had to feel the blues to sing the blues was stated, often in so many words, by just about every singer I've interviewed. Though all agreed that while you could perform light blues songs for dancing and entertainment, the lowdown blues, they believed, could only come from the personal experience of the singer. This could be a piece of folklore in itself, but it's borne out by many record executives. J. D. Miller ran a studio in Crowley, Louisiana; in the late 1950s his principal singer was Otis Hicks, known by his nickname of Lightnin' Slim. Miller understood that it was difficult to find an authentic blues singer:

> You never know how many you may get [of] these boys; you can't look at them and tell if they're gonna be good musicianers. Least you can with your higher-class musician, you can get a good idea, but not these blues boys. If you see an ole country boy, that's your bluesman; not

the other guy that knows his music on a higher level—
because he's not a bluesman no more. . . . I've had boys
come in here and sing and actually they had the blues so
bad they were cryin' when they got through. They really
had their heart and soul in it. And to my way of thinking, that's a good bluesman. That actually is the thing:
Slim seems to give out more of something real when he's
talkin' about either his girl or his wife has quite him or
he's lost his money. . . .

♪
(Excello 8000) 1957,
Crawley, LA

Slim's expressive performance of "FEELING AWFUL BLUES" is
typical of his popular recordings made for Miller. Blues songs
that were recorded before the late 1950s were issued as 78s and
marketed solely to black listeners, first as the "Race Records"
of the 1920s and '30s, and then as the "Rhythm and Blues"
releases of the early postwar years. But how did they communicate, and how did listeners respond to them? John Lee
Hooker commented,

> You can hear a certain type of record be playin'. You can
> be feelin' very normal, nothin' on your mind, period. But
> it's somethin' on that record hits you. It hits somethin'
> that have happened in your life. If it didn't happen to
> you, you still got a strong idea—you know those things
> is goin' on. So this is very touchable, and that develops
> into the blues.

That interview took place in 1960, when Hooker's fans were
the black workers of the Detroit automobile plants. He was
soon to adapt his blues to suit a new, white audience. Times
were changing in the blues, as they were in American society
as a whole. But for the previous half a century, blues singers
had expressed their perceptions of their world through song;
but they had also sung to—and for—the black community,
sharing their environments and their lives, giving voice to
their experiences.

In these programs, I'll be discussing the meaning in a number of blues 78s recorded during the segregation era, and I'll
be quoting some of the observations on them made by blues
singers themselves. My focus will be on subjects that have been
particularly prominent on record, and consequently, my examples will be drawn from the narrative and thematic blues rather
than from the earlier, random sequences of capsule stanzas.
Nonetheless, many moving blues records were of that type as
well, including a masterly performance by another singer from
Clarksdale, Eddie "Son" House, whose "MY BLACK MAMA"
was recorded in 1930.

♪
(Paramount 13042)
5/28/30, Grafton, WI

# 18

# Down the Dirt Road

First Broadcast: 6/2/91; Producer: Derek Drescher

Until the 1980s, the rural economy of the Deep South was still mainly based on the production of cotton. Though Blacks provided much of the labor force, only one in five owned the land they worked; the majority were sharecroppers or—just a little better off—tenant farmers. Those who were sharecroppers were held on the plantations in what was, in effect, peonage: They had to pay half of their earnings directly to the plantation boss. The other half was theirs, but from it they had to pay for their house and for their land rent. In addition, their "furnishings," which included food, seed, and tools, were charged against the balance of their earnings—at prices set by the landowners. In Clarksdale, Mississippi, a black barber, Wade Walton, explained to me the process when "settlement" came after the cotton crop had been picked: "When the final settlement come the white man have the pencil behind his ear and he figgered out. And he says, 'I'm gonna check you out. John, you did well, you made a damn good crop. Thirty-five bales, I feel that you did damn good. And a hundred dollars, a hundred and fifty dollars is what I think you cleared and I think you did good; don't you think you did good, John?'"

Breaking the cycle of debt wasn't easy. Blacks frequently had large families, which meant more hands to work in the fields, but also more mouths to feed. Many people became obsessive in their desire to produce more cotton, like the woman who was the subject

♪
(Bluebird B9036) 2/20/42,
Chicago, IL

of "Cotton Pikcin' Blues" by Robert Petway, from Yazoo in the Mississippi Delta. "She's a cotton pickin' woman, Lord, she do's it all the time," he sang, "if you don't stop pickin' cotton now baby, I believe you sure gonna lose your mind."

The women felt obliged to stay on the farms, to raise their families and to look after the two-roomed rented cabins. But during the "layoff" period, when there was little to do on the cotton farms, the men frequently left home to seek casual work. Without transport, movement was limited, as Robert Curtis Smith told me, in Wade Walton's Mississippi barbershop. Even in 1960 his miserable pay of three dollars per day was far below the state minimum. "You work from the time right after sun-up until sundown," he said. "Other words, in choppin' it's three dollars a day, and it's hard to make enough money to practically do anything. And if you don't you break even: the whole year's work gone and you ain't got nothin'."

There's a marked restlessness in the blues of all periods; the desire to get away is one of the most persistent themes. Thirty years before I spoke with Smith, the great Mississippi singer Charley Patton was living in the delta. Relatively speaking, he was better off than many black farmers, but his "Down the Dirt Road Blues" captures the feelings of them all. To a syncopated guitar rhythm, he sings in his heavy, regional accent that he has been to "the Nation" (the old name for the Indian Territory of Oklahoma), but he couldn't stay there. He continues, "Some people say the overseas blues ain't bad; it must not have been the overseas blues I had. Every day seems like murder here." He concluded, saying that he is "going to leave tomorrow," but he can't "go down this dark road" by himself.

♪
(Paramount 12854)
6/14/29, Richmond, IN

Apart from plantation labor, there was heavy manual work to be had. What were simply called "the jobs" were generally dangerous or unhealthy occupations, in the fertilizer or turpentine plants or the phosphate mines. I spoke with a blind street singer, Arvella Gray, who in earlier years had worked on many of the jobs. He was "just a roughneck all the way round," he said, who'd learned to play up to the Whites:

> I worked when I got ready, and then I didn't like that. Well, I worked for construction job. I did levee camp work; I worked in factories and things and I was a feller never did care for staying on a job, like marrying a job as I would call it in my way. I just jumped from job to job.

The levee camps, gravel camps, and logging camps were the most notorious of the jobs because the worksites were often remote, the conditions were rough, and the operators of the camps were well beyond the reach of the law. But many roughnecks relished their relative freedom to hobo a ride on a freight train in search of one job or another. Lewis Black, from Georgia, told of catching the back of a local train. He was going out on the "Q," the Chesapeake, Burlington, and Quincy line. "If I don't find no log camp, I'll find a gravel camp, sure," he sang in his "GRAVEL CAMP BLUES."

♪
(Columbia 144291)
12/10/27, Memphis, TN

Catching a freight train "on the fly" was hazardous. The hobo would swing on board as the train slowed down for a bend. If he could, he'd try to "ride the blinds," the side-door baggage cars that couldn't be easily reached by the brakemen. More dangerous still was "riding the rods"—lying across the brake linkages beneath the railroad car. Furry Lewis and Peg Leg Sam were just two of the blues singers who were crippled when they slipped as they tried to jump on a moving freight train, or as they called it, "nail a rattler." Apart from these dangers, the hobos frequently had to run the gauntlet of armed railroad police, as blues singer Speckled Red recalled: "I hoboed on trains—I'd catch a train right now, if I feel like it, go anywhere I want to go. My eyesight ain't too good and I couldn't see it very well but I could see it good enough. I wouldn't wait till it get started too much; catch it before it started off if I could, then I'd hobo my way. Well I got put off so many times—run like a rabbit! I've got shot at and everything at night."

Speckled Red's account confirms the details of a graphic narrative of hoboing a ride on the Illinois Central number 29 train from Cairo to East St. Louis, related musically in Wesley Wallace's piano blues narrative "NUMBER 29." This recording deserves its fame: With remarkable skill, Wesley Wallace set right-hand triplets against bass figures in 6/8 time. With these polyrhythms he captured the rolling impetus of the northbound train and suspended them as he described how he fell off and rolled down the embankment before waving the train good-bye.

♪
(Paramount 12958)
11/29, Grafton, WI

Those who were "on the bum" often spent their nights in the "hobo jungles," makeshift camps by the railroads made of tarpaulin and brushwood. They were dangerous places, but they were home to jobless men and homeless children. The migration from the South began during the First World War, but in the 1930s literally millions of transients of all kinds were moving from town to town, and from state to state. A high proportion of them were Blacks and their lives were hard. As Tennessee blues singer Son Bonds sang in his "OLD BACHELOR BLUES," "I'm a broken-hearted bachelor, traveling through this world all alone; it's the railroad for my pillow, the jungle is my happy home." There in the jungle, with cinders blowing in his face, he resolved to settle down.

♪
(Decca 7558) 4/22/38,
New York City

Many of these black transients would return home after the layoff period, but others were attracted by the relative freedom of the North. They were prepared to endure the hardships of a rigorous Chicago winter in order to get away from the "Jim Crow" discrimination of the South, where every facility—from drinking water fountains to lunch counters and seats in municipal buses—was strictly segregated. Yet it took great courage to leave the comparative security of a rural settlement in Arkansas or Alabama and strike out for a huge city like Chicago, a thousand miles away, with all the unknown problems of finding a job and somewhere to live. There was courage, yes, but also despair: "I'm tired of being Jim Crowed, gonna leave this Jim Crow town; dog-gone my black soul, I'm sweet Chicago bound," sang Charles "Cow Cow" Davenport in the unusually outspoken "JIM CROW BLUES." It seems to me that the conflicting emotions of anxiety and determination come together in his hesitant but compelling piano playing and deeply disappointed voice.

♪
(Paramount 12439) 1/27, Chicago, IL

# 19

# Black Cat's Bone
First Broadcast: 6/7/91; Producer: Derek Drescher

♪
(Columbia 14531)
4/23/30, Atlanta, GA

**I**n the last chapter, I discussed some aspects of the movement of Blacks through the South—the men in particular—and the migrations that took many of them to the North during the 1920s and 1930s. But, of course, the majority remained in, or soon returned to, their home states. Some felt trapped by the sharecropping system; others simply preferred to stay, as many a blues singer would sing, "where the weather suits my clothes." Life on the farms was arduous and monotonous. Picnics and dances and the occasional visits of the medicine shows broke the routine. But for the most part, such entertainment as was available was provided on a Saturday night in the local juke joint, where the guitarists played blues and the gamblers would shoot craps. Barbecue Bob met up with his brother Laughing Charlie for a spot of both, as they relate in their recording, "Darktown Gamblin'."

As Charlie remarked, Bob was now playing blues for a living; he played at a barbecue stand in Buckhead, a suburb of Atlanta, Georgia. Naturally enough, many blues singers hoped to augment their cash, if not make a living, from their playing. They were attracted by the saloons and gambling houses in the cities, places like the Monarch and the Panama on Beale Street in Memphis, as an old promoter, Robert Henry, recalled to me in his Beale Street pool hall, "The Monarch was a place wide open. This was on 340 Beale, and the Monarch was a place where we called it a gamblin' house at that particular time. They played piano there, blues goin' all the time. They searched you just like you would be if you were goin' to jail. It was a great time then, the streets were full of gamblin' houses where they shot craps."

Like a number of jazz musicians—Jelly Roll Morton, for instance—some blues singers thrived in the city joints by being both performers and professional gamblers. I spoke with one of them, James J. Harris, who got the nickname Shaky Jake from "rattling the bones"—that is, shaking the dice; as he told me, "I was a professional dice shooter, poker player for fifteen years. I used to get drunk, I used to drink a lot of whisky, brandy called Forbidden Fruit—I used to be a pretty rough boy. Well, every time I'd win a lot of money I'd tip off from the boys to keep from splittin' with them and I'd get stuck up."

Shaky Jake had sought the pickings in Chicago, but many of the big-time gamblers moved out to the rural areas after "settlement" in the fall, when the sharecroppers had a little money in their pockets. This was the time of the "skin game," when the gamblers fleeced the croppers. They traded on the desire of the farmers to double their money in the game, and on their superstitious belief in good luck, even in the luck of particular cards. In the lugubrious "Dice's Blues," "broke and hungry" Bob Campbell sang of being dealt the Queen, a "hard luck" card, while the gambler played the lucky Jack of Diamonds. That card could "turn your money green"—in other words, change cash into greenback dollar bills.

♪
(Vocalion 02830) 7/30/34, New York City

In the South, many Blacks would turn to the "conjures" to improve their fortunes. A conjure was (and in some parts still is) a person with magical powers. They went under various names—root doctors, conjure ladies, hoodoos, and gypsies—but they were all believed to be in touch with powerful supernatural forces. Voodoo, or hoodoo, has its origins in West African cult practices, and flourished in Haiti, Cuba, and elsewhere in the Caribbean as *voudun*. It was also very powerful in New Orleans, where the celebrated "Queen," Marie Leveau, was born in 1827. A century later, the most famous conjure was Aunt Caroline Dye, who lived in Newport News, Virginia. Will Shade, the leader of the Memphis Jug Band, went to consult her and made a blues about the visit called "Aunt Caroline Dyer Blues." Shade sang, "Aunt Caroline Dye she told me 'Son, you don't have to feel so rough, I'm gon' to fix you up a mojo, Lord, so you can strut your stuff.'" She made him a "mojo hand"—a powerful charm made of hair, fingernails, and such magic objects as "High John the Conqueror" root or a "black cat's bone," obtained from boiling down the carcass of a cat.

♪
(Vocalion 02830) 7/30/34, New York City

Shade was very impressed with Aunt Caroline Dye, as he told me many years later, in his barely furnished shotgun house off Fourth Street, behind Beale. "She was a two-headed woman," he said. "She had that much brains." I asked him how she compared with another celebrated hoodoo woman, Seven Sisters. "She break up all kinds of spells you had," he said, "she could have you walkin' like a hawg; any kinda whichaway, she could make you walk on two legs again. That's the kind of woman she was. Aunt Caroline Dye, she was the worst woman in the world . . . had that much sense. Seven Sisters ain't nowhere wit' Aunt Caroline Dye; she was the onliest one could break the record with the hoodoo."

There seems to have been more than one conjure who was known as Seven Sisters. There was Ida Carter, who had a considerable reputation in Hogansville, Alabama, in the 1930s; and in New Orleans there were, literally, Seven Sisters. They were visited by a Texas blues singer known as Funny Paper Smith, who was reputedly a plantation overseer. He wasn't wanting much, he explained in the remarkable, six-minute "SEVEN SISTERS BLUES." "They tell me they've been hung, been bled and been crucified; but I just want enough help to stand on the water and rule the tide," he sang on the first side of the two-part 78 recording.

♪
(Vocalion 1641) 7/10/31, Chicago, IL

If you picked up a black newspaper in the South in the 1950s, you'd see advertisements for many "sisters" who had occult powers. Any popular magazine aimed at the black community would carry advertisements for "loving powders," herb bags, holy oils, lodestones, and "goofer dust" (earth scraped from a grave). These were sold to those who were unlucky in love, who wanted to bewitch someone, or who needed protection against evil spells. But reading the signs, or recognizing the portents in natural phenomena, let alone the superstitions that certain actions would bring bad luck, were common knowledge. Migrants brought them to the North where they continued to believe in them, as is shown in songs like Jazz Gillum's "THE BLUES WHAT AM."

♪
(Victor 20-2580) 4/24/47, Chicago, IL

Out of the combination of popular superstition and the widespread desire to gamble arose the "policy game," a highly profitable enterprise—for a few. Sometimes called "playing the races" or "the numbers racket," it involved laying bets on sequences of numbers, generally three. The bets would be placed with a tout or "policy writer" who gave it to a "number runner," who worked for a "wheel." When the wheel was spun, a pointer indicated the numbers, and if the combination matched that placed by the gambler he could win a tidy sum.

While J. B. Lenoir picked at his guitar, Brother John Sellers told me how it worked:

> Policy, you know, it fed a lot of people during the Depression days in Chicago. Because that was their only hope. A lot of people wrote policy for their livin'. You know, they had policy stations, they had different wheels like the Red Devil, the Wisconsin, the Green Gable—they had all kinds of wheels. They had three drawin's—A.M., P.M., and midnight—and many people would win two fifty, three dollars, five. . . . some didn't win at all but this helped many people even though many people got rich on this type of numbers because it wasn't legal. It made a lot of people believe in policy game.

Although numbers could be obtained from many sources, the most common were the "dream books." These were compilations of words and names for people, animals, objects, events—anything, in fact, that might have significance for the gambler, especially when it came to him in a dream. Some of the number combinations were famous, and crop up frequently in blues, like 3–6–9, the number combination that signified feces, or the phallic 4–11–44, sometimes known as the "washwoman's gig." In "DREAM BOOK BLUES," Tommy Griffin from New Orleans tells about how he planned to purchase a Dream Book, so he could find out what his dreams meant, and what the numbers were. Mixing milk with cream was a good love symbol; so was his woman's crazy talking. He would probably have been advised by his Dream Book to play 58–40–55.

♪
(Bluebird BB B6756)
10/16/36,
New Orleans, LA

A West Indian, Caspar Holstein, organized the numbers racket in Harlem in the 1920s, while the Jones Boys operated in Chicago. They all lost out to big-time hoods like Dutch Schultz. But for the average person in the street placing a quarter on a gig with the Fast Mail wheel, it was the small-time racketeers that they had to deal with. The frustrations of the player, as the number writer urges him to commit more money, are evident in a blues in recitative style by Bumble Bee Slim called "POLICY DREAM BLUES." When Slim sang "policy is a racket and it's awful hard to beat; I played my last dime and I couldn't even eat," there were thousands of African Americans who knew just how he felt.

♪
(Vocalion 03090) 4/4/35,
Chicago, IL

# 20

# Tricks Ain't Walkin' No More

First Broadcast: 6/14/91; Producer: Derek Drescher

♪
(Paramount 12708)
11/28, Chicago, IL

♪
(Columbia 14514)
12/4/29, Dallas, TX

Some time in 1927, Willard Thomas, a singer from the Louisiana-Texas border whose restlessness earned him the name Ramblin' Thomas, tried his luck in Dallas. He was one of the many thousands of rural Blacks who had moved to the city. At the turn of the century there were fewer than ten thousand in Dallas, but by the time Thomas moved there the black population had multiplied five times. But he did not like the city, nor his treatment there, as he underlined in his recording of "Hard Dallas Blues": "And Dallas is hard, I don't care how you work there will be somebody comin' on your pay-day to collect."

If Ramblin' Thomas was disenchanted, others were attracted by the bright lights, the shops, the theaters, and the bars along Central Tracks—the bawdy, rowdy area that lined the Texas and Pacific Railroad tracks. Nearby Elm Street (known as "Deep Ellum"), was the heart of the red light district (such districts were often located in the black sector of a town). Texas Bill Day sang about it on "Elm Street Blues," while his companion, Billiken Johnson, made vocal effects based on the sounds of the Texas and Pacific trains. Bill Day advised him that "These Ellum Street women, Billiken, do not mean you no good. If you want to make a good woman, have to get on Haskell Avenue."

With the introduction of Prohibition in 1918, the manufacture and consumption of alcohol was made illegal. Inevitably, this promoted the illicit production of corn liquor, or crude substitutes

101

made from wood alcohol. In Texas and the Southwest, home-made liquor had been sold illegally to the Indians for many years. It was known as "chock"—short for Choctaw, the Oklahoma tribe that brewed it—and a secret saloon was called a "chock house." A native of Dallas, Whistling Alex Moore, collected junk with his mule and cart during the day and played piano in the chock houses on Elm Street at night. He recalled with amusement the raids by the police as they shot up the chock barrels and poured away the good homemade liquor:

> That was what you call chock-house days. You could go in them barrel chock houses, and police never used to do anything but run in there and raid it, and make them guys break up the chock barrel and throw it away. . . . And if it was a house had some of that home brew, man, they'd take it all out there and get all by one of them brick buildings and it sound like—"Wow, pow!" Every time they'd hit that barrel see they'd shoot. . . ."Pow! Pow-pow-pow!" Glass flyin'. "Pow! Pow!" and we'd be sittin' there, "Lawd, listen to that . . . they raidin' somewhere!" All that good brew.

Moonshine liquor, known also as White Mule, was full of impurities and often adulterated with tobacco. More damaging still was "canned heat," made by drawing off the methylated spirits from the solid fuel used for outdoor cooking, or from certain brands of boot polish. Tommy Johnson was one blues singer who was addicted to canned heat and sang about it. Addiction induced tremors known as the "limber leg," a partial paralysis known also as "Jake Leg," caused from drinking an illegal Jamaican liquor. Tommy Johnson's friend Willie "Poor Boy" Lofton seems to have been suffering from its effects when he recorded "JAKE LEG BLUES."

♪
(Decca 7076) 8/24/34, Chicago, IL

In the towns and cities, the saloons closed, but in their place gangsters opened up "speakeasies" that sold "bootleg" liquor at exorbitant prices. Only the so-called sporting class could afford it; most urban Blacks intent on drinking went to a "barrelhouse flat" improvised in domestic settings, where a plank set across a row of barrels of moonshine provided a bar. This was the period of the "rent parties," when someone who was short of rent money would produce a gallon of hooch and friends would each pay a dollar to join the party, knowing that when they were short of cash for their rent they could rely on the same support. To hide them from the police they'd be called "social whist parties." A boogie pianist playing for tips would provide the music—Charles Avery, perhaps, or Walter Roland,

♪
(Banner 32832) 7/19/33,
New York City

who in his "HOUSE LADY BLUES" reproached the "lady of the house" for neglecting him as he played all night.

As Prohibition showed every sign of being permanent, new establishments were set up. With a legitimate function in front, they'd have a bar at the rear, and good-time girls and gamblers offering further diversions in other rooms. Some were called "recreation parlors," while the innocent term *café* hid a variety of functions. The North Memphis Café, where Memphis Minnie played, was notorious in the early 1930s. "I tell all you people you can rest at ease, because the North Memphis Cafe has got everything you need" Minnie assured her hearers in her "NORTH MEMPHIS BLUES," using a 78 disc as useful medium for advertising. Her husband, Joe McCoy, playing second guitar, paced out the bass line.

♪
(Vocalion 1550) 10/11/30,
Chicago, IL

Untold numbers of blues singers learned their craft by playing in the good-time flats and sporting houses, or brothels. James "Stump" Johnson told me how he'd started out playing in those in St, Louis, between Deep Morgan Street and the Mississippi River levee, where the notorious Boots' joint was situated. Deep Morgan, by the way, had its name changed to Delmar Avenue after World War II in a city clean-up campaign, and the levee's now laid out with broad gardens below architect Eero Saarinen's gigantic arch. But when Stump Johnson was playing there it was very different. As he explained,

> The levee at St. Louis was known throughout the country as the origination of blues. When I was young I used to play around for the sporting houses and the only thing I would get would be fifty cents and a chance to be there and look at all the big-time sports comin' in and spendin' their money. And at that time there weren't many taverns, and very few saloons. They just had what they call the 'good-time houses,' and that's where you could find anybody 'in the life' in St. Louis, was at the sportin' houses.

Nostalgia for his youth doubtless lent a certain misty enchantment to Stump Johnson's recollections, for the Tenderloin in St. Louis was a very tough area indeed and it was there that a lot of blues singers lived. In a blues number recorded in 1932, frankly titled "NUT FACTORY," Hi-Henry Brown told an uncompromising story in rough accents. "Well it's down on Deep Morganjust above 16th Street. Well it's selling a business where the women do meet. Well it's down in a basement where they work so hard it's all on account of their husbands ain't got no job. Some draw checks babe some draw nothin' at all when they don't draw nothin' their husbands bust them in the jaw."

♪
(Vocalion 1692) 3/17/32,
New York City

Hi-Henry Brown's blues made clear that casual prostitution was a recourse of the poor; many of the "hustling" women who "turned tricks" did so when there was no other way of getting money. The statistics, if they can be relied upon, show that a quarter of all prostitutes were Black at a time when Blacks represented a tenth of the population. Yet, as the Depression hit hard, even this option was closed to them. Women who recorded blues songs tended to be tough; they had often made the decision to leave home and to work in the same joints as the bluesmen. They cannot be regarded as being representative of black women generally. Nevertheless, Lucille Bogan was voicing the frustration of many "hustlers" in her recording of "THEY AIN'T WALKIN' NO MORE," when she regretted that it was becoming harder to find "ramblin' men" with loose change willing to pay for their services; Charles Avery accompanied her on this disc.

(Brunswick 7186) 12/30, Chicago, IL

Dallas, Memphis, and St. Louis were only three of the cities that witnessed a rapid expansion of their populations as Blacks moved from the rural areas. Cincinnati, Louisville, and Indianapolis were among many others—apart, of course, from Chicago and Detroit. Each had several streets lined with "cribs" and "joints," which became more open following the repeal of Prohibition in 1934. With greater prosperity during the years of the Second World War and a relaxation of some of the local laws, a number of cities became celebrated for being "wide open"—places like Beaumont, Texas, or Nashville, Tennessee. Private Cecil Gant—known on some of his records as the "G. I. Singsation"—celebrated the nightbird's dens, or "OWL STEW," on Fourth Avenue in Nashville. He played the kind of powerful boogie blues that had kept the barrelhouses rocking for over twenty years.

(Decca 48231) 8/7/50, New York City

# 21

# Jail House Moan

First Broadcast: 6/21/91; Producer: Derek Drescher

Activities such as making moonshine liquor, running good-time flats, and hustling for purposes of prostitution on the streets were, and in many states still are, illegal. There's no doubt that early in the twentieth century, the criminal element in the South gravitated to the black sectors of such cities as New Orleans or Atlanta, sectors that were treated as "wide open" and virtually beyond the law. The gambling joints, saloons, and brothels provided employment for blues singers, and many were attracted by the possibility of getting away from the cotton fields and earning a living by playing their music. Memphis, Tennessee, located just north of Mississippi, was a natural magnet for musicians. Will Shade, a blues singer who'd lived all his life just off Beale Street in Memphis, recalled with relish its hedonistic past:

> There used to be a red light district; used to have wide open houses in them days. You could walk down the street in days of 1900 and like that and you could find a man wit' throat cut from y'ear to y'ear. Also you could find people layin' dead wit' not their throat cut, money took and everything in their pockets. Roustabouts on the boats would come in at three and four and five o'clock in the mornin', when the boats come in. . . . The *Katy Adams* they used to call that a boat, they used to call that a woman's boat on the water; all the women would foller that boat . . . jest pay fifty cents for

cabin fare and ride that boat from Memphis to Rosedale and that's the way they made they money—go up and down the river.

In such circumstances it isn't surprising that life was exciting, but also cheap, explaining perhaps the insouciance of another Memphis blues singer, Walter "Furry" Lewis, when he sang in his "Mr. Furry's Blues," "I believe I'll buy me a graveyard of my own—I'm going to kill everybody ever done me wrong. If you want to go to Nashville, man, and ain't got no fare, cut your good girl's throat—and the judge will send you there." Nashville was the Tennessee town where the main prison, known as the "Nashville Walls," was located.

Memphis in the 1920s was known as the "Murder Capital of America," with over a hundred homicides a year, 90 percent of the victims were Blacks. In the nation as a whole in the 1930s, Blacks accounted for a quarter of the convictions for assault, and 40 percent of those for homicide. But these somewhat suspect figures from J. Edgar Hoover's "Uniform Crime Reports" give no indication of the number murdered by Whites who were not brought to court, nor the large number of murders arising from gang warfare.

Violence figures prominently in the blues, and a number of singers were themselves the victims of cuttings and shootings. Guitarist and street singer Blind Gray was one of these victims; he was not born sightless, as he explained to me:

> See, by me gamblin' I went away from home and when I got back this feller Lamar Kilgore was in the house and they had the door locked. Part of it was glass and part was wood. Well I tried to put the key in the lock and it wouldn't unlock so then I knocked on the door. So while I was waitin' I struck a match on the door facin' and was lightin' a cigarette. And when I put the match up to my face they could see the flash of the match through the glass and they just blasted away at me, Lamar did.

Many assaults were crimes of passion, tempers flaring in the heat and humidity of the Southern summers. Others were motivated by jealousy, stimulated by the promiscuous and cramped conditions of two-room cabins and crowded tenements, and aggravated by raw liquor. Whistling Alex Moore, the Dallas junk collector and pianist whose recollections of his chock-house days were noted in the last program, was mystified as to why his woman had "trouble in her eyes." Then he saw her try to slip an ice pick from her dress; he described it in his "Ice Pick Blues," with humor used to dispel a potentially dangerous situation.

♪
(Vocalion 1115) 4/20/27, Chicago, IL

♪
(Columbia 14518) 12/5/29, Dallas, TX

It was an ice pick—or several—that ended the life, at the age of thirty, of the extremely popular blues singer John Lee "Sonny Boy" Williamson on June 1, 1948. Another blues singer, the celebrated Lonnie Johnson, had been with him at Chicago's Plantation Club, where he'd been working. Johnson related the story to me:

> He said, "Well, I'll see you after a while, when you get off. Come on 'round to the club." I say, "O.K." And about five minutes later a feller come round and say he's dead. And we thought he was kiddin', you know? He had seventeen holes in his head with an ice-pick. They ganged him. He was 'bout one of the finest fellers I know. . . . He worked to help the people with somethin' to eat and somethin' to drink. That's all he did, was work for them. And why they would kill a great guy like that I don't know, but they did. Don't know today who killed him.

Blues singers were probably more prone to being victims than others, because of the nature of the places where they played and the hours that they were obliged to keep. But some were also the perpetrators of crimes. Washington "Bukka" White was always somewhat reticent about the felonious assault that caused him to be sent to the notorious Mississippi penitentiary, Parchman Farm, in 1937. The 22,000-acre Parchman Farm complex was entirely worked by convicts, marked out by their black and white stripes. Bukka White described the brutal conditions there in his recording of "Parchman Farm Blues."

♪
(Okeh 05683) 3/7/40, Chicago, IL

Bukka White seems to have accepted his sentence philosophically, but he had a comparatively easy time of it, as the warders liked his playing and exempted him from heavy manual labor. Often the charges against Southern Blacks seemed to have been brought for the express purpose of keeping the prison farms operating. Alger "Texas" Alexander, who knew the penitentiary system from the inside, hollered in his song "Levee Camp Moan," "They got me accused of murder and I haven't harmed a man; they got me accused of forger and I cain't write my name." Then he turned to the mules who were overworked and beaten like the prisoners, and he couldn't find one with, as he put it, "his shoulder well."

♪
(Okeh 8494) 8/16/27, New York City

It wasn't difficult to get sent to prison in Texas; you could earn a month's sentence for playing cards on a passenger train. Many blues indicate that Blacks considered themselves to be arrested unfairly, to have been confused by the legal process, and to have been treated harshly when they were sentenced. This was the theme of a blues song by Hambone Willie Newbern, a singer from rural Tennessee, who was picked up at the bus station when he arrived from the Arkansas township of Marked Tree. "Lord the police arrested me, carried me before the judge," he sang, "Well the lawyers talk so fast didn't have no time to say not nary a word. Well the lawyer pleaded, and the judge he done wrote it down; says 'I'll give you ten days, buddy, out in little old Shelby town.'" Shelby was, and still is, where the county prison workhouse was located. "The guard said to the trustee, 'Put the shackles round his leg,' Lord," Willie complained, "the guards done treat me, like I was a low-down dog."

♪
(Okeh 8740) 3/13/29, Atlanta, GA

Hambone Willie's "Shelby County Workhouse Blues" would have found many sympathizers among Blacks who'd suffered similar treatment. Although Hambone Willie referred to the courtroom lawyers, it was rare for a black defense lawyer to work in the South; less than 1 percent of lawyers in the United States were Black in the 1930s. They had little status, and were themselves subject to segregation. In Mississippi there were only six at a time when statewide there were twelve hundred white lawyers. White lawyers were usually unwilling to take on cases in defense of Blacks, but there were exceptions. Sleepy John Estes sang about one of them, in his "Lawyer Clark Blues," "Boys y' know I like Mister Clark he really is my friend. He says if I just stay out of my grave he'll see that I won't go to the pen. Now Mister Clark is a good lawyer, good as I have seen. He's the first man that proved that water runs upstream."

♪
(Bluebird B8871) 9/24/41, Chicago, IL

High-spirited or frustrated black youths often found themselves arrested for minor offenses, and sentenced to work in a shackled team on the road gangs. Although such chain gangs recall the 1930s, the practice still continued in some States even thirty years later. Sam "Lightnin'" Hopkins had served time on a bridge-building chain gang and on a county road gang (see Program 4, "Go Down, Old Hannah"). The blues that told of crime and imprisonment were in one sense literally describing incidents and events within the experience of the singers and their audience. But I believe they performed another, more important function, serving as a vehicle for protest against social injustice and, in a subtle way, calling for freedom from oppression. As Lightnin' Hopkins sang in his "Jail House Blues," "Hey Mister jailer, will you please sir, bring me the key? I just want you to open the door because this ain't no place for me."

♪
(Arhoolie 2010) c. 1949, Houston, TX

# 22

# Let's Have a New Deal

First Broadcast: 6/21/91; Producer: Derek Drescher

**W**hen the Wall Street crash occurred at the end of October 1929, after an orgy of speculation on the stock market, sixteen million shares were sold in a single day. There were many stories of lost fortunes, of bankrupt financiers throwing themselves from skyscraper windows. But the real onus of the collapse of the economy was borne by the poor, and of these the Black population was the worst off. "Last hired, first fired," they used to say, and as steel mills ceased to operate and factories were closed down, thousands of workers, many of whom were seasonal employees, were laid off. Few were members of unions, and there was no protection against unemployment. President Herbert Hoover declared complacently that "no one has ever starved," while he ignored the bread lines. The shanty towns constructed from waste materials that sprang up around the cities were named "Hoovervilles" after him. In his song "IT'S HARD TIME," singer Joe Stone (J. D. Short) relates how he went down to the factory where he had worked for three years, but the boss man told him, "Man I ain't hiring here no more." Short continued, "Now we have a little city that we calls 'down in Hooverville.' Times have got so hard, people ain't got no place to live."

♪
(Bluebird B5169)
8/2/33, Chicago, IL

These were "hard times" for everyone: There were twelve million unemployed by 1932. Although Northern industry was immediately affected, in the Deep South conditions were also bad. Every farmer was hit by the Depression, but it was the

109

sharecroppers and their families, both Black and White, who suffered most. Tenant farmers faced rent demands, and in the Southern cities laborers were laid off by the thousands. With hungry families, they would try any kind of employment they could find or devise. Eugene "Buddy" Moss, a blues singer in Atlanta, explained how he bought a horse and coal wagon and shouted until his tonsils were sore. But his "HARD TIME BLUES" ended on a despairing note, as he considered letting the Depression take its own course.

♪
(Melotone M12665)
1/19/33, New York City

It was often the women who had the best chance of holding on to their jobs, because white Southern families were still dependent on their black staff and retained their maids and washerwomen as long as they could. It meant that many women were obliged both to work "in the white folk's yard" and try to feed and hold the family together in a period of extreme stress. In a cabin on Old Slaughter Road, near Zachary, Louisiana, I talked about those times with two veteran musicians, James Butch Cage and his animated friend, guitarist Willie Thomas. Thomas told me, "You see, a woman could get a job at that time, but a man couldn't hardly get it. Want a little money, had to get it from her. That's was in the time of the Depression. And it gave a man the blues: He's been the boss all the time and now the Depression come and she's washin' at the white folk's yard."

Franklin D. Roosevelt was inaugurated in March 1933. In the first hundred days of his administration, many remarkable measures were taken to combat the Depression; there was a cautious optimism in the air. The second part of the National Industrial Recovery Act in June allowed for the establishment of the Public Works Administration (PWA) for which over $3 billion was appropriated. PWA projects were largely engaged in construction: sewage plants, flood control, and bridge building among them. Blacks were doubtless confused, as was everyone else, by the "alphabet soup" of the new administrations—FERA, NTRA, CCC, AAA, CVA, PWA, and eventually, WPA and TVA—but many had reason to be grateful for the employment that the New Deal measures brought. In Chicago, where he had been able to exercise his right to vote, Jimmie Gordon pleaded in the song "DON'T TAKE AWAY MY PWA." To the president that he had helped to elect, "You can take away the alphabet, but please leave that PWA."

♪
(Decca 7230) 10/2/36,
Chicago, IL

♪
(Decca 7311) 3/30/37,
Chicago, IL

Further south, in East St. Louis, Peetie Wheatstraw had a somewhat more jaundiced, or perhaps a more realistic, view, for it was tough work. As he sang in his lugubrious voice in "WORKING ON THE PROJECT," which featured Kokomo Arnold on the slide guitar, "Working on the project, begging the relief for shoes, because the rock and concrete they've given my feet the blues."

Peetie Wheatstraw wrote several blues songs about the Works Progress Administration (WPA), which in 1935 was established to replace direct relief. The WPA projects built over half a million miles of roads, a hundred thousand bridges, and even more public buildings. For the workers, regular monthly pay meant the ability to obtain goods on credit: "Working on the project with pay-day three or four weeks away . . . Now, how can you make ends meet, ooh well, when you can't get no pay?"

Although many projects were very successful, some Blacks felt little benefit from the New Deal efforts and they were considerably disadvantaged in the relief program. In 1935 the Federal Emergency Relief Administration was liquidated and relief was administered locally. There is evidence to show that relief rates were often unequal: In some instances black families were getting only a third of the sums their white counterparts received. Carl Martin, from Knoxville, Tennessee, shared the widespread skepticism in his pointed song, "LET'S HAVE A NEW DEAL," a couplet-and-refrain blues number recorded that year: "Everybody's crying 'let's have a New Deal.' Relief stations closing down—I know just how you feel. If you went to the relief workers and put in a complaint, 8 times out of 10, you know, they'll say they cain't. They won't give you no dough, won't hardly pay your rent, and it ain't costin' them one dog-gone cent."

♪
(Decca 7114) 9/4/35, Chicago, IL

Project schemes like the PVA and the WPA hardly benefited black women directly, providing very little but domestic and indoor work for them. Some women, it seems, rather regretted the change of status with the coming of these projects. Until then, they were often the providers, and while they kept their men in food and clothes, they were sure of keeping them at home. When the men achieved financial independence with the WPA, the women felt threatened—or, at least, this was the ironic implication of Billie McKenzie's blues "THAT MAN ON THE WPA": "Be a friend to me girls; please try and see it my way—if you want a good man, don't get one on that WPA."

♪
(Vocalion 03385) 11/4/36, Chicago, IL

One problem of the 1930s that was the cause of great anxiety was the large number of homeless and abandoned children. It was estimated that over a quarter of a million were regularly hoboing across the nation, riding the rails and sleeping in the hobo jungles. The Civilian Conservation Corps (CCC) was set up within days of the inauguration of Roosevelt's

111

presidency, with a view to employing young men on forest-, soil-, and levee conservation projects. In all, some two and a half million youths were employed by the CCC. Even so, many were not considered eligible. In 1938, Robert Brown, known as Washboard Sam, sang of his frustrations when he attempted to sign on, in his "C.C.C. Blues." "I told her I need a job, and no Relief; On my rent day she sent me a can of beef. She said she'd give me a job, everything was nice and warm, Taking care of the dead in a Funeral Home."

♪
(Bluebird B7995)
December 16, 1938,
Aurora, IL

In spite of the stringency of the times, house parties were popular, helping people to forget their problems for a while. They brought in a little money for the blues singers who played for them. I spoke to one of them, B. K. Turner, who was known as the Black Ace. "Depression time. I couldn't get a li'l job nowhere," he told me. "So I would go aroun' play at house parties with this boy—make a dollar an' a half while other folks was gettin' that for one day's work on relief. Dollar an' a half for that one day. I get three or four parties, man—I made a lot of money. I was makin' somethin' playin' at li'l ole house parties. Dollar an' a half for fun!"

Later Turner obtained a job through the WPA, as a janitor in a photographic studio in Fort Worth, Texas. The achievements of the New Deal were real, but slow, and the benefits were unequally shared. It's probably fair to say that the long haul out of the Depression would never have been accomplished if it had not been for the outbreak of World War II. Even if the war did eventually ensure national economic recovery, the Depression still cast its long shadow. Its effects—the unemployment, the welfare programs, and the suffering of the poor and hungry—were not forgotten. Louis "Jelly Belly" Hayes and his companion, Guitar Slim (Alex Seward) expressed the anxieties of many black people as they faced the postwar years in their recording, "Keep straight blues": "We don't want no more war and no Depression at all. We don't know where the future lies whether it's dark or light."

♪
(Tru-Blue 102) 1948,
New York City

# 23

# High Water Everywhere

First Broadcast: 7/5/91; Producer: Derek Drescher

It's an inescapable fact that the poor suffer most in natural disasters. We may feel that catastrophes do not respect class or wealth, that everyone in an area prone to hazards, such as hurricanes, is equally at risk. But the rich live in the stronger houses and on the safer land, and they have more resources for recovery. In the Southern United States, Blacks (on the lowest rungs of the economic scale) have had to learn to live with the threat of disaster. How do they cope? One time-honored way is to joke and tell tall tales about the event.

Another way of coping with disaster is to sing about it. As I've shown in my book *Blues Fell This Morning*, there are blues songs about all kinds of disastrous events: floods, tornadoes, hurricanes, droughts, fires, epidemics, and so on. I believe that how the blues deals with catastrophes tells us a lot about its function, and the relation of the singers to their audience. These blues themes take the narrative form; quite possibly the best-known example, "BACK WATER BLUES," was recorded in February 1927. It was sung majestically by Bessie Smith, to impressionistic playing by the Harlem pianist James P. Johnson.

♪
(Columbia 14195)
2/17/27, New York City

Smith's "Back Water Blues" was notable for a number of reasons. It was made by the best-known jazz and blues singer of the time; it was one of the first important blues songs to tell a story in the narrative manner of a ballad; and it described in personal terms a tragic event, the Mississippi floods. Or so it seemed, for in fact either luck or prescience played a large part in its success; it was recorded a couple of months *before* the Mississippi River broke the levees. Columbia issued it at the time of the floods, and had an instant hit to which listeners could relate—in a general way. I say general because Bessie Smith's recording, although dramatically contrived, is quite unspecific. It probably referred to the earlier Ohio flood. Compare it with Mattie Delaney's straight-forward and dramatic song about the floods that occurred where the Tallahatchie and the Yazoo Rivers met in the Mississippi Delta region. She played her own guitar accompaniment, and it's a pity that "TALLAHATCHIE RIVER BLUES" was her only record.

♪
(Vocalion 1480) 2/21/30, Memphis, TN

There's no doubt in my mind that Delaney's "Tallahatchie River Blues" was sung from experience. The Mississippi floods were caused by early melting of snow in the northern mountains, and heavy rains in the Ohio Valley. In March 1927 the river was nearly 60 feet above normal; three quarters of a million homes were flooded, 600,000 people, half of them Black, were destitute; thousands of cattle and livestock were lost, and an untold number of people were drowned. The urgency of the situation was captured in a six-minute blues number, "HIGH WATER EVERYWHERE," recorded in a growling voice by Charley Patton: "The backwater done rose around Sumner, now, drove me down the line; Lord I tell the world the water done jumped through this town. Lord the whole round country, man is overflowed—I would go to the hill country, but they got me barred."

♪
(Paramount 12909) 10/29, Grafton, WI

When Patton sang that he would go to the hill country, but they had him "barred," he meant that he literally was prevented from escaping to high ground. The refugee camps discriminated against black victims of the flood; they were managed by the Red Cross, who in some cases even charged the destitute refugees for relief. Under armed guard, many Blacks were forced to rebuild the levees. Reluctantly, President Herbert Hoover appointed the Moton Committee to report on the mismanagement of the flood relief. Blacks bitterly resented their treatment, and when the Red Cross administered relief during the Depression in the early 1930s, the memory remained. Walter Roland complained bitterly in his "RED CROSS BLUES" that their relief workers "don't want to give you nothin', but two or three cans of beans." He sang, "No, I don't wanna go. I said 'you know I cannot go to hill, I got to go yonder to that Red Cross Store.'"

♪
(Melotone M12753) 7/17/33, New York City

Some months after the Mississippi floods had begun to subside, in September 1927, the city of St. Louis was struck by a cyclone. It cut a swathe of destruction through the poorer sectors, causing damage that even then was estimated at a hundred million dollars and killing eighty-four people, many of them Black. Blues singer Mary Johnson lived through it, but she didn't write a blues song about it. Instead, she recounted her experience to her husband, the guitarist Lonnie Johnson. Five days later he was in New York, and recorded "ST. LOUIS CYCLONE BLUES." He sang "The world was black as midnight, I never heard such a noise before. Sound like a million lions—when they're turned loose, they roar."

♪
(Okeh 8512) 10/3/27, New York City

A cover version of Johnson's song was made by a singer from Louisiana, Elzadie Robinson. Johnson himself made at least half a dozen recordings about floods, while others were made by singers as varied as Barbecue Bob, Big Bill Broonzy, Blind Lemon Jefferson, Joe Pullem, Sippie Wallace, and Casey Bill Weldon. I'm certain that many of them didn't experience the events themselves, even though they sang about them with conviction, as if they had. So, it seems, singers were projecting themselves into the situations they described, empathizing with those who had lived through the tragedies. I spoke about this to John Lee Hooker, who had himself recorded a blues about a flood in Tupelo, Mississippi. "It's not the manner that I had the hardships that a lot of people had throughout the South and other cities throughout the country, but I do know what they went through," he told me. "And so when you get the feelin' it's not only what happened to you—it's what happened to your foreparents and other people. And that's what makes the blues."

Immediate, and directly derived from personal experience, though the songs by Mattie Delaney and Charlie Patton might appear, even these were recorded two or three years *after* the events they described. Why did they sing about them so long after the events, and why in the Depression years were African Americans prepared to buy the discs? The reasons are complex, I think. The psychological wounds inflicted by the disasters, and by the treatment of African Americans at the time and after, went very deep. Singing or hearing the blues helped them to come to terms with the events. Through recordings they could share their experience with others who had endured the trauma, or who empathized with then. But what about the localized incidents that also crop up in the blues, which could only be known to a few of their listeners, such as the burning down of Martha Hardin's house on Wilson Street in Brownsville, Tennessee, described by Sleepy John Estes in his "FIRE DEPARTMENT BLUES"?

♪
(Decca 7571) 4/22/38, New York City

115

In this recording, Estes sings about a tragedy in the life of a hardworking but poor woman who has no money for insurance after she's paid her rent. Even if listeners knew nothing of Martha Hardin, nor of the country town in which she lived, they could still identify with her. There were many other blues songs about "manmade" disasters and accidents; like the rapid-impact natural disasters, they were sudden and violent. But there were also tragedies that crept up slowly, like poverty- or job-related diseases such as pellagra and silicosis. As a youth, Josh White saw the ravages of silicosis among the black workers in the Carolinas, Tennessee, and Virginia who'd contracted the disease in the iron ore mines and granite quarries or by tunneling for the railroads. He was just twenty when he recorded "Silicosis Is Killing Me" under the pseudonymn Pinewood Tom. White didn't suffer from silicosis, but he sang on behalf of those who did.

♪
(ARC 6-05-51) 2/26/36, n.p.

Blues records about disasters were very important to black listeners, as I hope I've shown. But at a deeper level it seems to me, the need for black solidarity in the face of events had symbolic parallels with their growing frustration with the social conditions of the time. Blues about disasters were occasionally recorded in the 1950s—but by then hundreds of thousands of African Americans had been engulfed by the international disaster of war.

# 24

# This World Is in a Tangle

First Broadcast: 7/12/91; Producer: Derek Drescher

♪

(Columbia 12-D)
10/2/23, New York City

**A**s many enthusiasts are well aware, the recording of jazz and blues didn't begin until 1920. It was the singer Mamie Smith whose records first showed that there was a considerable 1potential market in the black population. Yet she was more of a jazz than a blues singer, and the emphasis on cabaret and vaudeville entertainers continued for years. In the postwar euphoria of the 1920s there wasn't much room in the catalogs for records that looked back to World War I. However, as late as 1926, there were still some black soldiers waiting to be demobilized. In "UNCLE SAM BLUES," Clara Smith begs for the U.S. Army—in the guise of Uncle Sam—to send her man back home; noted jazz musician Fletcher Henderson plays piano on the recording.

Many black ex-servicemen were bitter about the discriminatory treatment that they had received during the First World War. Only 10 percent of draftees saw combat service overseas; the majority were drafted into the sanitary and labor corps. Those that went to France were unaware that an official document, "Secret Information Concerning Black American Troops," was circulated in Europe that insisted on segregation. I spoke with Professor Rayford Logan, a black veteran of the Western front, and a former officer, who told me:

> When we arrived in France at St. Lazaire, we found that about seventy-five or eighty colored officers were put in one

building, whereas the fifteen or twenty white officers had a building of approximately the same size for themselves. Our senior captain protested at an officers' meeting, the colonel finally granted our request, and permitted some of us to move over, but by the time the Negro officers had moved over to the white building, a curtain had been suspended to shield the white officers from the view of the Negro officers.

On another occasion, when we were closer to the front, I learned—and, incidentally, by that time I spoke French fairly well—that the same colonel had given orders to the French people in the town that they were not to associate with Negros, that we had only recently been released from jail, and we had only recently been emancipated from slavery.

Is the 1930s, when the Depression hit hard, ex-soldiers believed they were entitled to the payment of the bonus money promised to war veterans. In fact, it was due in 1945, but many joined the Bonus Expeditionary Force in a protest march on Washington, D.C., in 1932. They were stopped by the tanks and the tear gas of federal troops under General Douglas MacArthur. Even so, many Blacks looked forward to their "bonus money," and several wrote blues songs about it. Carl Martin wasn't impressed, and sang laconically in his "I'M GONNA HAVE MY FUN," "Lots of you are crippled, gassed, blind and cannot see—but we came back home with the Victory. So, when I get my bonus I'm gonna have my fun. I'm just sittin' here waitin', waitin' till my bonus come."

♪
(Champion 50074)
3/24/36, Chicago, IL

During the tough times of the 1930s there wasn't too much interest in what was happening overseas. American isolationism meant comparatively little to Blacks who were largely insulated from the dramatic events of the period. On the cotton farms, the only changes were for the worse, and they'd no reason to believe that winning the war had brought them any benefits. Among black intellectuals, the aggression of Benito Mussolini's forces against Emperor Haile Selaisse's Ethiopia was a symbol of Black oppression by Whites everywhere. But many rural Blacks felt that they were living in a crazy world that they couldn't understand, as is expressed in the aptly named record "THE COCKEYED WORLD": "It's war in Ethiopia and mama's feeling blue: I tell the cockeyed world—I don't know what to do." This was sung by Minnie Wallace from Jackson, Mississippi, fearing her man was going to be sent to fight in the war.

♪
(Vocalion 03106)
10/12/35, Jackson, MS

Cockeyed it may have been, but by the end of the decade the threat of American involvement in another war was common knowledge. Rural electrification programs had brought radio to Southern homes, and news of the Nazi invasion of Belgium and Holland, and by June 1940, of the fall of Paris, even reached the blues singer Ernest Blunt, known on disc as the Florida Kid. In "HITLER BLUES," he sang, "Hitler says some of our people are White says some are Brown and Black. But Hitler says all that matter to him they look just alike. Well, Hitler he's a bad man, tryin' to take every country now; well, before he takes this country, woman, please be my so-and-so. Well you mind how you get drunk be careful how you clown; you wake up some of these mornings—Hitler be right in your town."

♪
(Bluebird B8589) 11/7/40,
Chicago, IL

Yet the event that brought America into the war was the attack on the U.S. Navy base at Pearl Harbor. A battleship, three destroyers, and several other craft were sunk by Japanese dive bombers. The strike was timed to coincide with others at Guam, the Philippines, and elsewhere, which effectively paralyzed the American fleet in the Pacific. Every American, White or Black, raged in helpless fury over the undeclared act of war. There was anger and, under the circumstances, understandable racial hatred, in Peter "Doctor" Clayton's "PEARL HARBOR BLUES": "Some say the Japanese is hard fighters, but any dummy ought to know: a rattlesnake won't bite you in your back—he will warn you before he strikes his blow."

♪
(Bluebird B9003) 3/27/42,
Chicago, IL

Although General George Marshall had declared in 1940 that "there is no such thing as colored aviation," by the time of the outbreak of hostilities Blacks were training for flying duties. A number of blues singers recorded patriotic songs about the war—enough to make me wonder whether they were persuaded to do so, in the interests of inspiring Blacks to participate in the total war effort. A realistic awareness of the ironies of conscription was expressed in the high, icy voice of Arthur "Big Boy" Crudup from Mississippi in his recording of "GIVE ME A 32-20": "I've got my questionairy and they need me in the war. Now, if I feel murder—don't have to break the county law.

♪
(Bluebird B9019) 4/15/42,
Chicago, IL

Arthur "Big Boy" Crudup was aware of the dangers too, as he imagined dying with the stars and stripes waving in his hand. There was little to suggest patriotism in his closing words: "'Hero' is all I crave. Now, when I'm dead and gone write 'hero' on my grave."

If Arthur "Big Boy" Crudup would have been a reluctant hero, the heroism of the all-black 99th Pursuit Squadron in North Africa was legendary, as was the bravery of the 92nd

Division in Italy and the 761st Battalion in the Battle of the Bulge. But they were, indeed, all Black; it wasn't until July 1948 that President Harry S. Truman signed the Executive Order that was to ensure the desegregation of the U.S. Army. Even then it was opposed by the Chiefs of Staff. By that time forty Blacks had died at the hands of lynch mobs, and segregation persisted in the South as it did in the armed services. When the Korean War broke out in 1950, the courageous 24th Infantry Division was still all Black. There were blues songs about the Korean War, but no enthusiasm to participate in it. Mister Honey (David Edwards) summed up the mood in his song "BUILD A CAVE," a version of a protest blues: "This world is in a tangle, everybody singin' a song. They're fightin' across the water baby; ain't gonna be here long. I'm gonna build myself a cave so I can move down underground, so when I get into the Army darlin', won't be no more Reds around."

♪
(ARC 102) 1951,
Houston, TX

The complaint of Clara Smith and the phlegmatism of Carl Martin; the confusion of Minnie Wallace and the defeatism of the Florida Kid; the anger of Doctor Clayton, and the disillusion of Mister Honey—all these attitudes in relation to one broad theme illustrate the spectrum of emotions that can be found in the blues. They could have acted as a gauge of black feelings at the time—if more people had taken the trouble to listen to what the blues singers were saying within the black community.

# 25

# Blues with a Feeling

First Broadcast: 7/19/91; Producer: Derek Drescher

♪
(Decca 7171) 2/4/36, Chicago, IL

Although the range of themes in the blues—at any rate, between 1925 and 1960—was remarkably broad, there were some aspects of experience that did not figure prominently. At a time when black families were, on average, much larger than those of Whites, it's surprising that children were seldom even mentioned. Then again, the origins of the majority of blues singers were rural, even if they eventually migrated to the city. But in spite of the blues about natural disasters, there are very few blues songs that give so much as a passing mention to the landscape. Blues is principally about personal feelings and interpersonal relationships. When the natural world is referred to, it's usually as a metaphor. Even some emotions are rarely expressed—guilt or remorse, for instance. But they all come together occasionally, as on "CRYING MOTHER BLUES" by Red Nelson (Nelson Wilborn). "My mother's dead and gone to Glory" he sang, "only way to meet my mother, I will have to change my lowdown ways." He continued, "Tombstone's my pillow, graveyard gonna be bed; blue skies gonna be my blanket, and the pale moon gonna be my spread." There's no denying the poetic imagery of Nelson's lines: "Black cat crawls late hours at midnight, nightmares ride till the break of day. What's the use of loving some woman, some man done stole your love away?"

Blues verses encapsulate ideas so completely that they often seen too condensed, but with instrumental accompaniment they can reveal a poetic quality that is elusive when they're transcribed. Some blues singers were, unquestionably, folk poets whose use of language was unique and vivid. Take Willie "61" Blackwell, who recorded just one commercial session, in 1941. His "Four O'Clock Flower" conveys the heartache of a working man who's losing his wayward schoolgirl friend: "Four o'clock flowers bloom in the morning and close in the afternoon; they are only a summer beauty, so is my little Betty June." Blackwell was called "61" because he lived in Mississippi beside Highway 61, which eventually took him north.

♪
(Bluebird B8921) 7/3/41, Chicago, IL

A great many blues are about failing love affairs. James Oden, known as "St. Louis Jimmy," could have been speaking for many singers when I asked him how he got his ideas: "I got inspiration from writin', and looked at other people's troubles, and I writes from that, and I writes from my own troubles. Not from the other feller much—'cause I think I've had more than the other feller had. . . . I never sung no one's number but my own and I been writin' songs for the last thirty years."

Apart from the inevitable domestic stresses that occur in any culture, the black community until the late 1950s was the victim of overt racial discrimination. But there was more to it than legal segregation, because a divisive discrimination based on shades of color existed in what was then termed "Negro society." In 1927, Lillian Glinn recorded "Brown Skin Blues" in Dallas; sung in her warm contralto to the accompaniment of Willie Tyson on piano and an unknown twelve-string guitar player, the song affirmed her own dark skin color, and was addressed to the light-skinned girls with whom she'd been performing: "Now all you high yellers you ought to listen to me, a yellow man's sweet, a black man's neat. A brownskin man will take you clear off of your feet." "Brown Skin Blues" made her one of the most sought-after singers of the day.

♪
(Columbia 14275) 12/2/27, Dallas, TX

Many blues songs dwell on the attractions of the opposite sex, which sometimes reflected color prejudices within the black community, and also revealed unfashionable preferences for, in the direct language of the blues, "meat shaking on the bone," a partner who was "low and squatty" or another who might be "long and tall, like a cannonball." Hair straighteners were sold to women who aspired to film-star tresses but, as St. Louis Bessie (Bessie Mae Smith) dryly observed in her "Sweet Black Woman," "My hair is kinky but my baby do not care: any man's a fool, who wants a woman for her hair."

♪
(Okeh 8659) 12/5/28, Chicago, IL

St. Louis Bessie's somber, challenging posture in the record was not uncommon among the female singers who competed with the men on their own terms. Some of her recordings were aggressively sexual in character, but a great many blues numbers have a strong vein of sexuality in them. Singers drew upon a rich store of metaphors and allusions, based on a wide variety of domestic and farmyard analogies. Cooking—baking bread or biscuits, rolling dough, heating the oven, or turning down the damper on the stove—provided the basis for many such blues; so did the ponies, hogs, lowing heifers, and milk cows of the farm.

Yet the images were often far from pastoral, and many turned to technology for inspiration. Railroads and motorcycles offered modern alternatives to the persistent sexual metaphor of "riding" that formerly had been applied to horses, ponies, and even to the Shetland pony by none other than Charley Patton. It was the automobile that was to provide the most popular image, among the most powerful being that of the vaudeville singer Cleo Gibson in her risqué number "I'VE GOT FORD MOVEMENTS IN MY HIPS"; she bragged that she had "Ford engine movements" in her hips, which were "ten thousand miles guaranteed," and "You can have your Rolls Royal your Packard and such—it takes a Ford engine car to do your stuff."

♪
(Okeh 8700) 3/14/29, Atlanta, GA

The automobile was a resource for the youthful Mississippi philanderer Robert Johnson who, in 1936, found abundant sexual metaphors in the Hudson Terraplane, then new to the automobile market. In "TERRAPLANE BLUES," Johnson compared his woman to a poorly functioning car: The coils weren't buzzing, the generator wouldn't get a spark, and he advised this unspecified woman to get her batteries charged. Tragically, the good-humored lustfulness of the singer carried over into real life. Less than two years after he made that recording, he was murdered by a jealous lover at the Three Forks juke joint near Greenville, Mississippi. He was just twenty-seven years old.

♪
(Vocalion 03416) 11/23/36, San Antonio, TX

Johnson's brilliant but brief life has become the stuff of blues legend, but it underscores the fact that the places where blues singers played—the juke joints of the plantations and the barrelhouse of the job sites and sawmill camps—were often rough and violent. One such itinerant blues singer and pianist, Edwin "Buster" Pickens, told me about the music he played, and the barrelhouses in the sawmill camps where he worked. "They gambled, they drinked heavily and when there was a fight, there was a good one, but there was a reason for it. They didn't do things just right along so—imposin' on you. But in those days black people got along fine. But it could be rugged when it was; it was plenty rugged."

Only a few years after I interviewed Buster Pickens, he too, was killed in a juke joint in Houston, shot in an argument over a quarter. The stresses brought about by segregation, poverty, and the lack of opportunities were given some release in such games as Playing the Dozens, which was based on the capacity of the opposing players to withstand a stream of insults and abuse. I talked with Rufus Perryman, an albino known as Speckled Red who was nearly blind. He told me how he made "THE DIRTY DOZENS" into the keynote piano piece of the Southern barrelhouses:

♪
(Brunswick 7116)
9/22/29, Memphis, TN

> They used to have a word, they say "playin' the dozens." It was talking dirty you know, the boys be together and they'd try and outtalk one and the other till one feller would holler "You put me in the dozens!" because he couldn't think of no more to say. So I made a kind of a song out of the words, and I called it "The Dirty Dozens." But they was real bad words, you see; I was playing in one of them turpentine jukes where it didn't matter. Anything I said was all right in there, you see. I had to clean it up for the record, but it meaned the same thing but it was a different attitude.

Red's cleaned-up recording of that song, made in 1929, still captures something of the combination of raw sex and rough-house humor with musical inventiveness that helped black workers to cope.

# 26

# Three Ball Blues

**First Broadcast: 7/26/91; Producer: Derek Drescher**

♪
(Vocalion 05440)
3/6/40, New York City

**A**s I've tried to show in this series, the themes with which the blues are concerned are quite varied, and the layers of meaning in the blues are numerous and rich. Even so, there are popular myths about the blues that stem, it seems to me, from a desire to make them fit preconceived ideas. Among the most persistent is that of humor in the blues. There is, of course, humor in the blues, as has been evident in some of the examples I've mentioned. Sometimes it seems to arise out of a game with the censors in the record companies—particularly in the ingenious sexual metaphors used. Some singers, like Tampa Red or Bo Carter, were masters at double-entendre lyrics. But very few cast a humorous eye on their world as a whole. Humor in the blues is often ironic, used to point up a basically more serious theme. Take Blind Boy Fuller's "Three Ball Blues," about a visit to the pawnshop, for instance. In it, a destitute Fuller is driven to pawn anything he has—including his guitar—because he's broke, hungry, and cold. His boss won't advance him any money, so he goes to the pawnshop "with my shoes in my hand." The blues ends with this ironic exchange between Fuller and the pawnbroker: "Says I asked the pawnshop man, 'What the three balls doing hanging on that wall?' Says 'It's two to one buddy— you don't get your things back out of here at all.'"

This is gambling humor 2:1 odds.

It makes us feel a lot more comfortable, and dispels the feelings of guilt that the themes of the blues can inspire, if we can convince ourselves that the blues singer is really laughing at adversity. The very few singers who frequently sang humorous numbers—I can think of two: Cousin Joe Pleasants and Champion Jack Dupree—appear to have developed them while performing as entertainers for white audiences. I have never talked with a blues singer who so much as mentioned humor in the blues.

Even the blues songs that employ sexual metaphors frequently have an underlying strain of melancholy, or of frustration, or even of threat. Take "BLACK ACE BLUES," in which the singer explores the metaphoric possibilities of a deck of cards: "l am the Black Ace, I'm the boss card in your hand. I lays in your deck, mama—I lays close and tight, but I'll play for you, mama, if you treat me right."

The singer was Babe Kyro Turner, known as the Black Ace—not just to his friends or on record, but on radio too. In the late 1950s, he even had his own radio program, as he explained to me when I asked him how he developed his unusual style of playing the guitar flat across his knees while stroking the strings with a medicine bottle. He explained, "When I was around about thirty I run up on a feller they call Buddy Woods, but I call him Oscar Woods, and he was playin' git-tar—steel git-tar style—but he was playin' with a bottle. And I follered him around, lookin' at how he playin'. I always knowed how to make a few li'l chords on the git-tar but I never seen that kind of way of playin'. He was just messin' aroun' with it and I of course followed him on up and I learned how to play somethin' with that bottle."

"Black Ace Blues" was his signature theme on the radio, and its popularity suggests the possibility that his listeners may have read another meaning into the words: "I lays in your deck, mama, I lays close and tight, but I'll play for you, mama, if you treat me right . . ."

This raises the question of whether the blues functioned symbolically, as a vehicle for social protest. Although it is often regarded as a form of protest song, specifically targeted or overtly stated blues songs that protest against segregation, discrimination, and the many forms of social injustice that Blacks have endured are extremely rare. For rural Blacks there were also few role models to whom they could relate. Though blues borrowed the narrative form from ballads, there were almost no heroic figures in the blues, as there were in the ballads. Jesse Owens's triumph at the Olympic Games wasn't marked by any recording; the event was too distant.

♪
(Decca 7281) 2/15/37, Dallas, TX

The one exception was the boxer Joe Louis, whose battle to become World Champion was the subject of many blues numbers. After losing to Max Schmeling, Louis demolished the Nazi boxer on June 22, 1938. The day after, Bill Gaither recorded "CHAMP JOE LOUIS."

♪
(Decca 7476) 6/23/38,
New York City

With the disillusionment that set in after World War II as Blacks realized that the South intended to resist desegregation, blues might well have taken on a more political stance, and blues singers could have exhorted the black community to be more militant. But hardly any did. When Rosa Parks refused to take her seat in the rear of a bus in Alabama and by her defiance inspired so many to participate in the bus boycott, and eventually in the broader Civil Rights Movement, there were no songs about her, and none in support of the demonstrators or the heroic figure of Dr. Martin Luther King, Jr.

♪
(Blues Classics 12)
c. 1956, Detroit, MI

One slight exception to this was "ALABAMA BUS," recorded in Detroit by Brother Will Hairiston and accompanied by Washboard Willie, a song about the Alabama Bus Boycott. "You know they tell me a human being stepped on board," Hairston chanted, "the driver began to make a fuss. He says 'You know you're from the Negro race, and don't you know you're sittin' in the wrong place?'" The song is based on hearsay, and the details aren't incorrect, but the message is clear: "Stop the Alabama bus, I don't want to ride, Lord, an Alabama boy and I don't want to ride."

However, Brother Will Hairston was a gospel singer rather than a blues singer. Gospel singers *did* take up the challenge and many recorded songs on behalf of the Civil Rights campaign. It might be argued that, in a sense, they were protected by the churches they represented, but, in those violent times, being a member of a religious group in a peaceful demonstration was no guarantee of safety. On a busy street corner in St. Louis at the height of the Civil Rights demonstrations, I spoke with Marion Oldham, a young member of the Council on Racial Equality (CORE), who was picketing a hotel notorious for its discriminatory policies. She asked me what I was doing, and I explained, asking her how she felt about the blues. She answered, "I'm not an avid fan of blues singers or blues. As a Negro, I think that we have been stereotyped—that all Negroes like blues. I think that you might take a look at the noted Negro musicians, and those that have reached fame and popularity are not necessarily blues singers; I think the great majority are not. Radio stations that beam directly to the Negro community in St. Louis feel that they have to play blues records all day long, and this isn't so. I think this is a move back as far as the Negro is concerned."

The radio stations were indeed beaming blues to the large black audience, but it was not to last. As the Civil Rights Movement gathered momentum, it was not to blues but to gospel that the marchers turned. With great courage, church congregations and freedom choirs joined together, adapting traditional spirituals to tell new stories. In a recording of "THIS LITTLE LIGHT OF MINE" made in Selma, Alabama, the lyrics are changed so that the singer, Betty Mae Fikes, urges her listeners "to tell Jim Clark" (who was the sheriff of Selma) and "tell Al Lingo" (the leader of the Alabama State Troopers) that the oppressed Blacks were going to emerge from the darkness and let their light shine.

♪
(Smithsonian R023)
c. 1956, Selma, AL

# IV
## Documenting the Blues

# 27

# Creating the Documents

First Broadcast: 10/4/97; Producer: Derek Drescher

♪
(Victor 21279) 2/3/28,
Memphis, TN

"Cool Drink of Water Blues," recorded by Tommy Johnson, is one of the finest examples of Mississippi blues, with its haunting vocal, effortless falsetto, and superbly integrated accompaniment on two guitars. If we look for details in the blues collector's "bible," *Blues and Gospel Records, 1890–1943* we find that it was recorded at the Memphis Auditorium in Memphis, Tennessee, over seventy-five years ago, on Friday, February 3, 1928. Tommy Johnson played his own guitar, and was accompanied by Charlie McCoy on second guitar. Apparently this was the second "take" of the song; the first take was never issued and is unlikely to exist. This information doesn't necessarily add to our appreciation of the blues or its bitter theme—"I asked for water, and she gave me gasoline"—but it does help to place it in the story of the music.

Much has happened in the blues, and in African American music generally in the years since Tommy Johnson made that record. Blues became progressively more urbanized; then in the 1960s it began to decline as a black music, as Soul took its place. It was discovered by white enthusiasts, and in the past thirty years has become a major influence on popular music, to be sung and played all over the world. Gospel music flourished and its influence is felt in church music in much of the English-speaking world. With all this change and global expansion in blues and related music, it would be easy to forget their forms and development in the twentieth century up to World War II, when they were the creation of Blacks within a segregated society. How did it all begin?

The story has often been told—especially by himself—of how the black promoter Perry Bradford pushed the Harlem singer, Mamie Smith, until he succeeded in securing a recording date for Smith's that had been offered to the "last of the Red Hot Mommas," Sophie Tucker, singing "THAT THING CALLED LOVE." "Crazy Blues" was Smith's *second* record, but it was a tremendous hit with the black community, opening the way for scores—and eventually, thousands—of blues singers, gospel groups, preachers, and entertainers to be recorded. In the words of Alberta Hunter, sometime singer with Duke Ellington, "she made it possible for all of us." *Blues and Gospel Records*, however, lists recordings made only to the end of 1943, when the so-called Petrillo Ban of the American Federation of Musicians (imposed against recording by its members), the wartime rationing of shellac, and the last of the field recordings made for the Library of Congress, marked the cessation of recording of black music for some years.

♪
(Okeh 4113) 2/14/20,
New York City

Estelle "Mama" Yancey's version of "MAKE ME A PALLET ON THE FLOOR," accompanied by the blues piano of her husband, Jimmy Yancey, recorded in Chicago in December 1943, is among the very last records covered in the 1370-page *Blues and Gospel* discography. This remarkable work was first compiled in the early 1960s by Professor Robert M. W. Dixon, an anthropological linguist based in Australia, and a clerk in the Cardiff docks, John Godrich. They were brought together by their love for blues and gospel and their desire to establish all that was known, or could be found out, about the records. With the help of collectors in many countries, the first edition, covering 1902 to 1942, was published in 1964 and went through subsequent, enlarged editions. Tragically, Godrich died in 1991, but Dixon continued the work and Howard Rye, who replaced John Godrich, put the whole thing on computer. I asked Howard Rye to explain the purposes of discography, and to summarize some of the problems and the achievements of their work.

♪
(Session 12-003) 12/43,
Chicago, IL

> *H.R.* Discographies are accepted as guides for record collectors, to give information on who was playing on the records, as the record companies generally did not, and of course, to point them to other records in the same styles that they might want to acquire. But for any kind of scholarly work to be done, accurate documentation is essential. . . . Over the years, and especially with the

holdings of academic institutions, it would be fair to say that the provision of documentation for scholars has become more and more crucial in what we have been doing. But nonetheless, I think that probably the most typical user is still the record collector looking for information about records he's got, and what he might like to have.

What goes into a discography is *who* is on the records, *where* and *when* they were made, the titles of the items and the issue numbers—which, in our case, is generally the 78-rpm issue numbers—otherwise the book would become unmanageably large. We also, of course, include what are called the *matrix numbers*, which are the numbers originally allocated by the record companies to direct-cut recordings. Each of them is individually unique to a performance, so they are obviously important as a reference and they also give discographers clues about what was actually going on.

*P.O.* The first edition of *Blues and Gospel Records* came out about 1964, and this is the fourth edition, the new one, and it is certainly enlarged. So what are the principal differences between this and the previous ones?

*H.R.* The thing that people are most going to notice is the title index, for which there was a lot of demand after early editions but which, to be honest, was only feasible with the availability of computers. But there are about 150 new artists in the present edition, in three classes: jubilee vocal groups, which were previously left out because it was thought that they were aimed at the general market. I think the real reason was that they were never of interest to blues and jazz collectors, and that it's only recently that the demand of researchers in African American religious music as such has come to the fore and presented a real demand, making it worthwhile including this information.

We've also included some very early string bands and people on the fringes of minstrelsy, what some people would call "pre-blues" material. It's possibly of greater interest to researchers than to most record collectors. And we've had a very close look at the essentially arbitrary division between blues and jazz, which is a division imposed on African American music by record collectors, but which has no real significance in respect of the music at the margins. And we've tried to incorporate what *has* fallen between the two groups of record collectors.

*P.O.* What would be an example of a singer or artist who falls within that gap?

*H.R.* Well, there's Josephine Baker for one, who has been left out of both blues and jazz discographies in the past. When we decided that she was of sufficient interest to include, one of the titles we had in mind was "SKEEDLE UM."

♪
(French Odeon 49227)
11/26, Paris, France

*P.O.* Bearing in mind the vast amount of recording data you already have, what kind of information would you still like to see?

*H.R.* The greatest windfall we could possibly have would be, if the files of the Paramount Company or of one of the other small companies, whose files have disappeared over the years, were to somehow, miraculously, turn up. Being realistic, this is not going to happen at this stage. I'm sure that there's lots and lots of field recordings still out there, many of them undocumented by the institutions that hold them. And of course, our inclusion of such material is wholly dependent on the cataloging done by the institutions. But even at this late date, records are still turning up. Not only one of these numerous test pressings or takes still appearing from wherever they've been for the past sixty or seventy years. Another class of recordings that keep turning up are, what I believe are known as, *vanity recordings*—that is, records made on behalf of artists for sale at their gigs. And even from quite early in recording history we are still finding records of this type turning up—especially by religious artists, who presumably sold them in aid of church funds.

Listing all records made by African American artists, blues and religious, both issued and unissued, or known only through company ledgers, is a task of immense but indeterminate dimensions. Who knows what will be recovered from junkshops and discovered in files in the future?

However, all of this documentation is frustrating if the records cannot be heard. Yet now, to a very large extent, they can, thanks to the single-mindedness of an Austrian collector, Johnny Parth. Tommy Johnson's "Cool Drink of Water Blues," Mamie Smith's "Crazy Blues," Jimmy and Mama Yancey's "Pallet on the Floor Blues," and Josephine Baker's "Skeedle Um" are all on the Document 5000 Series of CDs. "Cool Drink of Water Blues" is in fact, the very first title in the series.

When Johnny Parth took a quick break from his recording equipment and came to England, I took the opportunity to discuss his extraordinary project with him. He has now issued on his various labels some 700 CDs in seven years—about two per week—and I wondered, how this was possible?

J.P. It's possible with a very tolerant wife who helps you as much as you need. And with a lot of love for the music. And you must work day and night, around the clock.

P.O. It seems to me that this is your third attempt at the comprehensive reissue of blues. I'm thinking of the Roots LP series, that you were doing some twenty-five years ago, the Blues Documents on LP, and now these Document CDs. What drives you to produce these?

J.P. I would like to have in my collection all the items listed in the Dixon and Godrich discography of *Blues and Gospel Records 1890–1943*, which is the most important book for the collector, I think. I'm sure that there are many people who think it's not necessary to have *all* this material. But these people can buy these *Best of . . .* CDs, and the mixed stuff with all this duplication. But people who want everything, they have to buy my series, because there are no others.

P.O. Nevertheless, relative newcomers to blues will have certain names they know. They might find some of them missing from your series. I'm thinking of Bessie Smith, Robert Johnson, or even Brownie McGhee, or, if they know a bit more about it, Henry Thomas. So why are they missing?

J.P. They are missing because they are already available in complete and chronological order, including alternative takes. So I think it isn't necessary to reissue them a second time.

P.O. Basically, what you are trying to see is everything available on CD. Not necessarily *your* doing it, but making sure that they are obtainable.

J.P. I'm glad when somebody else issues it, because I can retire at an earlier date. But you must understand my series is an academic one. I do not want to entertain with my records. I want to have everything available for serious research. And this is the reason why I call it Document Records.

P.O. Do you find that collectors *do* want everything by every artist? I'm thinking of fifteen CDs of Tampa Red; are there people who want all these—or nine CDs of Reverend Gates?

*J.P.* Well, there's a couple of people who want the complete Tampa Red, but definitely no one who wants the complete records of Reverend Gates! But when you do a work like this—a complete culture of the African American—you have to issue everything, whether you like it or not, and the preachers belong to this. If they don't sell, and I don't get the money I've spent, I have some profit with others.

*P.O.* In order to obtain many of these records, which are extraordinarily rare in some instances, you had to go to collectors who, it seems to me, have been extremely generous in loaning to you recordings, which often may exist only in one copy. How do you do that?

*J.P.* That's my charm! At first it was very difficult. There were some people—like Roger Misiewicz in Canada, and others—who were very interested in the project and so they began to ask all collectors, "Who has what?" And they send me tapes of the material, and the more records or CDs I put on the market, the more collectors went to the telephone and called me. Many of them didn't ask for anything, they gave it because they are friends.

The *Blues and Gospel Records* discography lists some 20,000 titles by over 3,000 blues and gospel singers and groups in discographical detail. Of these, perhaps 16,000 have been made available in chronological order and as completely as possible on the Document label and on certain other CDs. Most of the balance, including the majority of the U.S. Library of Congress Archive of Folk Music recordings, may never be isssued. But that's not all. Both gospel and the blues are essentially vocal musics; though there are instrumentals, of course, song, in various forms, is the basis of both these traditions. This has inspired a Scotsman, Robert Macleod, to undertake another daunting project: the transcription of the lyrics of every item in the Document catalog, which he is publishing in a series of volumes. I talked with him about this self-imposed task and asked him what his motivation was.

*R.M.* When I retired, in about '86 or '87, I had time on my hands, and I had a look at Charley Patton transcriptions in the various books—and thought that I could improve on some of them. That's when I started, and that ended up as *Yazoo 1–20.* I know at this stage there were many bloomers [blunders] in that book, and I wish there weren't. But the thing is done. My second book is a bit better, and during that time, Richard Metson and Bernard

Holland came in to help with the checking. Since I started on Document they've been checking every single item, and kept the books in a very satisfactory way, I'm quite pleased with all the Document books. Now why I did the Document books, was—when I finished the *Yazoo No. 2*— Roger Misiewicz, in Canada, he suggested the Document series, and that's how it started. So really, it's only been a planned operation since 1993.

*P.O.* I understand that you have introduced new methods to ensure a higher level of accuracy of transcription. I wonder if you could describe what those methods are.

*R.M.* It's really the machine. It looks as if it cost £50, but in fact it cost £500. It's an office dictation machine, and it has speeds from double speed down to virtually zero—which is a much wider range of speed than I would ever need. But I find it very useful to slow the thing down slightly, or speed it up to get a hint somewhere. Once I've got a hint of the meaning, I can go back to normal speed, and the words become quite clear. The other good feature on the machine is that there's a control to let it rewind slightly. It's a foot-operated machine, so, if I stop the machine and go back three seconds and then just simply switch it on, it repeats the last line or the last few words that I've set it for. I can go back and do this over and over again; maybe after the tenth time the meaning of the line becomes absolutely clear.

*P.O.* One thing that I've been wondering about is how you have coped with the problems of dialect and idiom, and their meaning—in recognizing their meaning and in writing up the transcriptions. For instance, you use "going to" rather than "gwine to," although several authorities would argue that this is Standard Black English, so that the terms that in the past would have been looked on as being rather "Uncle Tom" are in fact accurate, or fairly accurate ways of transcribing them. So I wondered how you arc coping with the problem of dialect?

*R.M.* Well, about half of my custom is non-English speaking; at least their, first language is not English; Japanese people, German, French, et cetera. So I thought it better, as far as I could, to have a standardized way of doing things. For that reason I say in the introduction that I use "gonna" when it could have been, say, "gon'" with an apostrophe and so on: "and" when it could have been "an'" with an apostrophe. I always use "and."

*P.O.* I also wondered if you felt in making the transcriptions whether you think that the arguments for blues as poetry are validated, or whether the majority of blues are not, in a sense, poetic.

*R.M.* I see the blues as a performance. That's to say, I see a single unit, with a lyric and a singer and maybe one or two instruments. If you extract the lyric and try to treat it as an item in its own right, I think you've lost almost everything. For example, "Some Summer Day" by Charley Patton: If you only read it, the whole thing is lost. I only appreciate it when you have a single item, which is a performance.

♪
(Paramount 13080)
5/28/30, Grafton, WI

It was late last spring, one summer day
Oh when he left here, he's gone to stay.
But now Harvey's gone, darlin' don't you worry
Because he'd kill again another day.

I'm worried and sinkin', out in the yard,
Catch me a freight train, good times got hard,
But now he's gone, darlin' don't you worry,
Because he'd kill again another day.

Some got six months, some got a year,
Purvis Harvey got lifetime here,
But now he's gone, darlin' I don't worry,
Because he'd kill again another day.

To sum up, we now have available to us all known recording data and all known issued recordings, together with a substantial proportion of lyric transcripts, of the entire corpus of African American music in the blues and gospel genres over the first half century of recording. It is equivalent to a complete *catalogue raissoné* of a school of artists, such as the Dutch genre painters of the seventeenth century. In no other branch of folk and popular music is so systematic a documentation in recording data, sound recordings, and lyric transcription to be found. But we're challenged by this documentation. Ramblin' Thomas may be unfamiliar to many who collect and study this music, but Tommy Johnson, Mamie Smith, and Jimmy Yancey are well known—too much so, perhaps, because it's evident that our enthusiasms are highly selective and that much African American music has been disregarded. In this book, I have examined the blues and one or two related traditions, attempted to answer some fundamental questions, and to reconsider some of our built-in assumptions, which have been brought to my attention by the wealth of secular material that is now available to us.

# 28

# Still to Be Documented

First Broadcast: 12/5/97; Producer: Derek Drescher

♪

(Paramount 12602)
1/28, Chicago, IL

In January 1928, the veteran minstrel show singer Charlie Jackson recorded the humorous ballad "LONG GONE, LOST JOHN" to his own banjo accompaniment. It told the story of a man on the run from the police, who eluded capture by various means: "Lost John made a pair of shoes of his own, just as good a shoes as ever were worn: Had heels in the front and heels behind, You couldn't tell which-away Lost John's gwine—now he's long, long gone." At the end of the song Charlie Jackson claimed authorship with a traditional verse: "Now, if anybody should ask you 'who composed this song?' Tell them 'Papa Charlie Jackson' and idle on—now we're long, we're long gone."

It's highly unlikely that he did compose the song, although the original Paramount issue did not give a composer credit. In text and tune it has similarities with W.C. Handy's "Long Gone," which was published in 1920, although Abbe Niles gave its date as 1913 and the author of the lyrics as Chris Smith, the composer of "Ballin' the Jack." But Niles agreed that it was "based on a folk song." If anyone should ask you who composed a great many blues songs, you'd be hard-pressed to name them. The earliest published blues song is reportedly "Baby Seals Blues," registered for copyright by Baby Seals on August 7, 1912; the registration gives his "nationality," at that early date, as "Afro-American." It was never recorded by any jazz, blues, or revue singer—or so it seemed, until Charles Anderson's

139

♪
(Okeh 8124) 10/24/23,
Chicago, IL

"SING 'EM BLUES," made in October 1923, with Eddie Heywood playing piano, was reissued by Document Records.

We don't need to hear too much of that to agree that Charles Anderson was no blues singer. But "Sing 'Em Blues" *is* "Baby Seals Blues," with music composed by the ragtime pianist Artie Matthews—though not, of course, credited to him. Interestingly, it included the lines: "Honey baby, mama, do-she, do-she, double-do love you."

♪
(Vocalion 03166)
10/20/35, Jackson, MS

This was derived from, or assimilated by, rural blues singers. The "Mississippi Moaner," Isaiah Nettles, for example, uses the line in his recording of "SO COLD IN CHINA." Regrettably, Nettles only recorded two titles. Perhaps he heard Blind Lemon Jefferson when the Texas singer visited Mississippi, because there's more than a hint of his influence there, but only those few words suggest a link with the earliest blues composition.

♪
(Victor 21135) 10/27/27,
Camden, NJ

A month after "Baby Seals Blues" was published, "Dallas Blues," written by white lyricist Hart Wand, was published in Oklahoma City. Just two days later, W. C. Handy published his "St. Louis Blues." "DALLAS BLUES" was recorded and issued just once by a revue artist, Maggie Jones, with a routine New York band. More surprising was the string-band version made by the South Street Trio, with Bobby Leecan on banjo, Alfred Martin on guitar, and harmonica player Robert Cooksey taking the vocal (somewhat uneasily, it must be admitted). The evidence of some of their titles suggests that Leecan and Cooksey came from Pennsylvania, but others consider that their origins were Southern.

These few examples only hint at the complexity of the relationships among composed blues, published sheet music, and recorded blues by professional and rural singers. One of the threads running through these programs has been the possible sources of blues phrases, such as in Barbecue Bob's "Chocolate to the Bone." The picture is further clouded by the fact that the song, which was recorded in Atlanta by a field unit, was credited on the record label to "Williams" and was notionally published by Clarence Williams. I say *notionally* because publication merely meant registration of the song with a few lead lines; sheet music was printed only if the song proved to be a hit. It's likely that Clarence Williams simply collected the royalties.

♪
(QRS R7043) 12/28,
Long Island, NY

Williams had his hand in publishing, recording, and accompanying various blues singers. He often shared "composer" credit with those he recorded, a not uncommon method used over the decades by record producers to take a cut of composition royalties. Blues singer Sara Martin recorded "Death Sting Me Blues," backed with "MEAN TIGHT MAMA," with

Clarence Williams and his Orchestra, featuring Joe "King" Oliver on trumpet, Cyrus St. Clair on tuba, Williams on piano, and an unidentified trombone player. The first title was co-credited to Williams and Martin; the second was credited to Andy Razaf, a young composer who wrote some fairly convincing blues songs, as well as a number of songs that gave a new meaning to the term *blue*, such as "My Handy Man" for Ethel Waters, and "I Ain't Your Hen, Mister Fly Rooster" for Martha Copeland. A mediocre singer himself, he made just one record under the name of Croonin' Andy Razaf, and then wisely kept to composing.

There were many other composers who wrote blues numbers for the major recording, vaudeville, revue, and show singers of the 1920s, like George W. Thomas, Tom Delaney, Chris Smith, and J. Guy Sudoth. A less familiar name, Sudoth who wrote "Blues and Booze" for Ma Rainey, "Graveyard Bound" for Ida Cox, and others for such singers as Ethel Waters and Sodarisa Miller. But unless you have the original 78-rpm records, or access to some rare record listings, you'll be hard pressed to find much information on these writers of blues and blues songs. This applies to blues in the 1930s, as well.

"BRING ME FLOWERS WHILE I'M LIVING," by Peetie Wheatstraw, was recorded in November 1941 at a session that also included "Hearse Man Blues," and Peetie's last recording, "Separation Day Blues." It was tragically prophetic because Wheatstraw was killed in a road accident a month later. Although it seems like an extraordinary premonition, the full story was even stranger, because Peetie did not write his own songs for the session. They had been written for him by James Oden, known as the blues singer "St. Louis Jimmy."

Clearly, we can learn a great deal about the interaction between blues writer and blues singer, of the operations of music publishers and recording agents, and of blues partnerships and blues poets from the composer credits on record labels. Not all 78s had them; sometimes they were entered in full, sometimes surnames only, sometimes not at all. But in my view, the authorship of blues lyrics is one of the least researched aspects of blues history, and the most inadequately documented. I have always felt that "composer credits" should be included in discographies and have urged the compilers of the discography *Blues and Gospel Records, 1890–1943*, Robert M. W. Dixon, John Godrich, and Howard Rye, to do so. The fourth edition includes a most valuable song-title index, but, to my regret, no composer credits were appended to them. Rye explained the position to me:

♪
(Decca 7886) 11/25/41, Chicago, IL

I have two wholly incompatible views on this. As a user, I think it would be a wonderful idea. As a compiler, I think mainly of the increased length. Even if the composer credits were to be added to the title index, it would still mean an extra line for every title, and that's not counting the cases where we would find that there are different composer credits attributed for the same title, and the numerous cases, especially where field recordings are concerned, where we wouldn't actually know if it was the same tune.

Perhaps Robert Macleod could include composer credits in future volumes of his invaluable series of transcripts, the Document Blues books. As the subject expands, and the distance in time from the recording of early blues gets greater, the original records become rarer and older. None of the recordings that we have discussed in this series of programs are less than fifty-five years old, and some were made a century ago. In the intervening years, many were broken or damaged, chipped, or simply worn grey with continual playing. Some cylinders could only be played half a dozen times before they deteriorated, while many wax recordings on 78s were pressed on inferior material, for the Race or chain store markets. Blues and Gospel collectors accept these limitations on quality and some even object to digital remastering that takes out the flaws as cosmeticizing the source material. But others find the imperfections hard to accept on CD. I asked the producer of Document Records, Johnny Parth, about this.

> *J.P.* When I started with the CDs, I tried to get the best possible copies of each record. I took all the tapes and records to the studio and we compared some six or seven versions and found out which one was the best. It is easy to produce a CD with clean copies, but if you do what I do, the complete chronological release of an artist, then you have to use titles of varying quality, and if this is the only known copy in the world, and is better than completely unplayable, you have to do something, so that it sounds like music.

> *P.O.* So, in other words what is really important [is] that it is available, and available to scholars, and you try to get the best quality that you can. Now, these records are sometimes seventy to a hundred years old. How is it that copies are being discovered even now?

> *J.P.* From junk shops, in the roofs, in cellars—mostly from collectors who are not very well known. Suddenly a letter

comes, from a guy who I have never heard of before, who writes to tell me he has found this title or alternative take, and he offers it and sends a tape and I put it on a *Too Late, Too Late* CD.

*P.O.* You've already got eight CDs of *Too Late, Too Late*.

♪
(Soundie 8103) 8/17/42, Hollywood, CA

An example of the type of material that continues to surface is "Spirit of Boogie Woogie," played with zest by Meade Lux Lewis. It was a recently discovered "soundie," or a recording for a sort of visual jukebox, made in August 1943. New discoveries like this will mean more work for the compilers of *Blues and Gospel Records 1890–1943*, Dixon and Rye. Similarly, if their discography continues to embrace aspects of African American entertainment that were not envisaged when the first editions were compiled, this will not only mean more work for the editors, and for Robert Macleod with his transcripts, it will mean the continuation of the Document series.

The aim of the producer of Document Records, Johnny Parth, is to ensure that all records listed in the discography are available on CD. Already there are discrepancies, as the discography includes titles made by the early African American entertainer Pete Hampton between 1903 and 1911, and the Coon Songs of Bert Williams made between 1901 and 1922. Over 250 items are known to have been made by them. Yet why the records made for Ajax by Chris Smith and Henry Troy—composers of "Ballin' the Jack," "Long Gone, Lost John," and "Cakewalkin' Babies from Home"—were omitted by Dixon and Rye still puzzles me. Even so, the Document series is nearing its end and I wondered what plans Johnny Parth has now.

*P.O.* Apart from the Document blues and gospel series that you are finishing now, you have issued Austrian folk music and started a series of country music. What are your future plans?

*J.P.* To retire some day—I'm 68 now, and I still have a lot of time, but I want to slow down; I'm near breakdown at times. I need a vacation, and that's what I said to people who wanted me to produce Country music. But with this exception, when I really want to retire, I want to be left alone. You wanted me to do a Calypso series? I don't think I can do so.

*P.O.* A Ragtime series, perhaps.

*J.P.* Mmm—perhaps. But now, what I have to do, is what I'm not so fond of doing—the last issues of the series, which are mainly gospel. But the more I hear it—and I have to hear it: I have to hear the master tapes; I have to listen to them in the studio, I have to listen to the pre-master CD when I come from the studio. I must listen to the first CD when it comes out from the pressing plant—and the more I hear it, the better I like it. And that's what I hope with the newcomers, the more they hear the music there will be more fans in the future—I hope.

*P.O.* You once told me that you weren't interested in the vocal quartets, though they figure prominently in *Blues and Gospel Records*, and you *had* to listen to them.

*J.P.* Yeah, I'm beginning to love them now. Also the preachers.

*P.O.* Anyone who strikes you especially as being of significance and interest?

*J.P.* Reverend Rice and Reverend McGee.

♪
(Victor 23401) 7/16/30, New York City

"FIFTY MILES OF ELBOW ROOM," featuring Reverend McGee and his congregation with trumpet, piano, guitar, and hand-clapped cross-rhythms, is just one of the hundreds of records of African American religious music now available on compact discs. They include the work of street evangelists, jack-leg, and storefront church preachers and their congregations, guitar evangelists, gospel quartets, and choruses, and even black shape-note singers. I haven't touched on the fields of early black entertainment, let alone the extensive range of gospel and other forms of religious music on record and now available, even though serious study of them is only in its infancy. Instead, I've concentrated on some of the neglected genres, some of the problems of classification, and some of the reconsiderations about black secular music that have been provoked in my mind by the comprehensive documentation that is now available to us. But as new discoveries are made new problems will doubtless arise. No one need fear that there is nothing that remains to be researched in documenting the blues!

# Discography

To accompany this book and to give examples of the blues and blues singers from the first half-century of the music, and the first three decades of its being recorded, a three-CD boxed set has been issued by Document Records: *Broadcasting the Blues* (DOCD 32-20-10). Sixty items—representing all the programs in this book—are reissued in full, and are indicated in bold type in the discography extracts from some of the cited interviews with blues singers are also included in the three-CD set.

Short discographic information, giving the original release number, date, and place of recording, was given for all the songs mentioned in the text in the margin of the book. This discography gives additional information for those who wish to research these recordings further.

I am especially indebted to the standard discographies of the blues—namely, Robert M. W. Dixon, John Godrich, and Howard Rye, *Blues and Gospel Records 1890–1943*, 4th ed. (Oxford: Clarendon Press, 1997); and Mike Leadbitter and Neil Slaven, *Blues Records 1943–1970* (London: Record Information Services, 1966). Supplementary data is included in the notes to a number of CD issues, those by Document Records, in particular. I am also indebted to Howard Rye and other specialists for additional material, including certain CD reissues. The information herein is listed in the following order: Name of the artist, title of item played in the program, and the original issue label and number. This is followed by the date and location of the recording, together with the relevant CD reissue catalog number. As Document is the most comprehensive of all reissue labels, its reissues are noted; alternatives are given where applicable.

## ABBREVIATIONS

The following abbreviations are used in the recording details:

alto saxophone: altsax
banjo: bjo
baritone saxophone: barsax
bass: bs
bass guitar: bs gtr
clarinet: clt
cornet: cor
drum, drums: dm, dms
electric guitar: el gtr

guitar: gtr
harmonica: hca
kazoo: kaz
mandolin: mand
organ: org
piano: pno
saxophone: sax
tenor sax: tensax
trombone: tmb
trumpet: tpt
twelve-string guitar: 12-st gtr
violin or fiddle: vln
vocal: vo
vocalized or imitation bass: vobs
washboard: wbd

## LABELS

The names of 78-rpm record labels are given in full, as are those of most of the LP records cited, the principal exception being the Library of Congress issues, listed here as LofC. As the majority of CDs listed are on the Document label, for these only the series number is given—i.e., DOCD 1000 series; DOCD 5000 series; MBCD 2000 series; BDCD 6000 series. Other CD label names are given in full, with the respective reissue numbers.

## INTERVIEWS

A number of extracts of interviews with blues singers are cited in the later programs. All the interviews quoted were made by myself in 1960. As they are necessarily brief, the extended, copyrighted extracts are quoted in my book *Conversation with the Blues* (1965; reprint, Cambridge: Cambridge University Press, 1997); the Cambridge edition includes a CD in which extracts from recorded interviews and performances by many blues singers can be heard. Some previously unissued interview extracts included in the programs can be heard in the three-CD Document Records set, DOCD 32-20-10.

## INTRODUCTION: THE DEVELOPMENT OF THE BLUES

Them, "Baby Please Don't Go"; Decca F12018; Deram CD.844132;
12/64, London, England
Van Morrison, vo, hca; Billy Harrison, gtr; Patrick McCauley, keyboards; Allan
   Henderson, bs.

Joe Williams, "Baby Please Don't Go"; Bluebird BB B6200; BDCD 6003; DOCD 32-20-10;
10/31/35, Chicago, IL
Joe Williams, vo, gtr, with the Washboard Blues Singers: Dad Tracy, vln; Chasey
   Collins, wbd

Discography

Willie Turner, "Another Man Done Gone"; Folkways FE 4474;
1/50, Livingstone, AL
Willie Turner, vo

Work Gang, "Katy Left Memphis"; Tradition 1020; Sequel NEXCD121;
1947, Parchman Farm, MS

Charles Berry, "Levee Camp Holler"; LofC unissued; DOCD 5320;
7/24/42, Stovall, MS
Charles Berry, vo

Son House, "Dry Spell Blues"; Paramount 12990; DOCD 5002;
5/28/30, Grafton, WI
Eddie "Son" House, vo, gtr

Blind Lemon Jefferson, "Match Box Blues"; Okeh 8455; DOCD 5018; DOCD 32-20-10;
3/14/27, Atlanta, GA
Blind Lemon Jefferson, vo, gtr

Lucille Hegamin, "The Jazz Me Blues"; Black Swan 2032; DOCD 5419;
11/20, New York City
Lucille Hegamin, vo; acc Her Blue Flame Syncopators: Wesley Johnson, tpt;
    Jim Reevy, tmb; unknown, cl; Clarence Harris, altsax; Bill Hegamin, pno;
    Ralph Escudero, bs; Kaiser Marshall, dms

Bessie Smith, "Baby Doll"; Columbia 14147-D; Frog DGF44;
5/4/26, New York City
Bessie Smith, vo; Joe Smith, cor; Fletcher Henderson, pno

Memphis Jug Band, "Kansas City Blues"; Victor 21185; DOCD 5021;
10/19/27, Atlanta, GA
Will Shade, hca; Ben Ramey vo, kaz; Will Weldon, vo, gtr; Vol Stevens, gtr

Romeo Nelson, "Head Rag Hop"; Vocalion 1447; DOCD 5103;
9/5/29, Chicago, IL
Romeo Nelson, vo, pno

Washboard Sam, "Levee Camp Blues"; Bluebird 88909; DOCD 5176;
6/26/41, Chicago, IL
Washboard Sam (Walter Brown), wbd; Big Bill Broonzy, gtr; Memphis Slim, pno;
    William Mitchell, vobs

Lightnin' Hopkins, "Short Haired Woman"; Aladdin 3005; Aladdin CDP7-96844-2;
8/15/47, Los Angeles, CA
Sam "Lightnin'" Hopkins, vo, gtr; Thunder Smith, pno

Dave Van Ronk, "St. James Infirmary"; Kicking Mule KM177; Fantasy FCD 24777-2;
1981, possibly Chicago, IL
Dave Van Ronk, vo, gtr

Paul Butterfield, "Born in Chicago"; Elektra Ekl 294;
5/66, Chicago, IL
Paul Butterfield, vo, hca; Mike Bloomfield, el gtr; Elvin Bishop, gtr; Jerome Arnold,
    bs gtr; Sam Lay, dms

Junior Wells, "Early in the Morning"; Delmark Dl 612;
1956, Chicago, IL
Junior Wells, vo, hca; Buddy Guy, el gtr; Jack Meyers, bs gtr; Billy Warren, dms

# 1. BLUES IN RETROSPECT

Bessie Smith, "Yellow Dog Blues"; Columbia 14075-D; Frog DGF 42; DOCD 32-20-10;
5/6/25, New York City
Bessie Smith, vo, with Henderson's Hot Six: Joe Smith, cor; Charlie Green,
    tmb; Buster Bailey, clt; Coleman Hawkins, tensax; Fletcher Henderson, pno;
    Charlie Dixon, bjo

Leadbelly, "Alberta"; Bluebird B8559; DOCD 5226;
6/15/40, New York City
Leadbelly (Huddie Ledbetter), vo, gtr

Muddy Waters, "I Feel Like Goin' Home"; Aristocrat 1305; Chess MCD09387;
1948, Chicago, IL
Muddy Waters (McKinley Morganfield), vo, gtr; Big Crawford, bs

Elmore James, "Dust My Broom"; Trumpet 146; ACE ABOX CD4;
5/62, Jackson, MS
Elmore James, vo, el gtr; Sonny Boy Williamson II, hca; Odie Johnson, bs gtr

Robert Johnson, "Walkin' Blues"; Vocalion 03601; Columbia C2K-46222;
    DOCD 32-20-10;
11/27/36, San Antonio, TX
Robert Johnson, vo, gtr

Tommy Johnson, "Big Road Blues"; Victor 21279; DOCD-5001;
2/3/28, Memphis, TN
Tommy Johnson, vo, gtr; Charlie McCoy, gtr

Charley Patton, "34 Blues"; Vocalion 02651; DOCD 5011;
1/31/34, New York City
Charley Patton, vo, gtr

# 2. ECHOES OF AFRICA

Fred McDowell, "Waiting For My Baby"; Testament T-2208; Testament TCD5019;
11/24/63, Como, MS
Fred McDowell, vo, gtr

Ladzekpo and Ewe Drum Orchestra, "Abkekor"; DOCD 32-20-1;
4/30/64, Legon, Ghana
Ladzekpo, *atsimeru*, two *sogo*, two *kidi* dms; *gong-gong* (clapperless bell)

Djuka Tribesmen, "Djuka Drums"; Folkways FE 4502;
1950s
Unidentified drummers Surinam

Mamprusi Tribesmen, "Ring Dance"; CBS 52799; DOCD 32-20-1; DOCD 32-20-10;
5/64, Navrongo, Ghana
Unidentified master drummer, calabash dm; dancers, flutes, rattles

Lonnie Young, "Hen Duck"; Atlantic SD 1346; London LTZ-K15209;
1959, Como, MS
Lonnie Young, vo, bass dm; Ed Young, cane fife; Lonnie Young Jr, snare dm

Austin Coleman, "My Soul as Witness"; LofC Lbc 1; DOCD 5312; DOCD 32-20-10;
7/34, Jennings, LA
Austin Coleman, vo; Joe Washington Brown, vo; with group, vo and percussion

Kunaal and Sosira, "Yarum (Praise Song)"; CBS 52799; DOCD 32-20-1;
5/64, Nangodi, Ghana
Sosira, vo, 2-string vln; Kunaal, vo, calabash rattle

Butch Cage and Willie Thomas, "44 Blues"; CBS 52799; DOCD 32-20-1;
8/9/60, Zachary, LA
James "Butch" Cage, vo, vln; Willie "Preacher" Thomas, gtr; Mrs. Thomas, dms

Yacouba Bukari, "Kouco Solo"; Nonesuch H-72074;
c. 1973, Gao, Mali
Yacouba Bukari, fretless lute

John Lawson Tyree, "Hop Along, Lou"; Blue Ridge Institute BRI 001;
1/13/77, Sontag, Virginia
John Lawson Tyree, bjo

Makai, "Babai"; CBS 52799;
3/7/63, Dogondoutchi, Niger
Makai, vo; *gouroumi* 3-string lute

# 3. GO DOWN, OLD HANNAH

C.B. and Axe-Gang, "Rosie"; Nixa Njl 11; Rounder CD1714;
1947, State Penitentiary, Parchman, MS
Unidentified convict group, vo

Diola Farmers, "Rice-Field Work Song"; Folkways FE4323;
c. 1963, Casamance, Senegal
Unidentified Diola-Fogny rice cultivators, vo

Joe Warner and Group, "Let's Move It"; Folkways FA 2659;
n.d, Demopolis, AL
Joe Warner, section boss, Frisco Line, vo; track-lining crew, vo response

Clyde Hill and Group, "Long Hot Summer Days"; LofC AFSL3; DOCD 5580;
   DOCD 32-20-10;
4/16/39, Clemens State Farm, Brazoria, TX
Clyde Hill, lead vo; group, vo

Tangle-Eye and Group, "Early in the Morning"; LofC Trad. 1020; Sequel NEXCA 121;
1947, Camp No. 10, State Penitentiary, Parchman, MS
Tangle-Eye, vo; group, vo

Charles Berry, "Cornfield Holler"; LofC AFS L59; DOCD 5320;
7/24/42, Clarksdale, MS
Charles Berry, vo

Ed Lewis, "Lucky Holler"; Atlantic LP 1346; DOCD 32-20-10;
c. 7/59, Lambert State Penitentiary, MS
Ed Lewis, vo

Texas Alexander, "Penitentiary Moan"; Okeh 8640; MBCD 2002; DOCD 32-20-10;
11/16/28, New York City
Alger "Texas" Alexander, vo; Lonnie Johnson, gtr

Robert Pete Williams, "Pardon Denied Again"; Folk-Lyric 109; Arhoolie CD394;
9/22/59, Angola State Penitentiary, LA
Robert Pete Williams, vo, gtr

# 4. OLD COUNTRY STOMP

Jimmie Strothers, "Thought I Heard My Banjo Say"; LofC FLYLP 256; DOCD 5575;
6/13/36, State Farm, Lynn, VA
Jimmie Strothers, vo, bjo

Henry Thomas, "Old Country Stomp"; Vocalion 1230; Yazoo CD1081; DOCD 32-20-10;
6/13/28, Chicago, IL
Henry "Ragtime Texas" Thomas, vo, quills, gtr

Mance Lipscomb, "Buck Dance"; Reprise R2012; Rhino RHM2-7829;
6/9/61, Houston, TX
Mance Lipscomb, vo, gtr

Blind Blake, "Dry Bone Shuffle"; Paramount, unissued; DOCD5062; DOCD 32-20-10;
c. 4/13/27, Chicago, IL
Blind Blake, vo, gtr; Cliff Moore, bones

Jim Jackson, "Bye Bye Policeman"; Victor V38505; DOCD 5115;
9/7/28, Memphis, TN
Jim Jackson, vo, gtr

Peg Leg Howell and Eddie Anthony, "Turkey Buzzard Blues"; Columbia 14382;
    MBCD 2005;
10/30/28, Atlanta, GA
Peg Leg Howell, vo, gtr; Eddie Anthony, vo, vln

Taylor's Kentucky Boys, "Gray Eagle"; Gennett 6130; DOCD 5167;
4/26/27, Richmond, IN
James Booker, vln; Marion Underwood, bjo; Willie Young, gtr

Mississippi Sheiks, "The Jazz Fiddler"; Okeh 45436; DOCD 5083;
2/17/30, Shreveport, LA
Walter Vincson, vo, gtr; Lonnie Chatman, vln

Dallas String Band, "The Hokum Blues"; Columbia 14389; DOCD 5162;
12/8/28, Dallas, TX
Coley Jones, vo, mand; Sam Harris, gtr; Marco Washington, bs

"Georgia Tom" Dorsey and Hannah May "Come On Mama"; Perfect 169;
    Wolf WBCH-011;
9/16/30, New York City
Famous Hokum Boys: "Georgia Tom" Dorsey, vo, pno; Big Bill Broonzy, gtr;
    Hannah May (Mozelle Anderson), vo

# 5. RAGTIME MILLIONAIRE

Sid Harkreader and Grady Moore, "I'm Looking for the Bully of the Town";
    Paramount 3022;
5/27, Chicago, IL
Sid Harkreader, vo, vln; Grady Moore, gtr

May Irwin, "The Bully Song"; Victor 31642;
5/20/07, New York City
May Irwin, vo, with Orchestra, unknown personnel

Kid West and Joe Harris, "Bully Of The Town"; LofC Flyright LP260; Traveling Man
    TMCD-09;
10/9/40, Shreveport, LA
Kid West, vo, mand; Joe Harris vo, gtr

Alec Johnson, "Mysterious Coon"; Columbia 14378; BDCD 6013; DOCD 32-20-10;
11/2/28, Atlanta, GA
Alec Johnson, vo, Bo Carter, vln; Charlie McCoy, mand; Joe McCoy, gtr;
    unknown, pno

Richard "Rabbit" Brown, "Never Let the Same Bee Sting You Twice"; Victor 24175;
    DOCD 5003;
3/11/27, New Orleans, LA
Richard Brown, vo, gtr

Lil McClintock, "Don't Think I'm Santa Claus"; Columbia 14575; DOCD5160;
    12/4/30, Atlanta , GA
Lil McClintock, vo, gtr

Henry Thomas, "Arkansas"; Vocalion 1286; DOCD 5665;
6/30/27, Chicago, IL
Henry Thomas (Ragtime Texas), vo, gtr

William Moore, "Ragtime Millionaire"; Paramount 12636; DOCD5062; DOCD 32-20-10;
1/28, Chicago, IL
Bill Moore, vo, gtr

Luke Jordan, "Traveling Coon"; Victor 20957; DOCD5045;
8/16/27, Charlotte, NC
Luke Jordan, vo, gtr

# 6. DOCTOR MEDICINE

Beale Street Sheiks, "You Shall"; Paramount 12518; DOCD5012; DOCD 32-20-10;
8/27, Chicago, IL
Frank Stokes, vo, gtr; Dan Sane, gtr

Earl McDonald's Original Louisville Jug Band, "She's in the Graveyard Now";
    Columbia 14255; JPCD 5102;
3/30/27, Atlanta, GA
Lucien Brown, altsax; Cal Smith, bjo; Benny Calvin, mand; Earl McDonald, vo, jug

Ma Rainey, "Ma Rainey's Black Bottom"; Paramount 12590; DOCD 5589;
12/27, Chicago, IL
Gertrude "Ma" Rainey, vo, with Her Georgia Band: Shirley Clay, cor; Al Wynn, tmb;
    Artie Starks, clt; unknown, pno, dms

Pink Anderson, "I've Got Mine"; Riverside RLP 12-611; Original Blues Classics
    OBCCD524-2;
5/29/50, Charlottesville, LA
Pink Anderson, vo, gtr

Speckled Red, "Right String, but the Wrong Yo-Yo"; Brunswick 7151; DOCD 5205;
4/8/30, Chicago, IL
Specklet Red (Rufus Perryman), vo, pno

Jim Jackson, "I Heard the Voice of a Pork Chop"; Victor 21387; DOCD 5114;
    DOCD 32-20-10;
1/30/28, Memphis, TN
Jim Jackson, vo, gtr

Peg Leg Sam, "Hand Me Down"; Flyright LP507-508;
9/15/72, Pittsboro, NC
Arthur "Peg Leg Sam" Jackson, vo, hca

# 7. JOHN HENRY AND THE BOLL WEEVIL

Blind Arvella Gray, "John Henry"; Heritage HLP 1004;
7/11/60, Chicago, IL
Blind Arvella Gray, vo, gtr


Mississippi John Hurt, "Spike Driver Blues"; Okeh 8692; DOCD 5003; DOCD 32-20-10;
12/28/28, New York City
John Hurt, vo, gtr


Furry Lewis, "Kassie Jones (Part Two)"; Victor 21664; DOCD 5004; DOCD 32-20-10;
8/28/28, Memphis, TN
Walter "Furry" Lewis, vo, gtr


Leadbelly, "Ella Speed"; Capitol H 369; DOCD 5310;
10/4/44, Hollywood, CA
Leadbelly (Huddie Ledbetter), vo, 12-str gtr; Paul Mason Howard, zither


Will Bennett, "Railroad Bill"; Vocalion 1464; DOCD 5106;
8/28/29, Knoxville, TN
Will Bennett, vo, gtr


Mance Lipscomb, "Ballad of the Boll Weevil"; Reprise 2012; Rhino RHM2-7829;
7/8/61, Houston, TX
Mance Lipscomb, vo, gtr


Pink Anderson, "The Ship Titanic"; Riverside RLP 12-611; Original Blues Classics
    OBC524-2;
5/29/50, Charlottesville, LA
Pink Anderson, vo, gtr


Down Home Boys, "Original Stack O' Lee Blues"; Black Patti 8030; DOCD 5236;
5/27, Chicago, IL
Papa Harvey Hull, vo; Long "Cleeve" Reed, gtr; unknown, gtr


# 8. YONDER COMES THE BLUES

Hambone Willie Newbern, "Nobody Knows (What the Good Deacon Does)";
    Okeh 8679; DOCD 5003;
3/13/29, Atlanta, GA
Willie Newbern, vo, gtr


Hambone Willie Newbern, "Hambone Willie's Dreamy-Eyed Woman"; Okeh 8693;
    DOCD 5003;
3/14/29, Atlanta, GA
Willie Newbern, vo, gtr

Josh White, "Dink's Blues"; Pye/Nixa NJL2; Castle CMETD 562;
1/31/56, London, England
Joshua White, vo, gtr

Joe Calicott, "Fare Thee Well Blues"; Brunswick 7166; DOCD 5002; DOCD 32-20-10;
2/20/30, Memphis, TN
Joe Calicott, vo, gtr

Gus Cannon, "Poor Boy, Long Ways from Home"; Paramount 12571; DOCD 5032;
    DOCD 32-20-10;
11/27, Chicago, IL
Gus Cannon, vo, bjo

Blind Willie McTell, "Travelin' Blues"; Columbia 14484-D; DOCD 5006; DOCD 32-20-10;
10/30/29, Atlanta, GA
Blind Willie McTell (as Blind Sammie), vo, gtr

Tommy Johnson, "Cool Drink of Water"; Victor 21279; DOCD 5001;
2/3/28, Memphis, TN
Tommy Johnson, vo, gtr

Mamie Smith, "Crazy Blues"; Okeh 4169; DOCD 5357;
8/10/20, New York City
Mamie Smith, vo, with Her Jazz Hounds: Johnny Dunn, cor; Dope Andrews, tmb;
    Ernest Elliott, clt; Leroy Parker, vln; Perry Bradford, pno

Ma Rainey, "Yonder Come the Blues"; Paramount 12357; Black Swan HCD 12002;
    DOCD 32-20-10;
12/25, New York City
Gertrude "Ma" Rainey, vo, with Her Georgia Jazz Band: Joe Smith, cor;
    Buster Bailey, clt; Coleman Hawkins, barsax; Charlie Dixon, bjo; Fletcher
    Henderson, pno

# 9. ANTICIPATIN' BLUES

Barbecue Bob, "Chocolate to the Bone"; Columbia 14331-D; DOCD 5046;
    DOCD 32-20-10;
4/13/28, Atlanta, GA
Robert Hicks, vo, gtr

Excelsior Quartette, "Kitchen Mechanic Blues"; Okeh 8033; DOCD 5288;
3/2/22, New York City
Vernon Jones, James C. Brown, tenor vo; Johnny Brown, baritone vo; B. B. Parker,
    bass vo

Unique Quartette, "Mama's Black Baby Boy"; Cylinder; DOCD 5288;
c. 1893, probably New York City
Joseph Moore, vo; possibly J. E. Settles, vo; Billy Carson, vo; and unknown, vo

Dinwiddie Colored Quartet, "Poor Mourner"; Monarch ; DOCD 5061;
c. 10/02, New York City
Sterling Rex, Clarence Meredith, tenor vo; Harry Cruder, Mantell Thomas, bass vo.

Old South Quartette, "Oysters and Wine at 2:00 A.M."; QRS R7006; DOCD 5061;
8/28, New York City
Unknown personnel, vo quartet with gtr; may include Randall Graves, vo; James L.
  Stamper, vo

Norfolk Jazz Quartette, "Sad Blues"; Paramount 12054; DOCD 5381; DOCD 32-20-10;
4/23, New York City
Otto Tutson, lead vo; James Butts, tenor vo; Delrose Hollins, baritone vo; Len
  Williams, bass vo

Monarch Jazz Quartet, "What's the Matter Now?"; Okeh 8736; DOCD 5546;
10/15/29, Richmond, VA
Unidentified vocal quartet

# 10. IN THE FIELD

Ernest Williams and Group, "Ain't No More Cane on This Brazos"; LofC AFS 13;
  DOCD 5580;
12/33, State Farm, Sugarland, TX
Ernest Williams, James "Iron Head" Baker, and convict group, vo

Mary C. Mann, "Finger Ring"; LofC AFS l68; DOCD 5576;
4/12/26, Merrian, GA
Mary C. Mann, vo

Jimmy Strothers, "Tennessee Dog"; LofC LBC 11; DOCD 5575; DOCD 32-20-10;
6/13/36, State Farm, Lynn, VA
Jimmy Strothers, vo, bjo; Joe Lee, vo

Richard Amerson, "Steamboat Days"; LofC AFS L53; DOCD 5578;
11/1/40, Livingston, AL
Richard Amerson, vo

Blind Jesse Harris, "Railroad Bill"; LofC, unissued; DOCD 5578;
7/24/37, Livingston, AL
Jesse Harris, vo, pno

Gabriel Brown, "Education Blues"; LofC Fly SDM257; DOCD 5587;
6/20/35, Eatonville, FL
Gabriel Brown, vo, gtr; Rochelle French, gtr

Nashville Washboard Band, "Old Joe"; LofC LBC3; DOCD 5461;
7/15/42, Nashville, TN
Frank Dalton, gtr; James Kelly, mand; Tom Carrol, bs; Theopolis Stokes, wbd

McKinley Morganfield, "Country Blues"; LofC TT 2210; DOCD 5146; DOCD 32-20-10;
7/22/42, Clarksdale, MS
McKinley "Muddy Waters" Morganfield, vo, gtr

Buster Ezell, "Roosevelt and Hitler"; LofC, unissued; DOCD 5576;
3/5/43, Fort Valley, GA
Buster Ezell, vo, gtr

# 11. PLAYING THE BOARDS

Washboard Rhythm Kings, "Tiger Rag"; Victor 24059; Vogue LAE12007;
7/6/32, Camden, NJ
Taft Jordan, tpt; Ben Smith, altsax; Carl Wade, tensax; Eddie Miles, pno; Steve
    Washington, bjo; Ghost Howell, bs; H. Smith, wbd

Blind Boy Fuller, "Step It Up and Go"; Columbia 37230; DOCD 5095;
3/5/40, New York City
Blind Boy Fuller, vo, gtr; George "Oh, Red" Washington, wbd

Brownie McGhee, "Key to My Door"; Okeh 06437; Columbia C2K52933;
5/22/41, Chicago, IL
Brownie McGhee, vo, gtr; Robert "Washboard Slim" Young, wbd

Sonny Terry's Washboard Band, "Sonny's Jump"; Folkways FLP 6;
1952, New York City
Sonny Terry (Sanders Terrell), vo, hca; J. C. Burris, hca; Alex Seward, washtub bs;
    Washboard Doc, wbd

Bobbie Leecan's Need-More Band, "Washboard Cut-Out"; Victor 20660;
    DOCD 5280; DOCD 32-20-10;
4/5/27, Camden, NJ
Bobbie Leecan, gtr; Robert Cooksey, hca; Al Martin, mand; Eddie Edinborough, wbd

Fowler's Washboard Wonders, "Salty Dog"; Columbia 14111d; RST JPCD 1520;
10/28/25, New York City
Seymor Trick, tpt; Percy Glascoe, clt, altsax; Lemuel Fowler, pno; A. Brunson, wbd

Blue Grass Footwarmers, "Charleston Hound"; Harmony 248-H; Classics 718;
6/16/26, New York City
Ed Allen, tpt; Benny Moten, clt; Clarence Williams, pno; Jasper Taylor, wbd

Clarence Williams Washboard Four, "Candy Lips"; Okeh 8440; Classics 718;
1/29/27, New York City
Ed Allen, cor; Benny Moten, clt; Clarence Williams, pno, vo; Floyd Casey, wbd

Beale Street Washboard Band, "Forty and Tight"; Vocalion V1016; Frog DGF9;
7/24/29, Chicago, IL
Herb Morand, cor; Johnny Dodds, clt; Frank Melrose, pno; Baby Dodds, wbd

McKinney's Cotton Pickers, "Milenberg Joys"; Victor 21611; Frog DGF25;
7/11/28, Chicago, IL
Don Redman, clt, arrangement; John Nesbitt, tpt; Langston Curl, tpt; Claude Jones,
tmb; Milton Senior cl; Todd Rhodes, pno; Dave Wilborn, bjo; Ralph Escudero, bs;
Cuba Austin, wbd

Washboard Sam, "Flying Crow Blues"; Bluebird B-8844; DOCD 5176; DOCD 32-20-10;
6/26/41, Chicago, IL
Big Bill Broonzy, gtr; Memphis Slim, pno; William Mitchell, vobs; Washboard Sam,
vo, wbd

Spike Jones' City Slickers, "Hotcha Cornia (Black Eyes)"; HMVBD 1099; CD: Paper
box 5;
11/12/43, Los Angeles, CA
Dell Porter, vo; Spike Jones, wbd; unknown tpt, tmb, clt, horns, bells; Willie Spicer,
sneezaphone Jones

Washboard Serenaders, "The Sheik of Araby"' Parlophone F425;
7/19/35, London, England
Harold Randolph, vo, kaz; Derek Neville, clt; Arthur Brooks, pno; Jerome Darr, gtr;
Len Harrison, bs; Bruce Johnson, vo, wbd

# 12. DECLASSIFYING THE CLASSIC BLUES

Hattie McDaniels, "Boo Hoo Blues"; Okeh 8434; DOCD 5516;
11/17/26, Chicago, IL
Hattie McDaniels, vo; with Lovie Austin's Serenaders: Shirley Clay, cor; Al Wynn
tmb; Artie Starks, altsax; Rip Basssett, bjo; Lovie Austin, pno

"Ma" Rainey, "See See Rider Blues"; Paramount 12252; Black Swan HCD 12002;
10/16/24, New York City
Gertrude "Ma" Rainey, vo, with Her Georgia Jazz Band: Louis Armstrong, cor;
Buster Bailey clt; Charlie Green, tmb; Fletcher Henderson, pno

Edith Wilson, "Rules and Regulations 'Signed Razor Jim'"; Columbia 3653; JPCD
1522; DOCD 32-20-10;
6/22, New York City
Edith Wilson, vo, with Johnny Dunn's Original Jazz Hounds: Johnny Dunn, cor;
Ernest Elliott, clt; Herb Fleming, tmb; poss. Dan Wilson, pno; John Mitchell, bjo

Butterbeans and Susie, "Mama Stayed Out the Whole Night Long"; Okeh 8319;
DOCD 5545;
3/10/26, New York City
Joe and Susie Edwards, vo; Eddie Heywood, pno

Lizzie Miles, "You're Always Messin' Round with My Man"; Vic 19083; DOCD
5459;
5/23/33, New York City
Lizzie Miles, vo; Clarence Johnson, pno

Hattie Hite, "Texas Twist"; Columbia 14503-D; DOCD 5513;
1/27/30, n.p.
Hattie Hite, vo; Cliff Jackson, pno

Gladys Bentley, "Ground Hog Blues"; Okeh 8610; DOCD 5349; DOCD 32-20-10;
8/8/28, New York City
Gladys Bentley, vo, pno

# 13. THE BLUES AS AN ART FORM, PART I: PLAYING THE BLUES

Peg Leg Howell, "Broke and Hungry Blues"; Columbia 14438; MBCD 2005;
    DOCD 32-20-10;
4/10/29, Atlanta, GA
Peg Leg Howell, vo, gtr; possibly Eddie Anthony, vln

Buddy Guy, "Leave My Girl Alone"; Chess 1936; Chess CHCD2-9337;
5/23/65, Chicago, IL
Buddy Guy, vo, el gtr; A. C. Reed, Milton Bland, tensax; Leonard Caston, org; Matt
    Murphy, el gtr; Leroy Stewart, bs gtr; unknown, dms

Pepe el de la Matrona, "Soleares"; Ducretet-Thomson TKL 43094;
c. 1958, possibly Seville, Spain
Pepe el de la Matrona, vo, gtr

John Lee Hooker, "Wednesday Evening"; Modern 20-746; Body and Soul 306787-2;
    DOCD 32-20-10;
1/50, Detroit, MI
John Lee Hooker, vo, gtr

Blind Lemon Jefferson, "Hangman's Blues"; Paramount 12679; DOCD 5019;
8/28, Chicago, IL
Blind Lemon Jefferson, vo, gtr

Fred McDowell, "Waiting for My Baby"; Testament T-2208; Testament TCD5019;
11/24/63, Como, MS
Fred McDowell, vo, gtr

Sonny Boy Williamson, "Do It if You Wanna"; Trumpet 139; Arhoolie CD310;
possibly 5/51, Jackson, MS
Sonny Boy Williamson, No. II (Alec Miller), vo, hca

Blind Boy Fuller, "Good Feeling Blues"; Okeh 06231; DOCD 5096;
3/7/40, New York City
Blind Boy Fuller (Fulton Allen), vo, gtr; Sonny Terry, hca; Oh, Red, wbd

Jimmy Yancey, "Eternal Blues"; Session 12-001; DOCD 5043;
12/43, Chicago, IL
Jimmy Yancey, pno

# 14. THE BLUES AND BLACK SOCIETY

Buster Pickens, "Colorado Springs Blues"; Decca LK 4664; CWTB/CUP;
7/60, Houston, TX
Edwin "Buster" Pickens, vo, pno

Robert Johnson, "Preachin' Blues"; Vocalion 04630; Columbia C2K-46222;
11/27/36, San Antonio, TX
Robert Johnson, vo, gtr

Sonny Boy Williamson, "My Black Name Blues"; Bluebird B8992; DOCD 5058;
7/30/42, Chicago, IL
John Lee "Sonny Boy" Williamson, vo, hca; Charlie McCoy, gtr; Blind John Davis,
    pno; Alfred Elkins, vobs; Washboard Sam, wbd

Robert Wilkins, "Falling Down Blues"; Brunswick 7125; DOCD 5014;
9/23/29, Memphis, TN
Robert Wilkins, vo, gtr

Barbecue Bob, "Brown-Skin Gal"; Columbia 14257-D; DOCD 5046;
6/15/27, New York City
Robert "Barbecue Bob" Hicks, vo, gtr

Jesse James, "Lonesome Day Blues"; Decca 7213; DOCD 5192; DOCD 32-20-10;
6/3/36, Chicago, IL
Jesse James, vo, pno

Henry Townsend, "Mistreated Blues"; Columbia 14491-D; DOCD 5147;
11/15/29, Chicago, IL
Henry Townsend, vo, gtr

Sleepy John Estes, "Brownsville Blues"; Decca 7473;
4/22/38, New York City
Sleepy John Estes, vo, gtr; Son Bonds, gtr

Gene Gilmore, "The Natchez Fire";
6/4/40, Chicago, IL
Gene Gilmore, vo; Leonard "Baby Doo" Caston, pno; Robert Lee McCoy, hca

Kokomo Arnold, "Mean Old Twister"; Decca 7347; DOCD 5040;
3/30/37, Chicago, IL
Kokomo Arnold, vo, gtr

Cripple Clarence Lofton, "Policy Blues"; Session 10-014; BDCD 6006;
12/43, Chicago, IL
"Cripple" Clarence Lofton, vo, pno

Texas Alexander, "Ninety-Eight Degree Blues"; Okeh 8705; MBCD 2002;
6/15/29, San Antonio, TX
Alger "Texas" Alexander, vo; Little Hat Jones, gtr

Bessie Jackson, "Shave 'Em Dry"; Melotone M13442; BDCD 6038;
3/5/35, New York City
Bessie Jackson (Lucille Bogan), vo; Walter Roland, pno

Sonny Boy Williamson, "Win the War Blues"; Bluebird 34-0722; DOCD 5058;
    DOCD 32-20-10;
12/14/44, Chicago, IL
John Lee "Sonny Boy" Williamson, vo, hca; Blind John Davis, pno; Ted Summitt,
    gtr; Armand "Jump" Jackson, dms

Jimmy Rodgers, "The World Is in a Tangle"; Chess 1453;
1950, Chicago, IL
Jimmy Rodgers, vo, gtr; Eddie Ware, pno; unknown, sax, bs, dms

J. B. Lenoir, "Eisenhower Blues"; Parrot 802;
1954, Chicago, IL
J. B. Lenoir, vo, gtr; Lorenzo Smith, tensax; Joe Montgomery, pno; Al Galvin, dms

Chuck Berry, "It Wasn't Me"; Chess CRL 4506;
9/1/65, Chicago, IL
Chuck Berry, vo, gtr; Paul Butterfield, hca; Johnny Johnson, pno; Mike Bloomfield,
    el gtr; Chuck Bernard, bs; Jasper Thomas, dms

Howling Wolf, "Smoke Stack Lightning"; Chess 1434;
1956, Chicago, IL
Charles "Howling Wolf" Burnett, vo, hca; Hubert Sumlin, el gtr; Hosea Lee Kennard,
    pno; Earl Phillips, dms

B. B. King, "Don't Answer the Door"; Bluesway 6001;
11/5/66, Chicago, IL
B. B. King, vo, el gtr; Kenny Sands, tpt; Bobby Forte, tensax; Duke Jethro, org; Louis
    Satterfield bs gtr; Sonny Freeman, dms

## 15. SINGING THE BLUES

Josh White, "Going Home Boys"; Pye GGL 0205; Elektra EKL158;
c. 1958, New York City
Josh White, vo, gtr

Josh White, "The House of the Rising Sun"; Keynote K452; DOCD 5572;
mid-1920s, New York City
Josh White, vo, gtr

Leadbelly, "In New Orleans"; Royale 18131; DOCD 5228;
1943, New York City
Leadbelly (Huddie Ledbetter), vo, gtr

Big Bill Broonzy, "John Henry"; Folkways FA 2328; Smithsonian Folkways
    CSSF40023;
1956, Chicago, IL
Big Bill Broonzy, vo, gtr; Pete Seeger, bjo

Sonny Terry and Brownie McGhee, "Fox Hunt"; Bluesville BVLP 1002;
 Ace CDCHD 247; DOCD 32-20-10;
12/59, Englewood Cliffs, NJ
Sonny Terry (Sanders Terrell), vo, hca; Brownie McGhee, gtr

Furry Lewis, "Casey Jones"; Folkways FS 3823;
10/3/59, Memphis, TN
Walter "Furry" Lewis, vo, gtr

Mance Lipscomb, "'Bout a Spoonful"; Arhoolie F1001; Arhoolie CD306;
8/13/60, Navasota, TX
Mance Lipscomb, vo, gtr

Mississippi John Hurt, "Candy Man Blues"; Piedmont PLP 13157; Rounder 1081;
3/26/63, Washington D.C.
Mississippi John Hurt, vo, gtr

Big Bill Broonzy, "Black, Brown and White"; Vogue 134; Frog DGF44; DOCD 32-20-10;
9/20/51, Paris, France
Big Bill Broonzy, vo, gtr

Mercy Dee, "Dark Muddy Bottom"; Specialty 481; Specialty CD7036;
10/4/53, Los Angeles, CA
Mercy Dee Walton, vo, pno; unknown, dms

Otis Spann, "Sad Day in Texas"; Testament S-01; Testament TCD5007;
c. 12/63, Chicago, IL
Otis Spann, vo, pno

John Lee Hooker, "Birmingham Blues"; Vee-Jay 538; Charly REDBOX6;
1963, Chicago, IL
John Lee Hooker, vo, gtr; unknown, sax, pno, bs, dms

Muddy Waters, "Mannish Boy"; Chess 1602; Chess CHD 9274;
5/24/62, Chicago, IL
Muddy Waters (McKinley Morganfield), vo, gtr; Junior Wells, hca;
 Jimmy Rogers, gtr; Willie Dixon, bs; Francis Clay, dms

# 16. THE BLUES AS AN ART FORM, PART II: EXPRESSING THE BLUES

Muddy Waters, "Forty Days and Forty Nights"; Chess 1620; Chess CHD 9380;
1/56, Chicago, IL
Chess CHD 9380
Muddy Waters (McKinley Morganfield), vo; Otis Spann, pno; Walter Horton, hca;
 Jimmy Rodgers, gtr; Willie Dixon, bs; Francey Clay, dms

Bertha "Chippie" Hill, "Pratt City Blues"; Okeh 8420; DOCD 5330; DOCD 32-20-10;
11/23/26, Chicago, IL
Bertha "Chippie" Hill, vo; Louis Armstrong, cor; Richard M. Jones, pno

Leroy Carr, "Blues before Sunrise"; Victor 02657; DOCD 5137; DOCD 32-20-10;
2/21/34, St. Louis, MO
Leroy Carr, vo, pno; Francis "Scrapper" Blackwell, gtr

Tommy Johnson, "Big Road Blues"; Victor 21279; DOCD 5001;
2/3/28, Memphis, TN
Tommy Johnson, vo, gtr

Blind James Brewer, "Big Road Blues"; Flyright LP549;
7/11/60, Chicago, IL
Blind James Brewer, vo, gtr; Charlie McCoy, gtr

Peetie Wheatstraw, "Long Lonesome Dive"; Vocalion 02712; DOCD 5242;
3/25/34, New York City
Peetie Wheatstraw (William Bunch), vo, pno; probably Charlie Jordan, gtr

Red Nelson, "Crying Mother Blues"; Decca 7171; Decca BDCD 6006;
2/4/36, Chicago, IL
Red Nelson (Nelson Wilborn), vo; "Cripple" Clarence Lofton, pno

Tommy McClennan, "Blues Trip Me This Morning"; Bluebird B9037; DOCD 5670;
    DOCD 32-20-10;
2/20/42, Chicago, IL
Tommy McClennan, vo, gtr; Ransom Knowling, bs

Gabriel Brown, "I'm Gonna Take It Easy"; Joe Davis 5015; Flyright FLYCD59;
9/13/44, New York City
Gabriel Brown, vo, gtr

Lonnie Johnson, "Hard Times Ain't Gone Nowhere"; Decca 3378; BDCD 6024;
11/8/37, Chicago, IL
Lonnie Johnson, vo, gtr

Bob Campbell, "Starvation Farm Blues"; Vocalion 02798; DOCD 5641;
8/1/34, New York City
Bob Campbell, vo, gtr

Zachary Child, "Rooster Blues"; unissued;
8/7/60, Zachary, LA
Butch Cage's grandchild Zachary, vo

Lightnin' Slim, "Rooster Blues"; Excello 2169;
9/59, Crowley, LA
Lightnin' Slim (Otis Hicks), vo, gtr; Lazy Lester, hca; Kenneth "Sam" Sample, dms

Georgia Talbert, "Boogie and Slow Blues"; unissued;
7/60, Clarksdale, MS
Georgia Talbert, pno

# 17. BLUES AND TROUBLE

John Lee Hooker, "Two White Horses"; Guest Star 2P1902;
7/7/61, Miami, FL
John Lee Hooker, vo, gtr

Robert Curtis Smith, "Council Spur Blues"; Bluesville 1064;
7/60, Clarksdale, MS
Robert Curtis Smith, vo, gtr

Henry Thomas, "Red River Blues"; Vocalion 1137; Yazoo CD 1080;
10/5/27, Chicago, IL
Henry Thomas (Ragtime Texas), vo, gtr, quills

Henry Townsend, "Poor Man Blues"; Columbia 14491; DOCD 5147; DOCD 32-20-10;
11/15/29, Chicago, IL
Henry Townsend, vo gtr

Lightnin' Slim, "Feelin' Awful Blue"; Excello 8000;
1957, Crowley, LA
Lightnin' Slim (Otis Hicks), vo, gtr

Son House, "My Black Mama, Part 1"; Paramount 13042; DOCD 5002;
5/28/30, Grafton, WI
Eddie "Son" House, vo, gtr

# 18. DOWN THE DIRT ROAD

Robert Petway, "Cotton Pickin' Blues"; Bluebird B9036; WBCD 005; DOCD 32-20-10;
2/20/42, Chicago, IL
Robert Petway, vo, gtr

Charley Patton, "Down the Dirt Road Blues"; Paramount 12854; DOCD 5009;
6/14/29, Richmond, IN
Charley Patton, vo, gtr

Lewis Black, "Gravel Camp Blues"; Columbia 144291; DOCD 5169;
12/10/27, Memphis, TN
Lewis Black, vo, gtr

Wesley Wallace, "Number 29"; Paramount 12958; DOCD 5104; DOCD 32-20-10;
11/29, Grafton, WI
Wesley Wallace, vo, pno

Son Bonds, "Old Bachelor Blues"; Decca 7558; WBCD 003;
4/22/38, New York City
Son Bonds, vo, gtr; Sleepy John Estes, gtr

Cow Cow Davenport, "Jim Crow Blues"; Paramount 12439; DOCD 5141;
    DOCD 32-20-10;
1/27, Chicago, IL
Charles "Cow Cow" Davenport, vo, pno

## 19. BLACK CAT'S BONE

Robert and Charlie Hicks, "Darktown Gamblin'"; Columbia 14531; DOCD 5048;
4/23/30, Atlanta, GA
Robert "Barbecue Bob" Hicks, vo, gtr; Charles Hicks, vo

Bob Campbell, "Dice's Blues"; Vocalion 02830; DOCD 5641;
7/30/34, New York City
Bob Campbell, vo, gtr

Memphis Jug Band, "Aunt Caroline Dyer Blues"; Victor 23347; DOCD 5023;
    DOCD 32-20-10;
5/29/30, Memphis, TN
Will Shade, vo, gtr; Ben Ramey, kaz; Charlie Burse, gtr; Hambone Lewis, jug

Funny Paper Smith, "Seven Sisters Blues"; Vocalion 1641; BDCD 6016;
7/10/31, Chicago, IL
J. T. "Funny Paper" Smith, vo, gtr

Jazz Gillum, "The Blues What Am"; Victor 20-2580; DOCD 5200;
4/24/47, Chicago, IL
William "Jazz" Gillum, vo, hca; Willie Lacey, gtr; Eddie Boyd, pno; Ransom
    Knowling bs, Judge Riley, dms

Tommy Griffin, "Dream Book Blues"; Bluebird BB86756; DOCD 5426;
10/16/36, New Orleans, LA
Tommy Griffin, vo; Walter Vinson, gtr; Ernest "44" Johnson, pno

Bumble Bee Slim, "Policy Dream Blues"; Vocalion 03090; DOCD 5264; DOCD 32-20-10;
4/4/35, Chicago, IL
Amos Easton "Bumble Bee Slim," vo; Myrtle Jenkins, pno; unknown, gtr

## 20. TRICKS AIN'T WALKIN' NO MORE

Ramblin' Thomas, "Hard Dallas Blues"; Paramount 12708; DOCD 5107;
11/28, Chicago, IL
Willard "Ramblin'" Thomas, vo, gtr

Texas Bill Day, "Elm Street Blues"; Columbia 14514; DOCD 52225;
12/4/29, Dallas, TX
Texas Bill Day, vo, possibly pno; Coley Jones, gtr

Poor Boy Lofton, "Jake Leg Blues"; Decca 7076; DOCD 5158;
8/24/34, Chicago, IL
Willie "Poor Boy" Lofton, vo, possibly gtr

Walter Roland, "House Lady Blues"; Banner 32832; DOCD 5144;
7/19/33, New York City
Walter Roland, vo, pno

Kansas Joe and Memphis Minnie, "North Memphis Blues"; Vocalion 1550; DOCD 5029;
    DOCD 32-20-10;
10/11/30, Chicago, IL
Kansas Joe McCoy, vo, gtr; Memphis Minnie McCoy, vo, gtr

Hi-Henry Brown, "Nut Factory"; Vocalion 1692; DOCD 5098;
3/17/32, New York City
Hi-Henry Brown, vo, gtr; Charlie Jordan, gtr

Lucille Bogan, "They Ain't Walkin' No More"; Brunswick 7186; DOCD 6037;
    DOCD 32-20-10;
12/30, Chicago, IL
Lucille Bogan, vo; possibly Charles Avery, pno

Cecil Gant, "Owl Stew"; Decca 48231;
8/7/50, New York City
Cecil Gant, vo, pno; unknown, bs, dms

# 21. Jail House Moan

Furry Lewis, "Mr. Furry's Blues'; Vocalion 1115; DOCD 5004;
4/20/27, Chicago, IL
Walter "Furry" Lewis, vo; Landers Waller, gtr; Charles Johnson, mand

Whistlin' Alex Moore, "Ice Pick Blues"; Columbia 14518; DOCD 5178; DOCD 32-20-10;
12/5/29, Dallas, TX
"Whistlin'" Alex Moore, vo, whistle, pno

Bukka White, "Parchman Farm Blues"; Okeh 05683; DOCD 5320; DOCD 32-20-10;
3/7/40, Chicago, IL
Washington "Bukka" White, vo, gtr; Washboard Sam, wbd

Texas Alexander, "Levee Camp Moan"; Okeh 8498; MBCD 2001;
8/16/27, New York City
Alger "Texas" Alexander, vo; Eddie Heywood, pno

Hambone Willie Newbern, "Shelby County Workhouse Blues"; Okeh 8740; DOCD 500;
    DOCD 32-20-10;
3/13/29, Atlanta, GA
"Hambone" Willie Newbern, vo, gtr

Sleepy John Estes, "Lawyer Clark Blues"; Bluebird B8871; DOCD 5016;
9/24/41, Chicago, IL
Adam "Sleepy John" Estes, vo, gtr; Son Bonds, gtr; Raymond Thomas, vobs

Lightnin' Hopkins, "Jail House Blues"; Gold Star 662; Arhoolie CD 337;
c. 1949, Houston, TX
Sam "Lightnin'" Hopkins, vo, gtr; Frankie Lee Sims, gtr

## 22. Let's Have a New Deal

Joe Stone, "It's Hard Time"; Bluebird B5169; DOCD 5147;
8/2/33, Chicago, IL
Joe Stone (possibly J. D. Short), vo, gtr

Buddy Moss, "Hard Times Blues"; Melotone M12665; DOCD 5123;
1/33, New York City
Eugene "Buddy" Moss, vo, gtr; Curly Weaver, gtr

Jimmy Gordon, "Don't Take Away my P.W.A."; Decca 7230; OTCD-01;
10/2/36, Chicago, IL
Jimmy Gordon, vo, possibly pno; Charlie McCoy, gtr; John Lindsay, bs

Peetie Wheatstraw, "Working on the Project"; Decca 7311; DOCD 5245; DOCD 32-20-10;
3/30/37, Chicago, IL
Peetie Wheatstraw (William Bunch), vo, pno; Kokomo Arnold, gtr

Carl Martin, "Let's Have a New Deal"; Decca 7114; DOCD 5229; DOCD 32-20-10;
9/4/35, Chicago, IL
Carl Martin, vo, gtr; Willie Bee James, gtr

Billie McKenzie, "That Man on the W.P.A."; Vocalion 03385; DOCD 5295;
11/4/36, Chicago, IL
Billie McKenzie, vo; unknown, clt, pno, bs

Washboard Sam, "C.C.C. Blues"; Bluebird B7995; DOCD 517;
12/16/38, Aurora, IL
Robert "Washboard Sam" Brown, vo, wbd; Big Bill Broonzy, gtr; Joshua Altheimer, pno; Bill Settles, bs

Guitar Slim and Jelly Belly, "Keep Straight Blues"; True-Blue 102; Arhoolie CD460;
1948, New York City (as "No More Hard Times")
Guitar Slim (Alec Seward), vo, gtr; Louis "Jelly Belly" Hayes, vo, gtr

## 23. High Water Everywhere

Bessie Smith, "Back Water Blues"; Columbia 14195; Frog DGF 44;
2/17/27, New York City
Bessie Smith, vo; James P. Johnson, pno

Mattie Delaney, "Tallahatchie River Blues"; Vocalion 1480; DOCD 5157;
 DOCD 32-20-10;
2/21/30, Memphis, TN
Mattie Delaney, vo, gtr

Charley Patton, "High Water Everywhere"; Paramount 12909; DOCD 5010;
10/29, Grafton, WI
Charley Patton, vo, gtr

Walter Roland, "Red Cross Blues"; Melotone M12753; DOCD 5144;
7/17/33, New York City
Walter Roland, vo, pno

Lonnie Johnson, "St. Louis Cyclone Blues"; Okeh 8512; DOCD 506; DOCD 32-20-10;
10/3/27, New York City
Lonnie Johnson, vo, gtr; Porter Grainger, pno

Sleepy John Estes, "Fire Department Blues"; Decca 7571; DOCD 5016; DOCD 32-20-10;
4/22/38, New York City
Adam "Sleepy John" Estes, vo, gtr; possibly Charlie Pickett, gtr

Pinewood Tom, "Silicosis Is Killin' Me"; Arc 6-05-51; DOCD 5196;
2/26/36, New York City
Joshua "Pinewood Tom" White, vo, gtr

# 24. THIS WORLD IS IN A TANGLE

Clara Smith, "Uncle Sam Blues"; Columbia 12-D; DOCD 5364;
10/2/23, New York City
Clara Smith, vo; Fletcher Henderson, pno

Carl Martin, "I'm Gonna Have My Fun"; Champion 50074; DOCD 5229;
3/24/36, Chicago, IL
Carl Martin, vo, gtr; Chuck Segar, pno

Minnie Wallace, "The Cockeyed World"; Vocalion 03106; BDCD 6028;
10/12/35, Jackson, MS
Minnie Wallace, vo, with Her Night Hawks: Will Shade, hca; Robert Wilkins, gtr;
 "Kid Spoons," spoons

Florida Kid, "Hitler Blues"; Bluebird B8589; DOCD 5427;
11/7/40, Chicago, IL
Ernest "Florida Kid" Blunt, vo; probably Bob White, gtr; unknown, vo, bs

Doctor Clayton, "Pearl Harbor Blues"; Bluebird B9003; DOCD 5179;
3/27/42, Chicago, IL
Peter "Doctor" Clayton, vo; Blind John Davis, pno; Alfred Elkins, vo, bs; Ransom
 Knowling, brass bs

Big Boy Crudup, "Give Me A 32-20"; Bluebird B9019; DOCD 5201; DOCD 32-20-10;
4/15/42, Chicago, IL
Arthur "Big Boy" Crudup, vo, el gtr; Ransom Knowling, bs

Mr. Honey, "Build a Cave"; Arc 102; DOCD 32-20-10;
1951, Houston, TX
David "Mr. Honey" Edwards, vo, gtr; Wilson "Thunder" Smith

## 25. BLUES WITH A FEELING

Red Nelson, "Crying Mother Blues"; Decca 7171; BDCD 6006; DOCD 32-20-10;
2/4/36, Chicago, IL
"Red Nelson" Wilborn, vo; "Cripple" Clarence Lofton, pno

Willie "61" Blackwell, "Four O'Clock Flower"; Bluebird B8921; DOCD 5229;
7/3/41, Chicago, IL
Willie "61" Blackwell, gtr; Alfred Elkins vo, bs

Lillian Glinn, "Brown Skin Blues"; Columbia 14275-D; DOCD 5184;
12/2/27, Dallas, TX
Lillian Glinn, vo; Willie Tyson, pno; unknown, gtr

St. Louis Bessie, "Sweet Black Woman"; Okeh 8659; DOCD 5290;
12/5/28, Chicago, IL
Blue Belle (Bessie Mae Smith), vo; unknown, pno

Cleo Gibson, "I've Got Ford Movements in My Hips"; Okeh 8700; DOCD 5471;
3/14/29, Atlanta, GA
Cleosephus Gibson, vo; Henry Mason, tpt; J. Neal Montgomery, pno; John Smith, gtr

Robert Johnson, "Terraplane Blues"; Vocalion 03416; Columbia C2K 46222;
11/23/36, San Antonio, TX
Robert Johnson, vo, gtr

Speckled Red, "The Dirty Dozen"; Brunswick 7116; DOCD 5205; DOCD 32-20-10;
9/22/29, Memphis, TN
Rufus "Speckled Red" Perryman, vo, pno

## 26. THREE BALL BLUES

Blind Boy Fuller, "Three Ball Blues"; Vocalion 05440; DOCD 5096; DOCD 32-20-10;
3/6/40, New York City
Blind Boy Fuller (Fulton Allen), vo, gtr; Sonny Terry, hca

Black Ace, "Black Ace Blues"; Decca 7281; DOCD 5143; DOCD 32-20-10;
2/15/37, Dallas, TX
Black Ace (Babe Kyro Turner), vo, gtr

Bill Gaither, "Champ Joe Louis"; Decca 7476; DOCD 5253;
6/23/38, New York City
William Gaither, vo, gtr; Edgar Saucier, altosax; Honey Hill, pno

Brother Will Hairiston, "Alabama Bus"; Blues Classics BC 12; Agram ABCD 2018;
c. 1956, Detroit, MI
Brother Will Hairiston, vo; unknown, pno; Washboard Willie, wbd

Betty Mae Fikes, "This Little Light of Mine"; Smithsonian RO23;
c. 1956, Selma, AL
Betty Mae Fikes, vo

# 27. CREATING THE DOCUMENTS

Tommy Johnson, "Cool Drink of Water Blues"; Victor 21279; DOCD 5001; DOCD 32-20-10;
2/3/28, Memphis, TN
Tommy Johnson, vo, gtr; Charlie McCoy, gtr

Mamie Smith, "That Thing Called Love"; Okeh 4113; DOCD 5357;
2/14/20, New York City
Mamie Smith, vo; Ed Cox, cor; Ernest Elliott, clt; Dope Andrews, tmb; Leroy Parker, vln; Willie "The Lion" Smith, pno; unkown, bs, sax

Mama Yancey, "Make Me a Pallet on the Floor"; Session 12-003; DOCD 5043;
(alternate take)
12/43, Chicago, IL
Estelle "Mama" Yancey, vo; Jimmy Yancey, pno

Josephine Baker, "Skeedle Um"; French Odeon 49227; DOCD 5652;
11/26, Paris, France
Josephine Baker, vo; unknown, vln; Jacques Fray, pno

Charley Patton, "Some Summer Day"; Paramount 13080; DOCD 5011; DOCD 32-20-10;
5/28/30, Grafton, WI
Charley Patton, vo, gtr

# 28. STILL TO BE DOCUMENTED

Charlie Jackson, "Long Gone, Lost John"; Paramount 12602; DOCD 5088; DOCD 32-20-10;
1/28, Chicago, IL
"Papa" Charlie Jackson, vo, bjo

Charles Anderson, "Sing 'Em Blues"; Okeh 8124; DOCD 5380;
10/24/23, Chicago, IL
Charles Anderson, vo; Eddie Heywood, pno

Mississippi Moaner, "So Cold in China"; Vocalion 03166; DOCD 5157;
10/20/35, Jackson, MS
Isaiah Nettles, the "Mississippi Moaner," vo, gtr

South Street Trio, "Dallas Blues"; Victor 21135; DOCD 5280;
10/27/27, Camden, NJ
Robert Cooksey, vo, hca; Bobby Leecan, bjo; Alfred Martin, gtr

Sara Martin, "Mean Tight Mama"; Q-RS R7043; Frog DGF49;
12/28, Long Island, NY
Sara Martin, vo, with Clarence Williams and His Orchestra: King Oliver, cor;
    unknown, tmb; Clarence Williams, pno; Arville Harris, clt; Cyrus St. Clair, tuba

Peetie Wheatstraw, "Bring Me Flowers While I'm Living"; Decca 7886; DOCD 5247;
11/25/41, Chicago, IL
"Peetie Wheatstraw" William Bunch, vo, pno; unknown, tensax, bs

Meade Lux Lewis, "Spirit of Boogie Woogie"; Soundie 8103; DOCD 32-20-10;
8/17/42, Hollywood, CA
Meade Lux Lewis, pno

Reverend F.W. McGee, "Fifty Miles of Elbow Room"; Victor 23401; DOCD 32-20-10;
7/16/30, New York City
Reverend Ford Washington McGee, sermon and lead vo, pno; unkown, tpt, gtr;
    members of the congregation, vo

# Name Index

Includes those singers and musicians whose records were played in the programs and are listed as entries in the Discography. References to cited recordings that can be heard on the three-CD set, *Broadcasting the Blues* on Document DOCD 32-20-10 are entered in **bold**. Accompanists who are listed only in the Discography are not entered.

Abbreviations: instruments are listed as they are in the Discography. Other abbreviations include:

auth: author
coll: field collector
comp: composer
discog: discographer
prod: radio producer
prom: promoter

## A

Ace, Johnny, vo, pno, 104
Ailey, Alvin, Dance Company, xi
Alderson, Mozelle (Hannah May, Jane Lucas), vo, 24
Alexander, Alger "Texas," vo, **19**, 71, 107
Allen, Fulton. *See* "Blind Boy Fuller"
Allen, Paul, comp, 26
Allen, Thomas, comp, 27
Amerson, Rich, vo, 49
Anderson, Charles, vo, pno, 39–140
Anderson, Pink, vo, gtr, 31, 36
Anthony, Eddie, vo, vln, 23
Armstrong, Louis, tpt, 56, 82
Arnold, Kokomo, vo, gtr, 70, 110
Ashanti (Asante) tribe, Ghana, 13, 14
Auden, W.H., auth, 83
Austin, Lovey, pno, 59
Avery, Charles, pno, 102, 104

## B

Baby Doo (Leonard Caston), vo, gtr, 70
Baker, Josephine, vo, 134
Baldwin, James, auth, 80
Banjo Joe. *See* Gus Cannon
Barbecue Bob (Robert Hicks), vo, gtr, **43**, 69, 140
Barber, Chris, tmb, viii
Barnicle, Mary Elizabeth, coll, 49
Bastin, Bruce, auth, coll, 32, 51
Beale Street Sheiks, **29;** see also Frank Stokes
Beale Street Washboard Band, 56
Bennett, Will, vo, gtr, 35
Bentley, Gladys, vo, pno, **62**
Berry, Charles, vo, 2,
Berry, Chuck, vo, gtr, 73
Black Ace, (B. K.Turner), **112**, **126**
Black, Lewis, vo, gtr, 95

Blackwell, Willie "61," vo, gtr, 122
Blake, Arthur "Blind," vo, gtr, **22**
Bland, James, comp, 27
Blesh, Rudi, auth, 60
Blue Grass Footwarmers (wbd band), 56
Blunt, Ernest. *See* Florida Kid
Bo Diddley, (Ellas McDaniel), vo, gtr, 73
Bogan, Lucille, vo, pno, 60, 71, **104**
Bonds, Son, vo, gtr, 95
Bowman, Elmer, comp, 26
Boogie Woogie Red (Vernon Harrison),
        vo, pno, 89, 90
Booker, James, vln, 23
Bracey, Ishman, vo, gtr, 26
Bradford, Perry, comp, pno, 30, 40
Brewer, Blind James, vo, gtr, 83
Bridson, D. G., prod, 11
Broonzy, Big Bill, vo, gtr, 6, 24, 57, 76–77, **78**,
        81, 115
Brown, Gabriel, vo, gtr, 50
Brown, Henry, pno, xi
Brown, Hi-Henry, vo, gtr, **103**–104
Brown, Richard "Rabbit," vo, gtr, 26
Brown, Sterling, auth, x, 83
Brown, Walter. *See* "Washboard Sam"
Bukari, Yacoubo, kouco (stringed
        instrument), 15
Bumble Bee Slim (Amos Easton), vo, pno,
        100
Bunch, William. *See* "Peetie Wheatstraw"
Burleson, Hattie, vo, prom, 62
Burnett, Charles. *See* "Howling Wolf"
Butterbeans and Susie, vo duet, 61
Butterfield, Paul, vo, gtr, 6

**C**

Cage, James Butch, vo, vln, gtr, 15
C.B. and Gang, vo, 17
Calicott, Joe, vo, gtr, **38**
Campbell, Bob, vo, gtr, 85, 98
Cannon, Gus "Banjo Joe," vo, bjo, jug, **31**, **39**
Casey, Floyd, wbd, 56
Carr, Leroy, vo, pno, 70, 71, **82**
Carter, Bo (Armenter Chatman), vo, gtr,
        vln, 23, 26

Caston, Leonard. *See* "Baby Doo"
Chatman, Lonnie, vo, vln, 23
Chatman, Peter. *See* Memphis Slim
Clayton, Peter Doc, vo, 70, 119, 120
Coleman, Austin, vo, **14**
Cooksey, Robert, vo, hca, 140
Cowley, John H., author, discog, 51
Cox, Ida, vo, vii, 62
Crudup, Arthur "Big Boy," vo, gtr, **119**
Curtis-Burlin, Natalie, auth, col, 45
Caston, "Baby Doo," vo, gtr, 70

**D**

Dabbs, Jack, prod, ix
Dandridge, Putney, pno, viii
Dallas String Band, 24
Davenport, Charles "Cow Cow," vo, pno,
        96
Davis, Walter, vo, pno, 69
Day, Texas Bill, vo, gtr, 101
Delaney, Mattie, vo, gtr, **114**, 115
Diddley, Bo (McDaniel), vo, gtr, 73
Dinwiddie Colored Quartet, vo group, 44
Diola farmers (Senegal), 18
Djuku tribesmen, 14
Dixon, Robert M.W., auth, discog, 132, 135,
        141, 143, 145
Dodds, Baby, dms, wbd, 56
Dodds, Johnny, clt, 56
Dorsey, Thomas A. *See* "Georgia Tom"
Down Home Boys. *See* Papa Harvey Hull
Drescher, Derek, prod, xiii, xiv
Dunn, Johnny, cornet, 40, 60, 61
Dupree, Champion Jack, vo, pno, viii, 126

**E**

Easton, Amos. *See* "Bumble Bee Slim"
Edwards, "Honey Boy," also "Mr.
        Honey," vo, gtr, **120**
Edwards, Joe and Susan, "Butterbeans and
        Susie," vo duet, 61
Ellington, Duke, pno, band-leader, vii, 132
Estes, Adam "Sleepy John," vo, gtr, 70, 108,
        **115**

# Title Index

Recordings mentioned in the text but not included in the Discography are also listed.

Records and extracts from interviews that were played in Programs and included in the Document three-CD set, DOCD 32-20-10 are indicated in **bold** numerals.

# General Index

## A

Abbreviations—instruments, 145–146
Africa
  Instruments, 15, 16
  Rainforest, xii, 13
  retentions, xii, 14–16, 35, 37, 66
  Savannah, xii
  Teaching in Ghana, xii
Alabama, 4, 18, 127
  Bus boycott, 127
Alcoholism, 49, 102
Alley fiddle, 23, 64
"Alphabet soup," 110
American Folk Blues Festivals, xi
Appalachian ballads, 34
Archaic Blues, 60
Art
  blues as, 63–65, 81–86
Arhoolie (Records), x
Asante (Ashanti; African tribe), 13
Atlanta, GA, 43
Audience, 73, 76, 77, 82, 84
Automobile imagery, 123
Axe-cutting song, 19

## B

Banjo, 15, 20, 21
  banjar, 15
Ballads, 33–36, 37, 70, 75, 126
Barbershop, 28, 94
Barnstorming, 61
Barrelhouses, 4, 24, 67, 123
Barrelhouse piano, 5, 69

Beale Street (Memphis), 97–98, 105
Begging, 33
Belly dance, 23, 51
Bent notes. *See* Blue Notes
Black Cat's Bone, 98
Black color, as epithet, 68; see also,
        Segregation
  stratification, 68–69
Blackface minstrels, 30
Blindness, 94
  blind singers, 22, 33, 94
Blinds (railroad cars), 95
Blue notes, 16, 64, 66
Blues
  Archaic, 60
  as art, 63–65, 81–86
  expression, 68, 73, 80, 81–86
  form, 9
  in jazz, 81
  mental state, 67, 91
  origins, 38–39
  styles, 64
*Blues and Gospel Records 1892–1943*
        (discography), xiii, xiv, 131–133,
        135–136, 143
*Blues Fell This Morning*, ix, xii, 113
*Blues Records 1943–1970* (Two vols.)
        (discography), 145
Boll weevil theme, 36, 79
Bones (as instrument), 30
Bonus money, 118
  March, 118
Boogie-woogie, 104, 143
  Slow boogie, 66

Declassification (of Classic Blues), 59–62
Decline of blues, 86
Delta, Mississippi, 10, 11
Department of Corrections, TX, 18
Depression (Era), The, 100, 110, 112, 115
Depression (state of mind), 91
Desegregation (of Army), 120
Detroit (Michigan), 85, 89, 92, 104
Dialect (in speech), 137
Dice games (gambling), 98
Diola (African tribe), 18
"Dirty Dozens" (game), 124
Disasters (theme), xviii, 70, 113
Discography, 132–134
    of records in programes, 146–168
Discrimination (Racial), 68, 96
Distribution (of recordings), 142
Djuka (Surinam), 14
Doctor Shows. *See* Medicine Shows
Document Records, xvii, 135
Documentation, xiv, 129–139
Double-cutting (logging), 19
Double-entendre, 35, 85, 125
Dream Books, 100
Drumming, 14, 56
Duets, 61

**E**

Earthquake, 64
Electric instruments, 76
Eight-bar blues/songs, 34, 36, 38
Eisenhower, Presidency, 72
Emancipation (from slavery), 29, 44
Employment, 85
Ethiopian War, 118
Europe, blues interest, xvii, 76
    Blues festivals/visitors, xiv, 7, 61
Ewe (African tribe), 13
Expression, blues, 68, 73, 80, 81–86

**F**

Falsetto (vocal), 131
Farming, 94; see also Cotton

Federal Emergency Relief Administration, 111
Federal Writers Project, 49
Feeling (blues as), 4, 5, 10, 67
Fiddle (violin), 15, 23–24, 26
Field Collecting (of songs and music), 47–51, 77
Field calls. *See* Hollers
Field recording, 48–51
Fife-and-drum (bands), 14
Forty Acres and a Mule, 19
Fire hazard, 115–116
Fisk Jubilee Singers, 75
Fisk University, TN, 75
Flamenco (Spanish music), 64
Flattened notes, 66; see also Blue Notes
Floating verses (in blues), 40, 82
Floods, Blues theme, 113, 114
    Ohio, 114
    Mississippi, 113–115
Florida, 50
Florida Cotton Blossoms (road show), 32
Folk blues, xi, 76, 77
Folk music clubs, 76, 78
Folk song, 1, 48, 78
    Blues as folk song, 56, 84, 139
Ford Motor Company, 28, 85
Fort Valley (folk festival), 50
Freedom. *See* Emancipation

**G**

Gambling, 97–98
Gandy-dancers (track-lining workers), 18
Gang labor, 17–19
Georgia (state)
    Sea Islands, 48
Ghana (West Africa), xii, 13
Gig (policy game), 100
Good-time houses, 103
Goofer dust (grave dust), 99
Gospel song, 6, 46, 64, 128, 131, 144
Gouroumi (lute, Niger), 16
Gravel camps, 95
Griots (West African musicians), xii, 14–16, 37